Endorsements

Jared is a storyteller! You will enjoy his stories of finding God in surprising places. Many people struggle to find God's purpose for their lives. Let Jared help you uncover how God is already speaking to you. As you read these real-life stories, you will discover the clues your Heavenly Father has been planting all around you. Follow these clues, and you just might bump into God's obvious purpose for your life.

~ *Charles Stock, Senior Pastor of Life Center in Harrisburg, PA*
Author of Glow in the Dark

Everyone has a story, and our stories are what connect us to each other. In Creation & Redemption, Jared beautifully intertwines his own story of brokenness and redemption with a message of hope. This book is a perfect example of vulnerability and truth, creating a powerful picture that no matter where you are in life, God can and will redeem!

~ *Polly Wright, Former Stripper and Founder of We Are Cherished Ministries*
Author of Cherished: Shattered Innocence. Restored Hope.

What I love about Jared's book is how real it is as he describes what it looks like to walk with God in the everyday and not-so-pretty stuff of life. In other words, the places where all of us live. Through his openness, vulnerability, and conversational writing style, Jared invites us into a moment-by-moment journey to know Jesus better.

~*Alan Kraft, Senior Pastor of Christ Community Church in Greeley, CO*
Author of More and Good News for Those Trying Harder

For such a young man, Jared has an amazing amount of tried and true wisdom. This is a book that will both encourage and challenge you to find out not just who you are in God, but who God is in you. Well done, Jared!

~ *Chris DuPré, Pastor, Speaker, and Songwriter*
Author of The Wild Love of God and The Love Project

Jared Stump is an excellent communicator, encourager, and practical theologian, and these characteristics are evident in Creation & Redemption. As I read this book, I felt as though I was listening to a story at the feet of God, the great story teller. Jared beautifully captures the Father's Heart while sharing his own story and the stories of others. It's clear to me that Jared spent much time in the presence of God as he worked on this project. Enjoy it and pass it on!

~ *Nic Billman, United Methodist Missionary to Brazil*
Author of Between the Flowers and the Broken

In Creation & Redemption, Jared Stump puts maturity and vulnerability on the same page. I don't mean to brag, but I have personally known Jared for the last five years. He possesses a teachable spirit, professional communication style, and a determination to fulfill the dreams of his heart. Jared is a BIG DEAL.

~ *Kyle Embry, Director of Youth Alive North Texas*
Author of Hidden in Plain Sight: America's Unreached Mission Field

It is an honor to recommend Creation & Redemption, written by my good friend, Jared Stump. His writing is passionate, insightful, and will provoke you to encounter the Father's love. From his lighthearted humor to raw, personal stories, Jared easily relates to those who have ever felt confused or alone. This book lucidly displays the invitation to encounter freedom and experience the power of redemption on a daily basis.

~ *Jessica Tripode, Student at Texas A&M University*

Creation & Redemption is a powerful story that challenges our perception of God's involvement in everyday life. Jared's recollection of events in his life make this a very relatable, intriguing, and challenging read. It will give hope to the hopeless and redirect our eyes to the wonder, majesty, and character of Jesus Christ.

~ *Kyle Callahan, Student at Abilene Christian University*

In fearless vulnerability, Jared details the universally awkward struggle of becoming in Creation & Redemption. This is not a theological work, but a recounting of how the Spirit of God writes on a human heart, how God enters our world so we can enter His. I recommend this book, a great read for all who aren't ashamed to let God meet them where they are.

~ *Josh McGready, Lead Janitor at Life Center in Harrisburg, PA*

Creation & Redemption is a wonderfully pure experience. Jared takes you on an observational journey through the catacombs of life's mundane moments and into the heart of God for a generation.

~ *Daniel Hazelwood, Husband, Father, Songwriter, and Sage*

I have known Jared for several years and have had the privilege of watching him discover his place in the world. Creation & Redemption is a poetic picture of God's heart for a generation. You need to read this book!

~ *Mark Royalty, Entrepreneur, Co-Owner of Pure Bean Coffee Roasters*

Jared's writing style is engaging and inspiring. We have known Jared for many years and have seen his growth in the Lord and His Kingdom come to life on many different levels. Creation & Redemption is a picture of that transformation and a call for us all to live our lives fully ALIVE.

~ *Henry & Michell Conner, Senior Pastors of Harvest Reign Church in Great Bend, KS*

There are people who are simply good "story tellers," and then there are those who *have* a story to tell. Jared Stump is a young man with a story to tell. His style of writing is as unique as he is, making Creation & Redemption an interesting and encouraging read. I'm sure I won't be around to see the fullness of Jared's life story, but it has been my pleasure to witness the miraculous transformation of his beginning.

~ *G.W. "Rocky" Ivy, Senior Minister at Open Gate Ministries in Austin, TX*

I first met Jared when he was 11 years old. When I see the man he is today, I couldn't be prouder! Jared has always had a passion for the Lord, and Creation & Redemption puts his compelling passion on display. I love this book!

~ *Glen Chmelar, Texas Oilman, Ordained Minister,*
and Former Player for the NFL's Houston Oilers

It is exciting to read about the discovery and exploration of God's Kingdom through the eyes of younger generations who are willing to step out into the unknown to see what God has in store for a "new now." We need fresh seers and thinkers in the Kingdom, and Jared is one of them. He speaks with an experience and wisdom beyond his age as he engages in the lost ministry of storytelling—a form of worship utilized by previous generations. God has invited us into The Story through personal stories of His people throughout the Scriptures. I believe He continues to do so through people willing to risk exposing themselves through their art. In this, Jared is a trail-blazer and pace-setter. I anticipate hearing more from him.

~ *Ron Beers, Retired Lutheran Minister who has pastored congregations*
across the United States and Canada

CREATION

&

REDEMPTION

FINDING YOUR PLACE

IN A FALLEN WORLD

JARED STUMP

Edited by Alana Stump and Chanel Worley
Cover Design by Christy McFerren
Interior Design by Kathrine Tripp

Published in Dallas, Texas, by Battle Ground Creative
First Edition

Battle Ground Creative is a faith-based publishing company with an emphasis on helping first-time authors find their voice. Named after an obscure city in Washington State, we currently operate offices in Dallas, Texas and Harrisburg, Pennsylvania. For a complete title list and bulk order information, please visit www.battlegroundcreative.com

ISBN-10: 0990873811
ISBN-13: 978-0-9908738-1-5
RELIGION / Spirituality / Christian Life

Printed in the United States of America

DEDICATION

To the different ones,
the misfits, the outsiders,
the square pegs trying to fit in round holes,
the ones who feel like they don't fit at all...
this one's for you.

TABLE OF CONTENTS

(continued...)

FOREWORD

I had known him as a regular, involved in Freedom Ministry classes at Gateway. I had known him in Texas, which is why it was so odd to bump into him on Fisherman's Wharf in San Francisco. This was an unusual and unexpected meeting, but I have come to realize that those words describe Jared quite well.

It is unusual and unexpected for someone of Jared's age to be able to engage in the journey he describes in this book, much less capture it for us to benefit from.

It is unusual and unexpected for any of us to find the connection between our little stories and The Big Story, but this is exactly what Jared has done. His engaging style and personal approach connects his story and yours to The Story that God is unfolding all around us.

I have watched Jared walk out his journey from creation to redemption, freely giving away what he receives along the path. I have been quite impressed by what I have seen, and occasionally thought the world would be a better place if we had more people like him. I think the thing I admire so much about Jared has been his journey to become his true self. I wish we had more people like him, but I am not proposing that anyone emulate Jared's unique characteristics, but rather that they might follow in his footsteps on a journey of their own, a unique pursuit of God and their true selves. It's the journey from birth to identity, or as Jared would say, the journey from creation to redemption.

I believe the value of this book is not simply what people might learn from what Jared himself has learned. Rather, I see it as a catalyst that will show those who read it *how* to learn, so that each might find their own unique story.

As I described above, I literally bumped into Jared one day, hundreds of miles from the normal setting where our paths cross. Jostling through the crowds of San Francisco, our shoulders made contact and our faces showed our surprise when we turned to face each other.

While reading this book, I couldn't help but see this "chance" meeting as a metaphor. We are all travelers; we are all on a journey. If you hold this book in your hands, you too, have likely bumped into Jared in the midst of his travels. Like me, you will be glad you did. And like me, while you may be on a different path at the moment, the words on these pages will show you that you are always prone to intersect with people whose journey, though different, can in many ways parallel your own.

Read this book, not just to know Jared's story or grab hold of the truths he has uncovered, but to bump into him on your journey, and perhaps discover your own story in the process.

Bob Hamp
Former Pastor of Freedom Ministry
Gateway Church in Southlake, TX
Author of *Think Differently, Live Differently: Keys to a Life of Freedom*

INTRODUCTION

←——————《 ✕ 》——————→

Let the redeemed of the Lord tell their story ...
~ Psalm 107:2

I went through a difficult time in my life recently, and I decided to start writing about it. This was the result. It's a collection of stories—true stories, the best kind there are. You could call it a Christian book, but it's not an account of how Jesus came into my life and instantly made everything better. Instead, it's about how He helped me re-build my life from the ground up. It's a bit dark at times, but it's also full of life and joy and many other beautiful things.

Creation & Redemption is about my story, your story, and the much larger Story that God is writing all around us. Sometimes, our stories struggle. Many of us have ripped out the pages that we can't bear to remember. For some of us, there's not much left.

We live in this place called earth surrounded by God's creation, and we know that He has promised redemption. He is in the process of making all things new, but all things are not yet new. There's a definite point where everything will become new, but at the same time that effect is currently taking place all around us. God's Kingdom is closer than the very air we breathe.

This is a book about life and death—and everything in-between. It is my hope that these somewhat random scenes will encourage you to begin writing a better story with your life—even if you feel like you're stuck somewhere between creation and redemption.

Come on, let's take this journey together.

Jared Stump
Providence Village, TX
February 17, 2012

ACT I

Begin

It began in mystery and it will end in mystery, but what a savage and beautiful country lies in between.

~ Diane Ackerman

CHAPTER 1

CREATION

I used to think I had all the right answers, but now I realize
I'm just beginning to ask the right questions.

I think one of my favorite parts of the Bible is *the beginning*. There's something about creation that ignites a fire in my bones. The first four words of God's story typically catch me by surprise.

In the beginning, God. [1]

We could stop right there and it would be enough, but that's not where The Story ends. I like how the Bible begins with God creating stuff. Throughout the core of The Story, there's more talk about creation, and also something called *redemption*. And then there's the end—the final page—where even though the pieces are beginning to come together, the puzzle is far from finished. The Story, as it turns out, cannot be bound within the cover of a book, not even the number-one bestseller of all time. But let's not get too far ahead of ourselves.

So here we are, at the beginning. The earth has been created, though not in full. Something is missing. Darkness is present—a mysterious void. But God is right there the whole time. He speaks, and life begins to invade the place where there was previously nothing. And then we end up with this lush garden and a man and a woman who live in this place of perfection, where there is no sickness or sorrow or shame.

The man doesn't lie awake at night wondering if he'll ever be good enough. He doesn't strive to live up to the expectations of a world that doesn't even know who

1

he is. He doesn't have to act tough and cool when he really wants to find a corner to hide in.

The woman doesn't stand in front of the mirror every morning and stare at the beauty that everyone else sees and wish that she could lose five pounds so she wouldn't be ugly anymore. She doesn't bury herself under the sheets in the middle of the day, struggling to survive her latest heartbreak because her heart is totally and completely unbroken.

Adventure abounds, and they don't have to live every day like it's the last day of their lives because they don't even know what death is. It's complete and utter bliss—until one day, when it all falls apart. The man and the woman had everything, but they believed the lie that they were not complete, that there was something else they needed. If they could grab ahold of this elusive thing, they would be complete and happy and everything that they already were. Though they were fully alive, they reached for something they thought would make them more alive, and it ended up killing them—in a slow and painful sort of way. Adam and Eve took the life that God had placed in them and exchanged it for death, and we've been doing the same thing ever since.

Once life was traded for death, blame, jealousy, and violence entered the world, causing it to become broken and messy.

A few thousand years passed. Jesus came and proclaimed the Kingdom of God. He was hung on a cross, died, was buried, came back from the dead, appeared to His followers, and ascended into Heaven. The Kingdom is breaking in all around us, but there is a stark contrast between the present reality of how broken this world is, and the future reality of how perfect things are going to be. Jesus bought back everything the human race lost in the garden. In the midst of the tension between the *now* and the *not yet*, He invites us to become a part of The Story, so that we may venture outside of ourselves and take part in the redemption that is unfolding all around us.

The only thing I don't understand is why God doesn't think the way I do. I say that with a bit of tongue in cheek, because I know God does not think like us, but He instead invites us to renew our minds so we may think like Him. But at the same time, I must admit that I don't understand His ways. I don't understand that the King who came to save the world was born a baby in a manger. I don't understand why He had to spend a couple of decades helping his dad pound nails into blocks of wood. I don't understand why He had to bleed and die on a tree in order to undo what Adam and Eve had done, but I understand that this act of love allows us to exchange the death in us for the life in Him. Above all else, I don't understand that even though *it is finished*, it really isn't.

I know that God is in the process of making all things new. I know that one day things will be very different than they are now. I know that Jesus has already won the ultimate victory that was necessary to make all things new and to reconnect us with our true Father. The strange thing is, even though I know and affirm these things to be true, I don't see them when I walk out my front door every day. In fact, I often see the exact opposite. I see a lot of hurt and pain and fear and death, and I know that none of those things belong in the Kingdom that God is building. It's strange to think that the Kingdom has come, but not in full. It's strange and awkward that I have to live with this taste of a world I cannot yet experience at the tip of my tongue. It's frustrating living in the gap between creation and redemption. Interestingly enough, God isn't worried about any of this, as I am. He is the same; He is unchanging, even when I am stuck in the gap between the now and the not yet. I guess that's why He's referred to as, *The One who is, and who was, and who is to come* (Revelation 1:8).

CHAPTER 2

THE STRUGGLE

I used to think I had life figured out,
but then I graduated from high school.

If you're alive and living in the world today, you're more than likely aware of *the struggle,* which affects us all at some point in our lives. It doesn't matter if you're a businessman in New York or a bartender in Atlanta. The struggle affects the farmer living on the plains of Kansas and the drifter living on the streets of San Francisco. The struggle is universal, transcending time and space. It affects everyone who has ever lived, and everyone who ever will live; it meets us between creation and redemption, seeking to rob us of everything good in our lives.

When Adam and Eve exchanged life for death back in the garden, it threw everything off balance, giving birth to the struggle. The remainder of Scripture chronicles what happened as a result of this one simple act, the exchange that started a war. This war rages all around us, and also inside each of us, surrounding us at every moment of every day—in every thought, every action, every decision—regardless of whether or not we are aware of it. All of creation is affected by this war. This war is the struggle.

Immediately after Adam and Eve blew it, the answer to the war they started was given. Jesus is first mentioned in Genesis 3:15, a few thousand years before He would live and die and rise again, defeating death and ending the war for good. All of this has happened; yet, the struggle continues—and will continue—until the end of the story, where all things are made new and the innocence of humanity is restored.

5

Why doesn't Jesus come and fix things now?

As He was hanging on the cross, His last words were, *It is Finished* (John 19:30).

Jesus doesn't need to get back up on the cross and die a second time. He has already fulfilled all the requirements to end the struggle—for good. According to 1 John 3:8, Jesus came to destroy the works of the devil; that is, to reverse the effects of everything that went wrong in the garden.

So why is the devil still at work if his works have been destroyed?

I don't know. I don't have all the answers. I'm not even sure I've figured out all the right questions. I know redemption is promised, it hasn't fully happened yet, but it's breaking in all around us. I know the Kingdom is coming, and it is already here.

As I write this, I find myself wondering: What if the end of the story—the point where the struggle ends—is really just the beginning? What if the story that God began was suspended when the war began, and Christ's return is not the end of the story, but the Father pressing "play" on the story that was paused some four thousand years ago?

✳ ✳ ✳

I know a guy named Alan who is a pastor. He's one of those deep, intellectual types—I guess you would call him a "theologian." This is fitting, since he always appears to be deep in thought.

Alan the Theologian says the resurrection of Jesus changed everything. It confirmed His identity as the Messiah, His provision for sin, His victory over the devil—not to mention death and the grave. Like the Old Testament events that pointed toward the incarnation, the resurrection points toward the resurrection that is yet to come. Because Christ is risen, we too will rise, and we will experience the fulfillment of all that has been promised. In the in-between, our world is broken, but the broken state of our world is what causes us to crave eternity. And I think that's how God wants it because we were created for eternity.

We all experience pain in our lives. We know we're broken, and we long for wholeness. We're always looking for answers and searching for something to heal our aching hearts. We aren't always aware that we're doing this, but most of us end up driving ourselves crazy searching for things to make us feel less empty. When we look for wholeness and meaning apart from God, we end up working out our own redemption through empty pursuits. [1]

When you see a beautiful plant on someone's front porch, you often don't look at the thing that's containing it. We don't notice the pots because they are so ordinary compared to what they contain. Of course, some people try to dress up the pots, try to make them nice and flashy so perhaps the eye will be drawn to them before the plant, but it is still ultimately the plant that remains the focal point.

It's beautiful how God takes our brokenness and exchanges it for His wholeness. He reminds us that our lives matter and we are deeply loved. He deposits His very nature inside of us, so that His love can radiate in our hearts and shine through us to the world around us, even though our physical bodies are a lot like ordinary clay pots. [2]

I've noticed that even after we've been made new, we still experience a lot of the same hurt and pain that we experienced before. When God comes into our lives, it doesn't instantly remove all of the crap; that often takes time. I suppose if we were immune to the struggle, we wouldn't be able to relate to people who feel like their lives are falling apart.

Sometimes, we forget who we are along the way. We feel like we've fallen asleep, so we do crazy things that we wouldn't normally do, attempting to wake ourselves up. Even though we've been made new, we're still capable of doing a lot of damage in the world—especially to the people closest to us. But God keeps loving us anyway, even when we find ourselves caught in the struggle. We are His kids; He is our dad. He is for us, even if it takes us our entire lives to wake up and realize who we are, who He created us to be.

I was feeling discouraged the other day, because although I have found clues that point to what I'm supposed to do with my life, the picture is still very blurry. I feel like a failure because I've never had a job that pays more than twelve thousand dollars a year, and I'm not sure what steps I need to take to reach my dreams. So I texted my friend Megan, who lives in Maryland, and she called me a few hours later when she got off work.

As I was explaining to her how I was feeling, I began to feel really silly, even guilty that I was letting something so trivial get me off track. Rather than letting the feeling remain internal, I put words to it. I told Megan that I felt silly saying these things out loud, and she responded with laughter, as she went on to tell me that she is in her mid-twenties and she still doesn't have things figured out either.

"Yeah, but at least you have a real job," I replied.

She chuckled again. "Not the one I dreamed I would have at this point in life."

Megan and I talked for another half hour, and then she prayed for me. As I hung up the phone, I didn't feel like I had any answers, but I knew I wasn't alone in the struggle, and that was enough.

Knowing that you are not the only one trying to make sense of the human experience is the only way to defeat the struggle. You can never run fast enough to escape it or achieve enough success to make the tension go away. Though you are a citizen of God's Kingdom, you are still a citizen of earth. As long as you are here on earth, as long as you live between creation and redemption, you will encounter the struggle. You don't defeat the struggle by making it go away; you defeat the struggle by becoming who God created you to be, right in the middle of it.

And while we are on our way toward discovering who God created us to be, while we are still looking for the clues that are often hidden in plain sight, we need to know that we are not alone. We need to be able to look someone in the eyes and tell them the struggle is weighing us down. Because chances are, they will breathe a huge sigh of relief, look us back in the eyes, and utter two powerful words: "Me too." Sometimes all it takes to push back the darkness that clouds our hearts is letting a little light in.

Though we try to run from reality, we are messed up people, living in a messed up world. But we don't have to wait until we have it together before we make a difference. The struggle is a normal part of the human experience, and it doesn't mean you have done something wrong, or that God is punishing you. Realize that you are not alone in the struggle, and that will give you the strength you need to move forward and do whatever you can to push back darkness.

CHAPTER 3

ME AND GOD ON A BEACH

I used to think God was off in the distance,
but now I know He wants to be close to me.

One morning last summer, I was walking through my near-empty church lobby, when a friend pulled me aside. He took me into the sanctuary, where two chairs were waiting off to the side, in the back corner of the room. We sat down, and he asked me to describe how I saw God and how I thought God saw me.

"I see myself on a beach," I said. "And God is off in the distance, walking toward me." The picture sounded great in my head, almost poetic and certainly cliché.

"Hmm," he replied. "Why do you think God is off in the distance?"

I didn't have an answer for that.

"You want to know what I think?"

I nodded.

He went on to tell me that, somewhere along the journey, the struggle had gotten the best of me. I had lost sight of the heart of God and how He felt about me. My friend told me that God didn't want to be off in the distance; He wanted to be close. He wanted us to walk down the beach together, arm in arm.

Tears began to form in my eyes as I told my friend that I longed for God to be close again, that I was thirsty for an encounter with the Father. I wanted us to walk down the beach together, get our feet wet in the ocean, and for Him to carry me when the waves grew too strong for me to stand up in.

As my friend looked at me, I could see the love in his eyes; I could sense his desire

9

for me to discover who I really was. "So, what's stopping you?" he asked quietly, a deep silence following his words.

Unsure how to respond, all I could do was shrug and shake my head.

CHAPTER 4

DEPRESSION AND WORSHIP

I used to think it was okay to take my time climbing the corporate ladder,
but now I realize I don't need to climb the ladder at all.

I began writing a book a few days before Christmas, which I titled *Confessions of a Struggling Evangelical.* [1] I was feeling a bit depressed at the time; this lasted for about a month. Over the past few years, I've noticed a pattern of depression creeping into my life. It begins in late September—not long after my birthday—and typically runs through Christmas and into the new year before lifting. But with each progressing year, the period of time I spend in a depressed state is noticeably shorter, as if God is breaking in on the scene and redeeming my story. This period of depression was the shortest by far, although it seemed like an eternity while I was in the middle of it. It was almost as if I spent a month sleepwalking. I wasn't daydreaming, because you have to be awake for that, and I didn't feel awake. With each passing day, I began to lose touch with reality, and I needed something to take my mind off the pain in my soul. That was when I started writing the book, which served as an outlet to talk about how the struggle was getting the best of me.

It was then that something unexpected happened.

It started out as just another Monday in the middle of the winter, the kind that you can't run away from. I got up before the sun met the sky, leaving the warmth of my house to go work at a coffee shop for a few hours. At the time, I typically worked a split shift on Mondays, which meant opening and closing with a five hour break in the middle. But that night, I had given my shift to a co-worker who was in need of extra hours, leaving the night wide open.

I'm a member of a large church in the Dallas/Fort Worth Metroplex. We have three campuses at the moment, but I know we'll have more by the time this book is published. Perhaps that's a bit presumptuous to say—that this book will someday be published. A friend once told me that no one will want to read my book until I've done something great in life. I'm not really sure what to do with that statement, because I think the "something great" might be something I write. Perhaps this is what God created me to do: to share my story in a way that connects with others and inspires them to share their stories.

I got off work shortly after lunch, and decided I would attend a class that my friend Bob the Freedom Guy was teaching that night at my church in Frisco. I live close to the Frisco campus, but I don't usually attend church there, because I'm weird. [2]

That night, Bob talked about walls we put up around our hearts. During the class, it felt like God walked into the room, right to where I was sitting, and began to peel back the layers around my heart. Some of the layers I'd created in vain attempts to protect myself, much like a three-sided wall around a city. Others were built up by negative life experiences, by the struggle. Regardless of how you look at it, I had enough layers built up to close off a portion of my heart.

The problem with protecting ourselves is it keeps God from doing His job. He wants to be the one who protects our hearts when we get caught in the struggle, but when we do it ourselves, it shuts Him out. The irony of this lies in the fact that by protecting ourselves, we shut out the only One who can truly protect us—which is God, of course.

As I drove home from church that night, I knew that God was doing a deep work inside of me. For a moment, the struggle seemed nonexistent. But that was before something even more unexpected happened.

※ ※ ※

I really enjoyed working at the coffee shop at first, even though it was a thirty mile drive from my house and most people thought I was crazy for working so far from home. After the first year, things started going downhill. I really liked the people I worked with, but the business structure was driving the people at the bottom crazy.

I only worked three or four days a week, but I dreaded those days every time they rolled around. Finally, after working there for a year and a half, I was let go at the end of January.

In the days that followed, even in the wake of losing my job, I began to realize that I was being less than honest by referring to myself as "struggling." Things were looking up, so I ditched that book altogether and started writing this one. I think things are going to turn out better this way.

I still have another job working with a youth outreach ministry, but it's a contract job that gives far more in experience than it does financial compensation. I have a significant[3] amount of money in the bank and still live with my parents, but for one reason or another, I worry about money like a single mom with two kids and a parakeet to feed. I graduated high school last year, and I'm not currently attending college. I'm not against college; I just don't feel like it's the best path for me at this point.

I spend my days writing and searching for adventure. I often find myself longing to change the world. I want to be a voice and make a difference and see a generation find out who they really are, as they begin to understand who God is and who He's created them to be.

Some days, I still struggle. Yesterday was one of them. I spent much of the day searching for jobs on the Internet, even though I felt like it wasn't what God wanted me to do. I feel like He wants me to wait for Him to open a door for me. Sometimes, God wants us to wait for Him to open a door; other times, He gives us the courage to try every locked door until we find the one that opens. It's not that I don't have a job; I just don't have a paying job. I feel like my job right now is supposed to be writing this book, but when I wake up every morning and sit down at the computer, it feels as though I don't have a "real job." Within a few minutes, I find myself online, looking for something else so I can feel like I'm worth something.

I think God is far more concerned about what's going on inside of us than what we're doing. I think that's why He wants me to trust Him and spend this season of life developing the gifts He put inside of me. We're supposed to work to support ourselves financially, but my job search at this point is more about distracting myself from developing the gifts God put inside of me. That's what often happens when something doesn't feel right inside of us; we make ourselves busier and busier, in an attempt to distract ourselves from the pain inside. When we're running at full speed, we don't realize our souls are slowly eroding. I love the way Pascal put it: *All of man's misfortune comes from one thing, which is not knowing how to sit quietly in a room.*[4]

I was lying in bed later that night, longing for God to come and break through the lies that were flooding my mind. In that moment, I felt His presence, as if He was right there in the room with me. I felt a peace wash over me, and the words, "Remember who you are," filled my mind. That simple phrase cut through all the static and lingered in my mind until I fell asleep.

We know that God is fully present in every place. That's why David said, *Where can I go from your Spirit? Where can I flee from your presence?* (Psalm 139:7). In other words, "It doesn't matter how hard I run, You're always right there with me."

God is fully present in every place, but what is often missing is our awareness of His presence. What would happen if we lived life fully aware that God is with us and will never leave us?

May He wrap you in His arms.

May you feel His embrace.

May He look you square in the face, with love in His eyes.

May you hear Him whisper your name in a way that makes you weak in the knees.

May you fall in love with the Father all over again, as if for the very first time.

※ ※ ※

In the Gospel of Mark [5], Jesus is talking with the disciples about how He must suffer and die and rise again. And then Peter—who is kind of like your obnoxious little brother—pulls Him aside and informs Him that he doesn't like this plan. Peter, being Jewish, lived under severe Roman tyranny in those days. He and the other disciples wanted Jesus to march into Rome and dismantle their governmental system. They had previously heard Jesus say that He would set the oppressed free (Luke 4:18), but they did not understand that the Kingdom He was bringing did not involve overthrowing the existing kingdoms by force. Because Peter and the other disciples did not understand that God's Kingdom is often completely backwards from man's way of thinking and doing things, they did not understand why someone as great and awesome as Jesus had to win by losing. That's why when Jesus responded to Peter, He told him he was acting like satan, because he was processing the situation through man's way of thinking instead of God's.

Apparently, a crowd had gathered, because Jesus called both the crowd and His disciples over and told them that if they try to live by their own systems, they will never find true life, but if they are willing to throw all of that aside and embrace Jesus' way of coming in first by coming in last, they would find the life they had been searching for, but could never seem to grab ahold of.

Then, these words rolled off Jesus' tongue, which you have probably seen on your friend's refrigerator: *For what does it profit a man to gain the whole world, and forfeit his soul? For what will a man give in exchange for his soul?* [6]

These questions are widely repeated in our world today, so it's not a surprise that they are widely misunderstood.

Jesus is not saying we can never be successful in the world's eyes. Rather, He is saying if we gain everything we think we need to amount to something, but forget who we are and neglect what is going on inside of us, we've already lost it all.

The second question speaks to the myth that it's okay for us to lose ourselves for a little while on the way to the top, because once we get there, we'll have enough resources to buy our souls back. Jesus is asking a rhetorical question, *What will a man give in exchange for his soul?*, to get us to realize that the most important things in life cannot be purchased, no matter how much wealth you have acquired.

In short, Jesus is saying it's okay to take a few years between high school and college to figure out who you are and how to write your story into God's larger and grander story. You don't have to hastily grab ahold of the bottom rung of the corporate ladder, ready to begin the lifelong journey of fighting your way to the top. It's not that it's bad to go into the corporate world and work your way up, or even get a job or go to college right out of high school, it's just that Jesus wants us to focus on our identity more than our activity. That's why when Jesus was baptized, God the Father looked down from heaven and audibly proclaimed that He was pleased with Him (Matthew 3:17), even though Jesus hadn't achieved anything great yet. He was about thirty years old, and had spent most of His life working with His dad in the construction business; He was not yet walking out the primary mission that God sent Him to earth to accomplish.

There was one time, right before He entered high school, when He joined His parents and their friends on a trip to Jerusalem, which was something they did every year. On the way back to their town of Nazareth, they realized Jesus had stayed behind, so they went back to look for Him. Three days later, they found Him in the temple, hanging out with a bunch of pastors. He was hanging on their every word, and asking them questions that caused them to scratch their heads, as if to say, *Who is this kid?* [7]

Long story short, Jesus returned with His parents to Nazareth, and we don't hear anything else about Him until eighteen years later, when He was baptized and God the Father gave Him two thumbs up. The only clue we have is, *Jesus grew in wisdom and stature, and in favor with God and man* (Luke 2:52). Jesus wasn't out performing a lot of miracles or even serving in formal ministry. We don't know whether He worked part-time or full-time in the construction business. We have no idea what He was doing; the Scriptures just tell us who He was, that He was wise beyond His years and had a great amount of favor on His life. What Jesus was doing during those years was irrelevant; the Father was pleased with Him on the basis of their relationship alone.

It's important to note that while Jesus was not concerned about achieving success or status, He was not sitting around doing nothing. In the same way, some of us (like myself) need to work part-time at a coffee shop after high school, rather than seeking a full-time job that will get us lost in the madness of trying to prove ourselves. I think that's why God led me away from looking for a "real job" at this point, because He knew it would be better for me in the long run, and He knew I needed to write this book, even if I'm only writing it for myself.

In the words of Ralph Waldo Emerson: *To be yourself in a world that is constantly trying to make you something else is the greatest accomplishment.*

※ ※ ※

It's March now, and I'm in Austin, the city I grew up in. My uncle is helping facilitate an event that consists of fifty hours of non-stop worship. We're nine hours in, and it's been really good so far, although I've come to realize that I connect with God easier when I'm alone in an empty room than I do in a crowd. I think the fact that I get distracted easily may have something to do with that. Quite often in the middle of corporate worship, I'll see something shiny and stop worshiping, even though I may still be singing the words on the screen. Worship is more than just words, you know. It's more about connecting to God, and sometimes words get in the way of actually doing that.

I remember one day, back in January, when I was feeling a little under the weather. I stayed in bed most of the day, until I remembered that we were having a special service at my church in Frisco that night. I didn't really want to go, but something told me I should, so I got up, took a shower, and put on my pointy shoes so I would look good for the Lord. I really like my pointy shoes because I feel like I'm somebody important when I wear them, and I sometimes get a big head about it. I didn't on this particular evening, which made me happy since I've been trying really hard to be humble lately.

By the time my family and I arrived at church, I had decided that we should sneak in on the back row, but we somehow ended up on the front row, next to all the important people. At that point, I was glad I wore my pointy shoes.

The service began. For once, I didn't see anything shiny and I was able to actually worship, which I assumed made God happy and not mad at me.

I occasionally like to kneel during worship, which is why I like to sit toward the back, so I can do so without anyone noticing. That night, toward the end of worship, I felt God tugging on my heart, and I immediately knew that I needed to kneel. I quickly informed God that kneeling was simply not practical, as I was about twelve feet from the stage, and there was an altar ministry box located directly in front of me. Kneeling would require taking several steps forward into the open altar area, in front of everyone. I did not want to do that, which is probably why I felt God leading me to do so.

As the song continued, I did what anyone else would do; I ignored God and kept singing. I felt really fake though, because my heart wasn't in it. I was thinking more about how I looked than anything else, which meant I wasn't worshiping, even though I was singing the words on the screen and even had my hands raised. I was hoping that if I just kept singing, God would leave me alone, which is kind of funny since the whole point of singing the song is to worship Him and thus position ourselves to encounter His presence.

The song was too fast to choreograph a perfect kneeling motion, and I told God that, but He didn't respond. I had almost made up my mind to obey God when the song suddenly ended. Usually, when you feel God leading you to do something you don't want to do, you just need to get over yourself and do it.

As the song came to an end, I immediately knew it was the last song in the worship set, which it was. But before I had a chance to feel any sort of regret, the worship leader burst into a refrain. All I remember after that is stepping forward, into the middle of the altar area. I remember kneeling, my eyes closed and arms outstretched. I remember God's presence overwhelming my heart as He met me there.

Less than a minute later, I managed to make my way back to my seat without tripping over my own feet, which was remarkable, since I could barely feel my pointy shoes. I didn't look at anyone, as I assumed everyone had seen how ridiculous I looked. But then I had the thought that maybe they had been worshiping, and were completely oblivious to what I was doing.

I don't know why we sometimes feel this way in church, but I think many of us do. I don't like feeling this way, and I wish God would fix me so that I won't feel this way anymore.

If you read the Bible, you'll find it talks a lot about letting go of our pride and being more concerned about pleasing God than pleasing people. Sometimes, in order to accomplish this, we need to physically do something, like kneel down in worship at church when no one else is doing so. That doesn't mean we go out of our way to draw attention to ourselves; it just means we let go of our need to always present a perfect public persona.

I once heard a pastor tell a story of a time when he was fixing something at the church during the week. He was down on his hands and knees, when a small group of people walked by. In that moment, he was embarrassed to be seen in such a lowly position. "That incident made me aware of my own pride," he said. "I was embarrassed, and I shouldn't have been, because Jesus calls us to go low and serve" (Luke 22:24-27). [8]

Over the past few months, I've noticed that when I try to kneel, God urges me to stand instead. It's almost as if He did fix me while I was on the floor, and now that

I've gotten over myself and what people think of me, I don't need to take that test anymore. Not that I will never kneel in worship again, but I think you get what I mean. Perhaps God is saying, "Well done, my son. You've gotten over your fear of what people will think of you. Now you can stand in confidence, not in yourself, but who I've made you to be."

The Apostle Paul tells us we are in a spiritual battle, not against our annoying neighbors that blast music at midnight or that person at work we don't like, but against unseen forces in the spiritual realm. He tells us that we should properly equip ourselves to fight this battle, but after we have done all we can do, we need to stand (Ephesians 6:12-13). We need to stand, not in our own strength, but in the strength God gives us. I have found that if I try to stand on my own, God will always make me kneel, but if I kneel on my own, He'll tell me to get up and stand.

CHAPTER 5

LONGING FOR ADVENTURE

I used to be afraid of growing up,
but now I realize I don't have to.

I get bored rather easily these days, which isn't normal for me. I think I want something—a new experience, a full schedule, an open schedule, a change of scenery—but when I get it, I grow tired of it after a day or two. Sometimes, all the things we think will bring us happiness end up having the opposite effect. One day, we're full of passion, finding joy and happiness waiting for us around every corner. But the next day, we can barely get out of bed.

I was talking to my dad a few weeks ago, and I told him I was considering disappearing for the day and leaving the state. I haven't actually done this yet, but the thought of it excites me. I have just enough of the drifter gene to cause me to be unsatisfied with remaining in one place for an extended period of time, but not enough to actually sell all of my belongings and wander the country like a nomad. I think there is something inside all of us that longs for an escape from the familiar, and I don't think this longing is restricted to a certain age group. We all want to live the lives we've dreamed of, before it's too late. Of course, we all have different definitions of what "too late" is, but at the end of our lives, I think we'll regret the things we didn't do more than the things we did do that got us in trouble.

I know a guy who is nearly fifty years old, who has a great marriage, multiple generations of children, a nice house, several cars, and all of the things we think will make us happy. He quit his job recently, and is traveling overseas with his wife for a few weeks. After that, the future is wide open.

I was talking to his wife the other day, as I stood in the kitchen of their suburban house in Central Texas. She told me that she hasn't felt this free in years. Aside from her job, they have nothing tying them down to this world. Many people would say they are being completely irresponsible, but I understand what is going on inside of them. They may have more life experience, but we share the same longing that drives us to break free from the familiar. At some point in our lives, we get to the place where we realize the things we think we need in order to be free, such as financial security, are actually the things that end up holding us back.

In one of his books, Donald Miller talks about how every good story has something in common—they all contain at least one character who wants something and overcomes conflict to get it. [1] It's like this in books, in movies, and in the stories we tell with our lives.

I watched a movie the other night about some characters who wanted something and overcame conflict to get it. But then the screen faded to black, the credits rolled, and it was over, causing something inside of me to wish the conflict had lasted longer, so the story would have lasted longer. Of course, there's always the sequels, but I've found that life isn't very exciting when you attempt to go back and reproduce it a second time. Reliving the same experiences is lame; something drives us to create new ones. Movie sequels are a perfect example of what happens when we take a good thing and try to make it more than it was ever intended to be.

We all have stories, we all want things, and we all seem to be wrapped up in some sort of conflict in our lives. Perhaps the conflict is good, because it lets us know that we're still alive and breathing, that we're still moving forward. Because when the conflict stops, it means we've either stopped trying or we've gotten everything we want, and if I know one thing for sure, it's that there is always more out there.

The first few chapters of our stories were written for us, depending on what family we were born into and what our upbringing was like. While we have some level of control over the in-between chapters, that control is often stripped away when a broken world slams us head on, turning our fantasies into tragedies. But the ending chapters are always within our grasp, to write as we see fit. As long as you are still breathing, you get to decide how your story will end, and it's never too late to re-write the script that will determine what you're remembered for

※ ※ ※

I was driving home from work one day, back when I still worked at the coffee shop, when I felt a longing for adventure begin to stir inside of me. In that moment, all I wanted was to continue driving past my exit, without giving a second thought to where I might end up. I had an appointment at 5:45, and it was already 5:15, so I exited off the freeway into the endless sea of suburbia. The closest I got to adventure that evening was tapping the gas pedal to the floor when a traffic signal turned yellow.

A few hours earlier, I had been holding down the afternoon shift with my friend, Nicole. We spent most of the shift talking, as it was an unusually slow day at the coffee shop. She told me about her honeymoon and how awful it had been because they couldn't afford to go someplace nice, and how she's tired of living in a tiny shack behind her parent's house in the suburbs.

I think a lot of us are tired of our shacks as well.

Nicole talked about how she and her husband are going to save up some money and finally take their dream trip. One of these days, Nicole and Jeremiah will stand on the rugged shoreline of the Oregon coast, staring at the massive rocks jutting out of the sand as waves crash all around them. In that moment, the memories of their first honeymoon will vanish and they'll feel fully alive—all because of adventure.

This same pursuit of adventure found me driving north on an Oklahoma highway late one night. Still struggling to figure out what the next chapter of my life would entail, I was headed to Missouri to spend a couple of weeks on my grandparent's farm.

My extended family isn't as close as I'd like for us to be. We love each other, of course, but there seems to be this awkward gap between us at times, and I'm not sure what to do about it. I wish God would fix my family so we would be tight-knit, like other families. I hear people say that everything will be okay as long as we have God and each other, but what if we don't have each other?

I think I'm beginning to understand why the Bible says there are friends that stick closer than brothers (Proverbs 18:24), because brothers aren't always close. Some of them only speak to each other because of the mutual blood flowing through their veins, while others turn their backs on each other when they need each other the most. But then your friends come along, pulling you close in those moments when your family fails you. Your world turns upright again, as you realize that it's so much better to let your guard down and let people in, even though you know some of them will hurt you eventually.

We all want picture-perfect families, complete with fake smiles and white picket fences. We want the kind of families that get together every Thanksgiving and Christmas without any drama, but have you noticed those types of families don't even exist on television? Some families just have rifts, and those rifts don't always go away, no matter how hard you try to fix them. But what if they aren't supposed to be fixed? Maybe we're just different people living different lives. Maybe if we viewed one another as people to love instead of people to fix, the rifts would settle down on their own. When we realize that we're all going through the same struggle and we all have baggage to deal with, we suddenly aren't so concerned with fixing one another anymore. But when we act like we don't have any baggage, when we smile and pretend that everything is okay (even though our lives are falling apart), we are setting ourselves up for conflict that only serves to deepen the rifts. We can pretend our problems don't exist for a short time, but we forget that all it takes is the slightest tension to bring them to the surface, which usually creates a bigger mess than dealing with them early on. This is why we must learn to create a safe place with one another, a place where it's okay to let our flaws show. Only then can we stop hiding behind anger and jealousy and truly relate to one another in the way we were originally designed to.

※ ※ ※

I talked to God that night, as I drove through Oklahoma, and I told Him that I was afraid. We're all afraid of things, but then there are those chronic fears that never seem to let us rest. My chronic fears in that moment centered on growing up. I was afraid that I didn't have what it takes, that my life just wouldn't work out, that I would soon end up a failure.

I think a lot of people are afraid of growing up, which explains why some never do. Perhaps that's why a seemingly happy man with a wife and two kids will abandon his family in pursuit of a younger woman who he claims makes him feel a certain way he never felt with his wife. What if his core problem isn't lust, but fear? Perhaps he's just afraid to grow up, to stop wondering *what if* and simply embrace *what is*.

When we know in our hearts that the future is secure, but believe in our heads that it is uncertain, it creates a war inside of us. And when we let the uncertainty of the future get the best of us, we stop moving forward and retreat to what we've always known. It may not be comfortable, but at least it's familiar. The only problem is we forfeit the future that God has for us when we settle for the familiar. We see this play out in real life when a woman runs back to a relationship with a man who abuses her. He's not safe, but he's familiar, and somehow that feels a lot safer than walking away into a new realm of uncertainty. We can't stand uncertainty, because it means we have to trust, and we don't like trusting in things we can't see and feel and touch. The idea of "faith" is completely foreign to many of us, even though we say we have faith in Jesus.

We can know that God has made us complete, but at the same time feel incomplete inside. When we lose sight of who we are, our default reaction is to reach for something to make us feel whole again. Sometimes this looks like relationships and sex; sometimes it looks like money, fame, and power, but if we were to peel back the layers, we would find the same internal unease driving these pursuits. This is why we must take all of our unrest, all of our angst, all of our pain and unfulfilled longings, and lay them at the feet of Jesus—the only one who can make us whole and complete. [2]

Have you ever wondered why the first thing babies do when they enter this world is cry? [3] Perhaps it's because they've just been shoved out of the only place they've ever known. In a moment, they are forced to embrace a world that is broken and messy, a place so unlike the place from which they came, with no turning back. They will never know the safety and security of their mother's womb ever again. And we can't understand why they won't stop crying. Selah.

CHAPTER 6

LIFE ON THE FARM

I used to try really hard to clean myself up for God, but now I realize
He loves me just as much when I'm covered in dirt.

My first day on the farm was a Wednesday. I awoke mid-morning and made my way into the kitchen, where I began brewing my morning coffee before settling into a cozy chair with my leather-bound Bible.

I opened to the Gospel of John and began reading about a guy named Nicodemus, who was one of the honchos of a religious group that didn't care much for Jesus. They were a bit put out by His claims that He was God, perhaps because they had their own opinions of what God made flesh should look like. So Nicodemus goes and finds Jesus in the middle of the night, while everyone else was asleep in their beds. Looking Him in the eyes, he tells Him that he knows He is more than just a man. How else could He perform such miraculous signs?

"That's right, Nicodemus," Jesus replied. "You understand exactly who I am, but unless you are born again, you won't be able to see or experience the Kingdom that I have come to establish."

That's when Nicodemus freaked out, because he couldn't get past the fact that Jesus said he had to be *born again*. How was he, a grown man, supposed to re-enter his mother's womb and be born a second time? Of course, Jesus was referring to spiritual birth, but Nicodemus didn't know that at the time.

Jesus goes on to explain the meaning of spiritual birth. His discourse with Nicodemus spans several verses, which is pretty impressive when you think that there are portions of the Bible where people are born and die within a verse or two. (I like that about Jesus, that He takes time to explain things to those who are struggling to wrap their minds around the vastness of The Story.) The dialogue includes those famous verses where Jesus talks about Himself in the third person—you know, the ones about God loving the world and sending Jesus to die so we could have eternal life. We find this message virtually everywhere, from billboards and church signs to shopping bags and soda cups. The record of their conversation cuts off shortly after that; we never find out what Nicodemus decides to do in regards to being born again. [1]

I'm not sure why the story ends so abruptly, but perhaps Jesus is trying to tell us that we shouldn't be too concerned with whether or not people decide to follow Him. What I mean by this is, perhaps we should focus more on loving and serving people, showing them the love of God through our actions, so they'll believe us when we tell them with our words. What they decide to do with that is up to them. Jesus never forced anyone to follow Him, and when people chose to walk away, He let them.

※ ※ ※

An hour or two passed before I got up from the chair and went into Grandpa's bathroom to take a shower. As I stood there aimlessly, I thought back to four years ago, when we almost lost him.

That year was a sad year for my family. I remember the whole family coming together over Labor Day weekend to celebrate his birthday. We had family pictures taken out in the barn against a backdrop of hay bales. We knew he would soon start chemotherapy, which would cause his hair to fall out and the color to drain from his face. What we didn't know was, in a few short months, he would be lying nearly lifeless in the ICU unit of a Springfield hospital.

As that weekend in Southwest Missouri came to a close, we drove home to Dallas. We settled back into our lives until November came, when we drove ten hours to Northwest Missouri to spend Thanksgiving with my mom's parents. That was the year the Great Recession would officially begin, though most Americans were still living under the mirage that all was well. My heart was made alive as we celebrated Thanksgiving together, talking and laughing and sharing in each other's company.

One day, Dad received a call from his sister, and we quickly drove across the state to his parent's farm. We spent the night there, in their empty house, while they were struggling to fall asleep in a hospital a hundred miles away. The house was cold and lonely without them there, and the drive to Springfield the next morning was even more static. When we arrived at the hospital where I had taken my first breaths fifteen years prior, we were told that Grandpa Stump had barely made it through the night, but he had been regaining his strength as the morning progressed, enough that he had been moved out of the ICU.

The elevator ride to his floor seemed to go on for hours. I felt as though we were moving in slow motion when the doors finally opened and we stepped into the hall. We located his room and lingered a moment before entering, unable to avoid the impending waves of emotion any longer.

Grandpa turned to face us as we entered the room without a word. Dad and I walked over to the edge of his bed and just stood there, as he gripped our hands in his. Tears flowed freely from our eyes; it was the only time I'd ever seen him cry. He asked to hold Mom's hand, and she stepped forward to meet him. He took her small, smooth hand in his large, rough hand. As he gripped it tightly, he quietly remarked, "Alana's hands always were cold."

Mom had brought her flute with her, and it wasn't long before the room was filled with the gentle sounds of worship. You could feel the sting of death exit the room as the presence of Life entered. That's something I've noticed about death—that it's a spirit before it's a condition. It can creep into our lives while we're still living, and it can hang in the air over a room. But when Life comes and releases aliveness into the atmosphere, death has nowhere to hide.

Grandpa continued to grow stronger as the days turned into weeks. He was finally able to return home, and appeared to be alive again when we visited him at the farm a month later. An ice storm had just swept across the Midwest, leaving a slew of downed tree limbs in their yard and the surrounding fields. They would later have to cut down six of the nine trees that once towered over their house. Today, the shade is gone and a few stumps are all that remains, but Grandpa Stump is alive and well.

Upon exiting the shower, I got dressed and went outside. It was technically still winter, but the temperature had reached a comfortable seventy degrees. I entered the big silver barn, where Grandpa was working. He dropped what he was doing when he saw me, and we climbed into one of his trucks and began driving. As we turned out of the driveway, I glanced out the window, and was nearly lost in the beauty of the green fields set against a backdrop of brown trees, void of their leaves. The line of trees followed the horizon as far as the eye could see, swelling up and down to form a line of gentle rolling hills.

We drove down the road to another relative's house, where a tornado had swept through a few days before. One of their barns was collapsed and three others were damaged, but my grandparent's property a mile away was untouched. Grandpa told me that more than seventy people had come from miles around to help clean up on the Saturday following the storm. He had cleared his schedule for an entire week so that he could help from dawn to dusk. This is one of the things I find beautiful about Middle America: people don't think twice about throwing their lives out the window to help their neighbors.

I followed Grandpa inside the house, where my great-aunt and uncle were sitting at the kitchen table, buried in insurance paperwork. I headed back outside moments later to survey the damage. The feeling was bittersweet. While the destruction was untimely, it was beautiful to see how everyone had come together to help put things back together, a reminder that there is life after wreckage.

※ ※ ※

We spent the second half of the afternoon gathering scrap metal, which would be loaded onto a truck and taken to a recycling center in Springfield to be sold. The longer we worked, the more I realized how much I disliked working outside all day and getting my hands dirty. I enjoyed being close to my grandpa and spending time with him, I just didn't want to be like him; I didn't want to be a farmer. And a thought crossed my mind: I wonder how many of us want to be close to Jesus without actually becoming like Him?

I used to really like doing work around the farm when I was younger. I still do at times, but I've realized I only like it on my terms. I like the idea of working with my hands, but I don't like it as much when it comes time to actually do it. I like the idea of waking up early and doing work on the farm from dawn to dusk, until it comes time to actually do it—and then get up the next day and do it all over again. And I'm realizing that it's okay that I don't like this and other people do. I don't have to be a carbon copy of someone to be close to them. But when I think of this in terms of my faith, I realize I can't be close to Jesus without becoming like Him, and there is a part of me that likes His ideas in theory, but when I actually have to love someone I want to hate ... well, those are the moments when I find myself wondering if I really want to follow Jesus at all. The answer is still "yes," of course, but there are still moments where I feel in over my head, moments where I wonder if I would have said "yes" to Jesus if I had known about everything that would entail.

I think the first disciples may have felt this way too sometimes. Most of them simply responded to Jesus' request to follow Him, not knowing that His Kingdom would come through death on a cross, rather than a violent military takeover. When we read through the Gospels, we see that as Jesus' final hour was approaching, the disciples ended up scattered and disillusioned, and those who once followed Him made statements like, "We had hoped that he was the one who was going to redeem Israel" (Luke 24:21).

After awhile, Grandpa and I took a break from our work and drove a couple of miles to a small country store. As we entered, I noticed that the walls were covered with Bible verses and what some would call "inspirational artwork," but what I call "crap on the wall."

It was apparent that the owners of the store were Christians, but I think they might have been a little stuck in the past, and not just because they didn't accept credit cards. Four or five sheets of paper were taped to the wall behind the cash register. Written on each sheet of paper were the names of people who had written bad checks, the city they lived in, and the amount of money they owed. There were about a dozen names posted on the wall in chronological order; the first entry was more than a decade old. I also noticed that some of the people had come in after the fact and repaid the money they owed, but for one reason or another were still subject to this public shaming.

I stared at the wall while Grandpa paid with cash. There was something about the scene that just didn't seem right to me. I couldn't help but think of the time when Jesus said He wouldn't forgive us unless we choose to forgive others (Matthew 6:14-15).

If there's one thing I know, it's that I need to be forgiven—not just of the things I did before I knew Jesus, but of the things I've done since. I know I need forgiveness on even my best days, and I'll likely need forgiveness tomorrow. Because I've realized my own need, forgiving others is a whole lot easier than it used to be.

※ ※ ※

I awoke the next day to find winter had returned. Dark clouds hugged the sky overhead, as sleet fell to the ground intermittently, until late in the afternoon, when the clouds parted, allowing light to shine on the green grass and blossoms of the bradford pear trees behind the house. I walked toward the front window, as afternoon light filtered in through the curtains. Standing over the furnace vent, I allowed the air to warm my toes as I looked out at the blue sky that was emerging overhead.

It was then that I remembered that the sky is always blue, even when you can't see it through the clouds, [2] and I think our lives are often like that as well.

I stood at the window for awhile, drinking life in. It was a beautiful moment, one I never want to forget.

※ ※ ※

One afternoon, I decided to take Grandpa's truck for a drive through the fields. I didn't ask permission, which was probably my first mistake. I entered the open-air garage and opened the door of the truck, where I found the keys in the ignition. After backing out of the garage, I drove across the cattle guard into the first field, then across another cattle guard into a second field. I crossed over a dry creek bed and through a gate into a third field, and over a low water crossing into a fourth, and then I got stuck in the mud.

Grandpa was four fields away, working in one of the barns, and I knew he would be upset if he had to stop working to pull his truck out of the mud, so I tried frantically to get the truck unstuck by myself. I shifted through all of the gears and in and out of all-wheel drive for about twenty minutes, but my efforts only resulted in the tires getting buried deeper in the mud. After awhile, I did the only logical thing left to do—I gave up and walked a mile back to the house in shame.

I broke the news to Grandma before sitting down on the couch to wait for

Grandpa. When he entered the house an hour later, she helped me break the news to him as gently as possible.

"You're across the creek? You know I sold that land to Ogden, right?"

I played dumb, grateful that we had averted the real issue of my taking the truck without permission.

We exited the house and made the short walk to the silver barn in silence. Grandpa poked around in the dark for awhile, until he found a heavy-duty chain. We exited the barn and climbed up on to the tractor. He was in the seat; I was on top of the right wheel well, just like when I was a kid. We backed out of the barn and Uncle Paul joined us, taking a seat on top of the opposite wheel well. Without a word, we drove into the field, across both of the cattle guards, dry creek bed, low water crossing, and through the mud until we reached the truck, which was apparently on Kenny Ogden's land.

Grandpa and Uncle Paul climbed down from the tractor and began to hook the chain to the truck. I didn't move from my seat on top of the tractor. Most of the time, when you get yourself into a mess, you aren't qualified to get yourself out.

Within minutes, the truck was not only out of the mud, but the damage I had caused in my frantic attempts to fix the mess I had created had been reversed as well. I kept waiting for Grandpa to get angry, but he never did. He simply fixed my mess, and then life went on as normal.

I think we often try to get out of our messes on our own because we're afraid of bringing them to God. And I think the reason why we're afraid is because we have this picture of God as harsh and angry; we're afraid He'll get mad at us if He sees our brokenness. Which is kind of funny, since He already sees all of our junk and loves us in spite of it. We often think that God is mad at us, when all He wants to do is fix our mess and help us keep from getting stuck in the mud the next time around.

Nothing was said about my mess that night, but the next morning I was told to go outside and wash the truck within minutes of my feet hitting the floor. I splashed water on my face, pulled on my boots, and exited the house without coffee. As I approached the truck, I realized it was much dirtier than I had thought, but that didn't matter so much; I was just grateful it wasn't stuck anymore. As I took a brush and began to scrub the mud off, I realized the truck wouldn't have been nearly as muddy if I would have asked for help the moment it got stuck. Ironically, it was my efforts to fix and cover up my mess that made it all the more visible.

This world is a messy place. Sometimes, we get dirty. It's unavoidable, really, regardless of how hard we try to keep ourselves clean and spotless and pure. We simply don't possess any of those qualities, and we're not capable of obtaining them on our own. We're not innocent. We're not blameless. We're not pure. This is the reality of the human condition, and the reason why Jesus came. He was clean, spotless, pure, and blameless. He was innocent when we were guilty. We were without hope, but something remarkable happened—Jesus took the weight of our sin, guilt, and shame on Himself. But He didn't stop there—He took His innocence and wrapped it around us, clothing us in His righteousness. This is what it means to "be made new" (2 Corinthians 5:17). Just like Grandpa Stump used the tractor to pull the truck out of the mud without getting stuck himself, Jesus came to us while we were stuck in the mud. He got down in the mud with us, pulled us out, and cleaned us off—all without getting mud on Himself. Jesus took our death upon Himself, so that we could be made alive. [3]

I remember when I came alive for the first time. One moment, I was dirty. The next, I was clean. I felt so spotless, so pure—but that feeling didn't last long.

As long as we're living between creation and redemption, we're going to get dirty. I think that's why the Apostle Paul felt compelled to write a letter to the Christians who lived in Galatia, to tell them to stay on the path that led them to the Kingdom to begin with (Galatians 3:3), to keep coming back to Jesus.

You were made alive when you surrendered your life to Jesus for the first time. In that moment, He didn't just wash off your dirt, He made you new. There is no need to be made new more than once. You don't have to get saved again every Sunday morning and Wednesday night. Just keep coming back to Jesus, so He can wash off the dirt that continues to accumulate as we go through life.

I stood in the shower moments later, letting the water wash over me. It cleaned off all the dirt, and reminded me of the time when Jesus got down in the dirt and washed the crud of the world off the feet of His friends (John 13:3-14). And I thought back to that morning, when I awoke to the sweet presence filling the house, as though God had moved a few steps further into my awareness. I had opened my ears to the birds chirping outside the open window, breathing in the scent of spring as my eyes adjusted to the light. The grass was green, the trees were budding, the flowers were blooming; new life was showing its face as far as the eye could see. I have yet to find a feeling in this world that compares to waking up to God's presence. I've experienced this feeling in a variety of places, from a Missouri farmhouse to the mountains of Colorado. But I've also experienced it at home in Texas, in the middle of the mundane. Sometimes it's harder to recognize the feeling when life is in the way, but if you're still, you can almost taste it: The King of the Universe, sitting beside your bed, waiting for you to wake up so He can enjoy creation with you.

Even if it's just going to be another day at the office, there's so much beauty all around us. If only we could clear our minds of all the stuff that doesn't really matter and allow God to tune our hearts to sing His praise. Then our eyes might be opened, so that we can see His work of redemption unfolding all around us, and even join in the process. Perhaps then we could escape the concrete jungle we often find ourselves caught in. It's possible to live a life of adventure without ever physically taking flight, without abandoning those closest to us in search of what has been right in front of us all along.

※ ※ ※

I was sitting in the living room with Grandma one afternoon when the phone rang. Moments later, I was sent outside to let Grandpa know there was a man waiting to talk to him. I tried the garage first, but it was empty, so I headed for the barn. He wasn't there either, but I found him in the field behind the barn, loading scrap metal onto the tractor. He looked up as I approached.

"Grandpa, there's a guy on the phone for you."

"Huh?" he yelled, in typical fashion.

"There's a guy on the phone for you!" I yelled, louder this time.

He nodded, motioning toward the tractor.

Grandpa followed me as I climbed on top of the wheel well, claiming the tattered leather seat. He pulled down on the throttle, and we sped off toward the house. I remembered when I was a kid, climbing up on his knee to go for a ride on the tractor. I remember being afraid of the massive wheels, which seemed even larger back then. As we made our way back to the house, I held on tight, until I realized I wasn't afraid anymore.

CHAPTER 7

WHERE DEATH MEETS LIFE

I used to think I needed to feel new to be new,
but now I know faith isn't about how I feel.

I awoke early on Sunday morning, slowly making my way out of bed. Grandpa was already wide awake, of course, sitting in his chair in the living room as I entered. Continuing into the kitchen, I started my coffee before taking a seat at the table with a book. It wasn't long before the rain made its way from heaven to earth, falling steadily but gently to the ground below.

A few hours later, I was on my way to Springfield to catch the last of three services at my former church, James River Assembly. It's been years since my family attended there, so I don't remember it, but I like to attend church there as often as I can.

I was only a few miles away from the farm when the rain stopped and the sun poked its head out from behind the clouds, shining down on the earth below as colors danced across the fields. I passed few cars the first hour, so I assumed everyone was either already at church or sleeping off their hangover from the night before. Isn't it interesting how quick we are to make such broad judgements? I do this a lot, and I should probably stop.

The light was gone by the time I made it to Springfield. I entered the church and found a seat in one of the back corners of the sanctuary. Before the service, a commercial played for spontaneous water baptism, which would take place after the service.

Have you ever had one of those moments where you just knew you needed to do something, even though you couldn't explain why? This was one of those moments for me. I had been baptized a few times before, but it didn't mean much to me back then. I remembered that my pastor back in Dallas says you should be baptized *after* you truly believe in Jesus, and I wasn't sure if I had done that or not, because I don't remember the exact moment when I began to believe.

After the service ended, I approached an authority figure and told him I would like to be baptized. I was given a change of clothes, and was led backstage with a small group of people, most of whom had just made the decision to follow Jesus during the service. I was the last of five to be immersed in the baptismal tank. When I came up, I felt new. I also felt cold, so I quickly changed clothes before heading to my car.

As I approached the front door of the church, I was surprised to find that it was raining again. This time, however, it was absolutely pouring. I stood there in my dry clothes for a moment before casually walking to my car, which was located toward the back of the near empty parking lot. Soaking wet, I climbed inside my car and dried off with some old napkins that I found in the glove compartment. I sat there in silence for a moment, soaking in the feelings of newness. I cannot describe these feelings, other than I felt the love of God washing over every part of me. It reminded me of the place in Scripture where Jesus said, *Indeed, the water I give them will become in them a spring of water welling up to eternal life* (John 4:14b).

I didn't know how long the feeling would last, and I wanted to treasure it in my heart and never let it go. It wasn't until later that I realized the newness wasn't just a feeling I was experiencing in the moment—it was actually me! It was a picture of who I had become, and I felt as though I was coming alive for the very first time.

Bob the Freedom Guy says Jesus died to exchange the life in Him for the death in us. He came to make all things new—creation and all created things. He breathes life into dead places and speaks things into existence that did not previously exist (Romans 4:17).

We like new. New changes us. I think that's why God offers us new mercies every morning (Lamentations 3:22-23), because each day is different. It isn't that yesterday's mercies are inadequate, they were just for—well, yesterday.

My baptism wasn't really a big deal on the surface level. None of my family or friends were there, so I didn't know any of the people who were crowded around the baptismal tank. But for some reason, I felt like I was surrounded by family. I didn't know the man who led me under the water and brought me up again, but I felt that he loved me, as if we had grown up together. I hope I get to see him again someday. I guess we'll have plenty of time in eternity to trade stories of our lives on earth. We'll talk about that rainy day in Springfield when I walked into that church building, not far from where my physical birth took place. We'll talk about how fitting it was that our paths crossed there, about the fresh experience of new life he immersed me into. There are some things in our lives that don't seem like much at the time; it's only later that we are hit with the reality that everything has changed.

※ ※ ※

Like with any feeling, the newness began to fade. A few days later, I found myself feeling like I needed to be made new all over again. I decided that getting out of the house for a few hours might help, so I got in my car, made my way down the driveway, and turned toward Lamar, where I would purchase a few items I didn't need from the local Walmart. I have this problem where I buy things I don't need when I'm feeling stressed or depressed, and this time was no exception. Some people medicate their pain with drugs or alcohol; I drive to Walmart and wander aimlessly. This isn't the only way I deal with my pain, just one of the more socially acceptable methods.

As I made the ten-mile drive into the town of four thousand, I passed a tiny clapboard house, where a man who would one day become a U.S. President was born. As I drove the streets of the small Missouri town, I thought of all the people who have accomplished great things in this world, and how many of them have come from obscure places like this. I suppose this is why Jesus came from Nazareth, a place that people thought was incapable of producing anything good (John 1:46). Interestingly enough, that seemingly insignificant town would produce the greatest game changer this world has ever seen.

I arrived back at the farm feeling accomplished after my trip into town. I don't remember what I bought, which just proves how much I didn't need it. Grandma and I sat down in the living room and she began telling me a story about a guy named Rick, who used to live on a neighboring farm a few miles down the road. He grew up in Southwest Missouri before making his way to college at Purdue in Indiana.

Marilyn, a native of the Hoosier State, naturally chose Purdue as well, and it wasn't long before their paths crossed. They married soon after, and he brought her home to Missouri, where they lived in the big house with the pond and gazebo for decades. They had a family and grew old and navigated their way through the ups and downs of life, until one day, when Rick found a tumor on his shoulder.

Life changed after that, as the cancer spread. Rick began to grow weaker and weaker, and it became more and more apparent that his time on this side of eternity was limited. Sometimes, he would get in his truck and drive down to my grandparent's house, knock on their door, and sit down with them in their living room. They would share stories, talking about everything but the cancer. He loved coming there because they helped him forget the pain for a few hours.

Rick and Marilyn's son had left home years earlier and joined the Army. He dated a girl off and on for nearly eight years, before casually asking if she would marry him. She said "yes," and they began planning the wedding.

Rick had always wanted to see his son get married. His body quickly failing, he and Marilyn made the drive from Missouri to Indiana, where they laughed and cried with their son and his new bride, helping them celebrate the best day of their lives. A few months after the wedding, Rick slipped into eternity.

That was a year ago. Today, Marilyn spends her days alone in the big house, while the rest of her family goes about their lives, hundreds of miles away in Indiana.

As I sat there, in the same chair where Rick used to sit to forget all that was wrong in the world, I remembered that Jesus calls us to care for the widows and orphans (James 1:27), to visit them and be present with them in their pain. He calls us to do what we can to correct the injustice in their world, even while we're waiting for Him to correct the injustice in our own. He calls us to love them until they make it to eternity, until they make it to the Wedding Day.

CHAPTER 8

WRESTLING WITH GOD

*I used to get my identity from what I did, but now I know
that God wants to be the one to tell me who I am.*

I left the farm early the following Sunday morning, hours before the sun came up.
I crossed the state line and ventured across the plains, into Central Kansas. I was
planning on surprising my friends Henry and Michell, who pastor a church in a town
called Great Bend, but when I arrived three hundred miles later, I was informed that
they were on a beach somewhere in Texas.

I was a little disappointed as I walked through the doors of their church,
knowing they wouldn't be there. The service wasn't very well attended. There were
only eighteen of us, and I didn't know anyone, but the entire congregation soon
introduced themselves. One lady even remembered my name from a brief meeting
six months earlier, even though I didn't remember hers.

We drank coffee, sang a few songs, prayed for one another, and then a guy named
Rick—who was a biker—got up and preached for nearly an hour. I could tell he
really loved Jesus, because he cried when he prayed. Tears flowed freely down his
cheeks and into his thick biker beard.

The church may not have had big numbers in terms of attendance, but the people
who were there had big hearts. It was obvious that they really loved Jesus, and each
other as well. I think they might have loved me too, even though they had no clue
who I was an hour before.

I remember one woman who was struggling under the weight of a physical pain of some sort. She cried as she talked about how she just wished the pain would go away. She had read in her Bible about Jesus healing people and longed to be healed herself. After several weeks of prayer with no results, she grew so frustrated that she threw her Bible on the ground. It fell open to Isaiah 58, where she read about light breaking forth like the dawn and healing appearing quickly. [1]

Another man stood up and talked about a time when he got so mad at God that he burned his Bible. As the best-selling book of all time went up in flames, he said he sensed God telling him, "You can burn that book, but you can't burn My Word."

While I don't concur with his decision in the moment, I appreciate that he was honest enough to talk about his struggles. He has another Bible now—which he hasn't burned—and while he still struggles at times, He's fully convinced that God cares about the smallest details of his life.

Two hours later, the service was over. I lingered for a bit before driving a few blocks to Henry and Michell's house. I pulled into their driveway and climbed over the two-foot fence into their backyard. As I sat down on the back steps of their empty house, I knew there wasn't much I could do but laugh at the situation.

I've known Henry and Michell for most of my life. I grew up alongside their kids in Austin for several years, before we scattered across the Midwest. We ended up in North Dallas; they ended up in Central Kansas. I know parts of their story that the general public doesn't, such as the fact that they rarely ever leave town for extended periods of time. I was glad they were finally taking a vacation; I just wished it hadn't come at the same time as my surprise visit. I sat on their back steps for awhile, taking in the rhythms of grace that saturated the property.

I had taken the time to plan everything perfectly, down to the smallest details. I would surprise my friends and perhaps spend a few days with them. I had even picked up a bag of coffee when I stopped for breakfast in Wichita. The night before, I was so excited; I couldn't sleep. I was excited to see my friends, excited for the adventure of driving across the plains in the middle of the night on two hours of sleep, and excited about this new season of life that I had stumbled upon. But when the moment came, things turned out nothing like how I had planned. I was quite disappointed, and even considered wrestling with God a little myself, until I realized that I had gotten exactly what I wanted: to be spontaneous. I had even spent considerable amounts of time planning to be spontaneous with my surprise visit to Kansas, but I guess the real surprise was on me.

I think sometimes we say we want to live by faith and trust God, when we really don't at all. We think our lives are boring, and we need to escape on some sort of adventure in order to break free, but I dare to question if it is possible for us to find adventure and live unscripted in the familiar and mundane places of our lives.

I was only in Great Bend for three hours before I called my friend Josh in Oklahoma and told him I was driving another three hundred miles to Shawnee that night. He was expecting me to drop in later in the week, but we quickly adjusted our plans to align with my unfolding adventure.

Josh is a few years older than I am, and runs a successful web design business from home. He has been married to Elizabeth since shortly after their high school graduation, and they have two young, naturally caffeinated kids. Josh told me one of the reasons he loves working from home is he never misses anything; he's always there with his wife and kids in their small shotgun house, which he affectionately refers to as *the circus*.

I remember going to the circus once as a kid, but I can't remember if I liked it or not. I guess we don't remember all of our adventures.

I'm not sure how Josh maintains his sanity, since he spends the bulk of his time at home. If it were me, I'd have to get out at least once a week and find some adventure or something, but perhaps that is actually part of the problem. What I mean is, we live in a society where we always have to be doing things in order to be considered important. But what if God created us to live and move and have our being in Him alone? What if He desires to be our source of identity, rather than the things we put on our resumes? What if the primary reason we were created was not to create, but simply to be?

We were made in the image of a God who is complete in Himself, but still took on the work of creation. God created us and everything around us in six days, and then took a day off. While some argue about whether these seven days were metaphorical or literal, we can see from the account in Genesis that God took on and finished a creative project that brought Him deep joy. Because He was complete in Himself, God didn't need to take on this project, but I think it brought Him a deep sense of satisfaction. Not a "I've finally done something to prove I'm valuable" sort of satisfaction, but the type of satisfaction that stems from creating out of a place of security, rather than trying to produce something to redeem yourself.

So we have a God who is completely secure and doesn't need anything, but decides to create the world and everything in it, including two people who live in unbroken relationship with Him. His original plan was for these two people—Adam and Eve—to reproduce and fill the earth with offspring that shared this unbroken fellowship with the Creator. Adam and Eve were in perfect relationship with God, which means they would reproduce His nature in full, not just fragments of His nature.

God is secure in His identity, and He designed us to receive our identity from Him. He likes to create for the sheer joy of creating, and we were made in His image. The only problem is, our connection with God was broken, and even though we've since been reconnected, the rope that holds us together is often twisted and frayed. We're still made in the image of God, so we still have this thing in us that longs to create, but a drivenness that wasn't there before now accompanies it. Now, instead of creating just to create, we create because we feel we have to produce. In fact, for many of us, the whole creative process has been reduced to production-focused formulas, and has become quite stressful and even lifeless at times. Instead of creating because we're in relationship with God and that's what we do, we drive ourselves to produce because we're seeking to redeem ourselves and somehow recapture what Adam and Eve lost. Because our activity is flowing from hearts lacking identity, instead of hearts fully alive in God's love, everything we produce is flawed, and it doesn't satisfy us. And when we do actually feel satisfaction from our work, it's fleeting. Our motives are jacked up, we're not satisfied, and we don't even consider taking a day off. On top of all of this, we have no idea how we got so disconnected from God in the first place, and we're still trying to figure out how to reconnect ourselves.

In Genesis 1, we keep seeing the phrase *And God saw that it was good* repeated time after time, which tells us that creating things is not the core problem. The core problem is this: We were designed to receive our identity from the top down, not the bottom up. God never intended for us to create things and then look to them for our identity. But we do this all the time, which is why we have a bunch of Christians running around doing things in God's name without His heart.

We, as humans, are wired in a way where we need something outside of us to tell us who we are, to affirm our identity. We know this to be true, whether consciously or not, because we are always looking to different things to tell us who we are. We rarely ever look inside ourselves, and when we do, we often don't find anything. This is because the human race became empty when Adam and Eve exchanged life for death. Around that time, we began looking for meaning in created things, rather than the Creator.

What I am trying to say is we need something outside of us to tell us who we are—not just something, but Someone. When we restore our broken relationship with God, He tells us who we are, He becomes the source of our identity, and then we can get back to creating for the right reasons again. Work is a gift from God, an act of worship—until we make it our identity, and thus turn it into an idol. When we form idols in our hearts, we look to them to define us. We begin to receive our sense of value from how much we can produce, which is why we work fourteen-hour days and are still connected to the office like a crash victim on life support when we walk through our front doors at night. Work is good, and certainly necessary, but if it becomes our primary focus and source of identity rather than God Himself, it will eventually destroy us.

Getting rid of the idolatrous portion of work doesn't mean we stop our work altogether, but that we start getting our identity from the right place again. This way, everything we do flows from a place of knowing who we are—sons and daughters of the King. Everything we do should start from this place, whether it is vocational work or the "good works" we do to reveal the Father to a tired and burnt out generation.

Of course, not everyone has the luxury of working from home, as my friend Josh does. Going to an office each day and putting in long hours doesn't mean work is your god. Sometimes you've got to take calls at night, and that doesn't automatically make your heart full of idols. It's all about where we get our identity from, and I've learned that I'm better off when I focus on being a child of God who happens to work as a writer, rather than a writer who happens to be a child of God.

We live in a society that lies to us an awful lot. It tells us it's not enough to live a simple story, to first and foremost be good husbands and fathers. It tells us we must do something big before we can become someone big. But my friend Josh is perfectly content with staying in his house all day because he's realized that his highest calling is to be a child of God, a husband, and a father. He doesn't have to go out looking for adventure, because his wife and kids are his adventure.

This is all very easy to read about, and even theologically affirm. The real challenge comes in the trenches of life, when our identity as children of God is challenged by the systems of the world—this present age of chaos and darkness.

Life is a long and brutal assault on your heart by the one [satan] who knows what you can be and fears it. [2]

✳ ✳ ✳

There's a guy at my church named Mark, who I deeply respect. Mark works full-time building sets that we use in our services and for special events. I worked with him in the warehouse once. He spent much of the morning covered in sawdust and dripping sweat, as he hammered nails into blocks of wood. It reminded me of Jesus, and how He spent decades working with His dad as a carpenter and only three years in full-time ministry.

It's interesting how the Bible doesn't tell us a whole lot about Jesus' early days. I wonder if there just wasn't much to tell? The early years of His existence may have been boring and mundane. When we read through the Gospels, we find that Mark and John skip Jesus' birth and childhood entirely. Matthew tells us a little about His birth, but doesn't tell us much after that, except that his family moved around a lot before finally settling down in Nazareth. The story then abruptly cuts off, as Matthew skips a few decades. When he does resume writing, it isn't about Jesus, but a pastor named John who was apparently a Baptist. [3]

Only Luke gives us the full backstory of Jesus' birth—at least, all that is recorded in Scripture. I wonder what prompted Luke to pay attention to these details? I imagine the four of them—Matthew, Mark, Luke, and John—sitting around in a coffee house somewhere, discussing how they should tell The Story. Luke started bringing up the backstory about Jesus' birth—the little details, such as Him and the Baptist named John being cousins. The other guys must have looked at him like he was crazy, and perhaps patted him on the head and said something like, "Alright, Luke. You write about that stuff. We'll stick to the parts of The Story that people will actually care about."

Little did they know that Luke would pen profound words like, *For my eyes have seen your salvation,* and *Glory to God in the highest heaven, and on earth peace to those on whom his favor rests,*[4] words that are still echoing around the world today.

Luke told the parts of The Story that the others left out, and then joined in to talk about the Baptist pastor who lived in the desert and ate bugs, who was given more airtime than the Savior entering the world. God wrapped Himself in flesh, entered our world, grew up in a normal home around normal people, followed in His earthly father's footsteps, and then used a guy who ate bugs to proclaim that He was the Savior of the world. Am I missing something?

I think sometimes, in the evangelical world, we're told to take things at face value and believe them simply because they're in the Bible, even if we don't understand them. I like the idea that The Story is full of mystery and there are some things we will never fully understand, but the danger of this is we often believe things simply because we know we're supposed to, without taking the time to actually think about them. I'm not saying we shouldn't believe the things we learn in church, but I've noticed that far too often, pastors expect the people they are teaching to simply take their word for it, without thinking about it for themselves. Pastors are people, just like us. Hopefully yours is one of the good ones who gets things right most of the time, but if they are human, there is a good chance they miss it every now and then.

I was in the home of a pastor in Salt Lake City once, talking about the ups and downs of ministry. He is originally from South Africa, and told me that very few pastors in the West teach their congregation to think critically. Instead, they expect them to take whatever they say at face value and "apply it to their lives," without ever searching the Scriptures for themselves. It's not so much that critical thinking is discouraged, it just isn't encouraged. The reasons for this vary, but I think a lot of pastors are insecure and don't want people to question them. They think (often subconsciously) that questioning will lead to rebellion, which is interesting, because I have found that not allowing questions is a much quicker way to start a riot than welcoming them.

Welcoming questions and allowing people to respectfully challenge what you are teaching communicates that you don't think you have all the answers.

People don't like people who act like they have all the answers. They come across as larger than life, and it's hard to trust people who act like they're better than you, even if they don't do it on purpose. Admitting that you don't have all the answers and welcoming questions creates a culture of vulnerability, which leads to connection and trust. When people feel they can trust you, they're able to be vulnerable as well.

When we don't encourage people to ask questions, we deny them the opportunity to have their own experience with God. Perhaps this is why so many people walk away from the faith when they enter college and don't return until years later—if they return at all.

If you read the Gospels for more than five minutes, you'll see that Jesus rarely answered questions directly. He often told stories, or answered questions with another question. I think this is because He wanted people to still be pondering the things He talked about when they went home. I think He wanted them to have their own encounter with the Father, and perhaps even wrestle with Him a little.

It's okay to struggle and wrestle with God. He doesn't expect you to take everything you're told about Him at face value. Even if your beliefs are misguided, He invites you to wrestle with Him, because He knows that you have to be close to Him in order to do so.

I love the story of the man who brought his son who had been sick from childhood to Jesus.

Jesus simply looked at him and said that He could heal his son if he would just believe.

The man began to cry. "Lord, I believe, but help my unbelief!" he exclaimed through tears.

This man was struggling. There was a war going on within him; he was wrestling with God. He wanted to believe, but for some reason could not. At least, not fully. I think it's interesting that Jesus' response was not, "Go get rid of your doubts and come back when you really believe." Rather, He responded to his honest statement by healing his son. I don't think the man wrestled with God as much after that.[5]

⚹ ⚹ ⚹

I was lying on the couch at Josh and Elizabeth's house when their dog, Cookie, suddenly ran across the room and jumped into my lap. She didn't really seem to care what I was doing, all she knew was that she wanted to play. We began to wrestle. She bit my finger and I threw her up in the air and caught her. I couldn't tell if she really liked wrestling, or if it just made her mad. Josh told me she loved it, but I think it was a little of both. After a few minutes, Cookie abruptly stopped wrestling. Lying down at my side, she stretched her neck across my chest and closed her eyes. In a moment, she went from wrestling to completely at peace at my side.

I think there are times when we have to stop striving to get our questions answered and simply lay our heads on God's chest and receive the perfect peace that only He can give.

Cookie is one of those little dogs who thinks she's a big dog. I think a lot of us are that way, too. We think we're big and strong and independent, that we can get by on our own, while God looks at us and sees us as cute, but weak animals who don't really know what we're doing. I think this is why God consistently refers to us as "sheep" throughout Scripture. If you know anything about sheep, you know that they aren't the most intelligent animals; they require constant guidance and aren't able to carry heavy loads. I think a lot of us are afraid to admit that we don't have everything figured out, that we need constant guidance, and that we've been carrying things we were never intended to carry. But when God calls us sheep, He's not insulting us. It's not like He is looking at us and saying, "Oh, those poor, stupid humans. What would they do without Me?" Rather, I think He calls us sheep so that we'll realize that it's okay to be fragile, weak, and dependent on Him.

I remember one night, when it was pouring rain. Elizabeth and the kids had already gone to bed, but Josh and I were still wide awake in the living room. We became so lost in conversation that we forgot about Cookie, who was tied up on her leash outside, completely exposed to the elements. When Josh realized Cookie was still outside, he abandoned our conversation and ran out the back door. He returned moments later, soaking wet and holding an even wetter dog, who was covered in mud and shivering from the cold. Taking her directly to the bathtub, he washed the mud away and wrapped her in a warm towel, then handed her to me to hold. It wasn't long before she jumped out of my arms and ran to the back door, begging to go outside and get muddy all over again.

I think many of us have forgotten about those stormy nights when we were stuck in the mud. We've forgotten how Jesus came and rescued us, how He cleaned us up and wrapped us in His loving embrace. A thought enters our minds, or we see something that catches our eye, and we jump out of His arms to go play in the mud again. Before long, we realize we're dirty and helpless, so we cry out for Jesus to come and rescue us again. And He does, of course, because He is faithful to us, even when we're not faithful to Him. This is one of the most beautiful truths about grace.

I don't understand why God doesn't get frustrated with us and leave us in the mud, or why He doesn't condemn or accuse us. It's probably a good thing that we don't get to make up the terms for grace. If we did, we'd probably set a point where it runs out, but God's ways are higher than our ways. He doesn't condemn or accuse us because it's not who He is. Besides, the enemy of our souls is already pretty good at that.

God's love is perfect, and He is not like our earthly fathers, who could only offer us the best of their broken, fragmented love. If you've had a father that was less than perfect, it's okay; they all are. When you stop expecting them to be perfect, you'll set them up to surprise you—just like my grandpa did when I got the truck stuck in the mud back on the farm. There will be moments like these, when the fathers we know capture and display the Father's heart, but there will also be moments when they wound us deeply. That's the way the cards will fall, because we're all still in the process of learning to love well.

⚹ ⚹ ⚹

It's basically a sin to talk about wrestling with God without talking about Jacob, so turn with me in your Bible to Genesis 28 and 32.

In Genesis 28, Jacob had just tricked his father, Isaac, into blessing him by dressing up as his brother, Esau. Since Isaac was old and couldn't see very well, Jacob's plan worked—until Esau found out and tried to kill him. So Jacob skipped town, traveling until nightfall. He then found a rock, which made a great pillow, and fell asleep. While Jacob was sleeping, God appeared to him in a dream and told him that He was going to bless everyone on the planet through his family line (Genesis 28:14). Then God told Jacob, *I am with you and will watch over you wherever you go, and I will bring you back to this land. I will not leave you until I have done what I have promised you* (Genesis 28:15).

Suddenly, Jacob awoke from his dream, and said aloud, "I didn't realize this before, but God is here!" He was scared, so he said aloud, "Wow, this place is awesome! This is the house of God, the place where heaven and earth meet."

He then went back to sleep. What an odd thing to say.

The next morning, Jacob took his pillow (which was a rock), and poured oil on top of it. Then, he changed the name of the city from Luz to Bethel, which means "House of God."[6] It appears that Jacob was trying to buddy up to God, because his manipulative nature surfaces in what he did next.

Jacob made a promise to God, that if God would watch over him on his journey, give him food and clothing, and allow him to return safely to his home (where his brother was waiting to kill him), then Jacob would give God ten percent of everything he received, which is kind of like what we do today when we tithe. The only difference is, Jacob wasn't doing this to worship God, which should be our motive. Instead, he was essentially saying, "Hey God, let's make a deal."

It's important to note that God had already said He would watch over Jacob, but Jacob added the part about food and clothing. He might as well have said something like, "Hey God, if you make sure I have food to eat and clothes to wear, then I'll give you ten percent. (Side Note: Any time "You do *this*; I'll do *that*," language is used, we're likely being manipulative.) For Jacob's grandfather Abraham, who initiated the practice of tithing[7], giving ten percent to God was an act of worship, a statement of belief and trust in God. But Jacob manipulated it for his own purposes, which was really no different than twisting God's arm. Jacob also inserted the ability to return home as if he had never wronged his brother into the deal. In essence, he wanted back what he had lost due to his sin, but without repentance. God told Jacob that He would bring him back to the land where he had the dream; He never said anything about Jacob returning home.

What is even more shocking than Jacob's audacity (he tried to manipulate God in the same way he manipulated his father and brother), is that God did not object.

Brian Zahnd, who pastors a church in Missouri, says that God was not giving in to Jacob's manipulation; rather, He was getting His foot in the door in Jacob's life. This would not be Jacob's last encounter with God.[8]

Jacob continued on his journey, got married (to two women, actually, but we don't have time to get into that part of the story), and ended up on the short end of an unhealthy relationship with his father-in-law. Sometime around two decades after his dream and "deal" with God, God told him to return home (Genesis 31:3). It's interesting that Jacob returning home was never part of God's initial promise to Jacob, but because Jacob put it in his deal with God, God held him to it.

We now find ourselves in Genesis 32, with Jacob on his way home. He sent messengers ahead of him, to his brother Esau, which was probably a good idea. Showing up unannounced after twenty years might not have gone over so well. In today's culture, we would send an email or a tweet, but they didn't have the Internet back then, because Al Gore hadn't invented it yet. [9]

Jacob also told the messengers to tell Esau that he had acquired great wealth and possessions over the years, which at first glance could mean he either wanted to bribe Esau or simply brag. [10] But when we read on to Genesis 32:20, we see that Jacob's intention was to bribe his brother. I love the way the messengers responded when they returned to Jacob: *We went to your brother Esau, and now he is coming to meet you, and four hundred men are with him.* (Genesis 32:6).

This scared Jacob, as it should have, so he divided his traveling party into two groups. His logic was that if Esau came and attacked one group, perhaps the other group would escape unharmed. After that, Jacob prayed. It's pretty easy for us, safe in our homes, snuggled up by the fireplace with our Bibles, to look at that and say, "Well there's the problem—if he would have only prayed first" ... but let's be honest, if you and I heard that an army was coming to attack us, we would probably split the group too, only to later realize that even our most well-crafted schemes are useless if God isn't with us.

We can see in Jacob's prayer, found in Genesis 32:9-12, that he is beginning to be transformed. That's often what happens when you come to the end of your rope.

All of the discipleship methods in the world can only give *information*; it takes coming to the end of yourself and having a true encounter with God to produce *transformation*. And as we journey on with God, as we learn to trust Him more deeply, that is how we become more like Him. The Apostle Paul makes it very clear that only God can produce both our initial and ongoing transformation. [11] Information—books, sermons, Bible studies, *Creation & Redemption*—are good and helpful, but only if they lead us to a place of deeper trust in Jesus. Otherwise, we're just wasting our time.

Jacob's prayer reveals that he is coming to the end of his rope, though not fully. His heart is being softened, but he has not reached the peak of initial transformation yet.

I am unworthy of all the kindness and faithfulness you have shown your servant. I had only my staff when I crossed this Jordan, but now I have become two camps. Save me, I pray, from the hand of my brother Esau, for I am afraid he will come and attack me, and also the mothers with their children (Genesis 32:10-11).

Jacob had a realization that everything good in his life had been given to him by the grace of God, coupled with a revelation that he was not worthy of any of it. So many different religions (and many Christians) focus on worthiness and being "good enough" to get to God, but in reality, we cannot be saved unless we first realize we are not worthy. The Gospel is not about us going up to God, but about God coming down to us. Upon realizing that he was not worthy, Jacob cried out to God to save him. Four thousand years later, this is the same manner in which we get saved. Salvation is not about raising your hand, coming to an altar, eating a cupcake, signing up for a class, or joining a church. There is nothing wrong with those methods, but there are countless Christians who have done all of this without coming to the end of their rope, crying out to God, and making the decision to trust Him with their lives until they see Him face-to-face. It would be fair to say that many who claim the title of "Christian" have encountered religion, even put their trust in religion, but never encountered Jesus.

We can also note from Jacob's prayer that he was not just concerned about his own life any longer, but also about the people around him. Innocent people would perish with him, for his sins, should Esau attack the caravan. But I have a feeling his primary concern was himself, and the mothers and children were an afterthought. It's pretty easy to sound spiritual, when you're really just a scoundrel who needs Jesus to save you from yourself.

The more obvious manipulative parts of Jacob's prayer are revealed at the beginning and the end. I like how the parts that revealed his transformation are right there in the middle—sandwiched in manipulation, if you will. I think a lot of us try to twist God's arm in a similar manner when we pray, and we should probably stop.

But we'll save that for another time.

Jacob then prayed, *"O God of my father Abraham, God of my father Isaac, Lord, you who said to me, 'Go back to your country and your relatives, and I will make you prosper'* (Genesis 32:9).

But you have said, 'I will surely make you prosper and will make your descendants like the sand of the sea, which cannot be counted'" (Genesis 32:12).

While there is nothing wrong with reminding God of what He has promised, it appears that Jacob is using an accusatory tone here. He's essentially saying, "What's the deal, God? You said that if I did this, then you would make me prosper. Well, I did this, but you don't seem to be keeping your end of the deal."

It should be noted that Jacob is reminding God of the parts of the deal that he added, not the parts that God initially offered him. God told Jacob that He would give him the land at Bethel, but Jacob took it a step further when he added in the part about returning to his *father's* land. It's amazing how God will give us what we want at times, simply because it's what we want.

I know this section is a bit more theological than the rest of this book has been, but it's the only way I know how to explain it. For the sake of time, I'll cut to the chase.

Jacob sent all of his people ahead of him to wine and dine Esau, so perhaps Esau would be merciful to him. Jacob was left alone, at the back of the caravan, in the middle of the night, when a strange man appeared and began wrestling with him (Genesis 32:22-24). When the man saw that he was not going to overpower Jacob, he reached out and touched his hip, immediately dislocating it. The two continued to wrestle.

"Let me go!" the man exclaimed.

"No," Jacob replied firmly, "I will not let you go until you bless me."

The two stopped wrestling. The man looked at Jacob. "Who are you?" he asked.

In that moment, the shame Jacob had struggled with all of his life came rushing back. He turned his eyes away from the man, hung his head, and quietly admitted, "I'm a deceiver."

The man shook his head. "Not anymore. From this moment on, you will be called 'Israel,' for you are a Prince with God and will share in His inheritance. You have wrestled with God and with men, and you have prevailed." He then blessed Jacob, and vanished as quickly as he had appeared.

Stunned by what had just happened, literally overnight, Jacob heard himself say aloud, "I have seen God face-to-face ... and my life is preserved."

You could almost add a question mark after Jacob said, "My life is preserved." I know if it had been me, I would have expected God to kill me over saving me; I would have doubted that His unconditional love was truly unconditional.

This whole time, Jacob had been wheeling and dealing with God, trying to get the better end of the deal, always fighting for control. Perhaps he had assumed he needed to earn God's favor before he could look Him in the eye. This would explain why Jacob was afraid at Bethel when He realized that God was present with him.

Jacob paused for a moment and gazed out over the horizon, as the light of a new day began to shine upon him. And then he left to go find the rest of his caravan, limping from his hip that was still dislocated.

I don't know if the man he wrestled with was actually God in the flesh or just an angel of some sort, but I do know that Jacob wrestled with God, and it saved his life.

Like most of us, Jacob had done a pretty good job of ruining His life. That's why God came to give him true life, because he couldn't obtain it on his own. Yet, Jacob thought there had to be conditions to God's unconditional offer, which is why he added to it. He wanted God's blessings, but he didn't trust that God was who He said He was. It was through wrestling with God that Jacob grabbed ahold of the true heart of the Father.

C.S. Lewis once said that *God sometimes seems to speak to us most intimately when He catches us, as it were, off our guard*[12], which is what He did to Jacob that night. I love when God does this, when He comes and cuts through the crap, right to the chase, when He shifts my perspective in a moment and leaves me completely speechless and in awe of who He is.

I wonder why the man blessed Jacob but didn't heal the hip he had dislocated. Perhaps he wanted to leave him with a scar that would always remind him of this part of his story; perhaps he wanted him to remember who he was before he encountered God, before his past was healed and his future secured.

This life is quickly fading, like a flower that is here today and gone tomorrow.

Don't be afraid to show emotion, to ask questions, to struggle, to believe, to dream, to feel. Embrace the story that God is writing through you. Don't seek to be anyone else. Remain aware of the fact that, at every waking moment, God is with you and He is for you. Take advantage of every opportunity to stand still in awe and wonder. Take in the beauty of the universe. Open up your heart and simply live. Don't allow yourself to become numb. Don't allow yourself to get swept away by the experiences of life. God wants to bless you, but you may have to fight for it. Not because God is holding out on you, but because He wants you to take hold of your true identity and leave the past behind.

CHAPTER 9

SEASONS

I used to think I had to figure out my path before leaving home,
but now I know it's okay to choose your direction at the intersection.

I talked to my friend, Christina, a few weeks ago, at a time when her story was struggling. Christina lives in a small town on the beach in Florida, though she recently spent five months in Africa, where she attended a Bible school for missionaries in training. We talked about her life, about how she's bored of living in Florida. She feels like she doesn't belong there, and she wants to escape to a place where she fits in better. She's doesn't want to slip into the mundaneness of a 9:00 to 5:00 job, her hopes and dreams buried somewhere out of sight. She longs to wake up in the morning without the uncertainty of the future slapping her in the face. She's really not asking for much, just to live a full life and not be afraid all the time.

We also talked about her life overseas, how it was so much different than life in America. The people in Africa don't have all the things that we have to fill our lives with. Many of them don't have much more than God and each other. Christina told me something changes inside of you when you go from a wealthy community in Florida to an impoverished community in Africa, only to find that the people there are actually happier than they are back home. It made her realize how fake and shallow she can be at times. It was the experience of a lifetime, though it nearly ate her alive. Upon returning home, Christina realized that she's not called to be a missionary to Africa at this point in her life.

We often have to discover who we are not before we can discover who we are.

God sometimes tells us how our stories are going to unfold, but most of the time, He just gives us clues along the way. It would be a lot easier to make decisions if God just told us what to do to make our stories align with His will, but I don't think that's what He wants. I think He would rather us embark on a journey with Him, into the great unknown, where we will learn to trust Him as our lives unfold. I'm glad God doesn't require us to always get things right the first time around. In fact, the Apostle Paul tells us that sometimes we have to try out a few different avenues before we discover what path God wants us to take (Romans 12:2b).

※ ※ ※

This past winter was unusually warm, even for Texas. We welcomed the mild weather, as we had just finished one of the hottest summers on record. The heat had taken its toll on the Lone Star State. Long before the first cold front arrived, the fields surrounding my neighborhood were brown and lifeless. It was hard to look out the window and see how thirsty the ground was from the prolonged dry season, and I think it hurt so much because it reminded me of my own life.

January slipped in through the side door, and it was then that something unusual happened—the fields began to turn green. Life was springing up all around us, at a time when everything was supposed to be dead.

I have learned that God likes to breathe life into dead places. He takes the dry, dirty places of our hearts, the places where we ache to be alive, the places where we've tried everything in our power to obtain that sense of aliveness, and in a moment, He breathes life into us that we could never obtain on our own.

※ ※ ※

I attended the young adults service at my church in Southlake the other night. I was with some friends, and we entered the sanctuary for what we thought would be just another service. We were wrong.

Jesus usually shows up when we gather to worship Him, but that night He showed up in a special way. At one point, the guy who was leading worship sang a song about how beautiful Jesus is, about how His eyes explode with light and sound and color, and we see His face in every sunrise. [1]

I closed my eyes during the song, and when I did, I saw myself on top of a ridge in the mountains of Colorado. I scanned the horizon, looking out across the vast, blue sky. Looking down, I saw the valley I used to walk in. I began to soar through the air, taking in the view of the valley below. I could see myself at various stages of life, trudging through the seemingly endless valley, unsure of whether or not I'd ever reach the mountain top. Somewhere along the journey, I had unknowingly begun climbing. Until one day, when I reached the top of the ridge, and looked down at where I had come from. The next thing I knew, I was back at church in Southlake. All of that happened during one worship song, which is why you should show up for church on time and take worship seriously.

※ ※ ※

My parents recently purchased new furniture for our living room. They put it on layaway, making weekly payments for a month or so. They knew they had to get rid of the old to make room for the new, so one Saturday morning, I awoke to find our living room was completely empty. I quickly ruled out the possibility that they had moved without telling me. When I went downstairs in search of coffee, I learned that a man from church had picked up our old couches while I was sleeping.

It was a bittersweet moment. The couches that had been the focal point of every home I had lived in for the past two decades were gone. The new was coming—it had been bought and paid for—but it had not yet arrived. Our old couches were making their way to a new home; the man from church was planning on giving them to his son, who was spreading his wings wider than ever before, as he prepared to move out on his own for the first time. The couches that once graced our home in our early days would now grace his apartment for his early days. New seasons were beginning, new memories would be made—both for us and for him.

※ ※ ※

Yesterday was a masterpiece, one of those days filled with all the things we so easily miss when we become tangled in routine. I spent the day with my family by my side, as we laughed and dreamed and let our hearts come alive again.

God came close and met me in a special way—not just once, but at numerous points throughout the day. Interestingly enough, I never opened the Bible once on that day. I didn't read any of the written story about creation and redemption, as I normally do. Instead, it came and knocked on my door. I experienced the redemption the Bible speaks of. In those ordinary, but holy moments, I couldn't remember any of the pain that life had thrown my way. Late in the afternoon, I found myself in the living room with my family. Our new couches had yet to arrive, so all the room contained was two chairs and a stereo system. A worship album was playing in the background, and I began to sing along. It was under my breath at first, but I found myself singing louder and louder, until I reached the top of my vocal range.

Something about this experience changed me in ways I can't quite put to words. It may not seem like much, but this was the first time in years I had sung in front of other people, even if it was only my family. In a moment, another one of the walls I had put up to hide who I really was came crashing to the ground.

I remember when my family used to drive to this little town in East Texas every month, back when we lived in Austin. Near the end of each visit, I would get up on stage at our friend's church and sing a song about Jesus. This was back before video cameras were commonplace, so we don't have any documentation, which is probably a good thing. I assume I was an average singer. Not good, but not bad either. Regardless of how I sounded, people loved listening to an eight-year-old sing about the Jesus he loved and longed to know. It was all just theory for me back then. I didn't have a relationship with Jesus; that wouldn't come until later on. But whatever I had, it was real, even though I didn't understand it.

I guess people loved when I sang was because of the sheer innocence of it. I didn't care how I looked or sounded; I just sang. I had been beaten down by life to some extent, but I didn't yet know what it meant to hide and be afraid all the time; I hadn't arrived at the place where I lived life wrapped in shame. When we see people living out of a place of innocence, it creates a deep longing to regain our own innocence, to go back in time to before life took its toll on us.

Though the memories have all but faded, I remember one girl in particular. While I don't recall the details of her story—or even her name—I remember that she was in the process of walking out of a troubled life of shame and shattered dreams. She heard me sing one day at the church in the little town in East Texas, and the next day she got up and sang a song of her own, which was a big deal for her. I had inspired someone to step out of their comfort zone, without even realizing it. How much more could I inspire others to greatness if I lived life on purpose? You don't have to be great to inspire someone to greatness, you just have to be intentional.

※ ※ ※

Christina is doing better now. In the last couple of weeks, she has started a new job and given her room a fresh coat of paint. She never packed up and moved away from the beachfront town near Jacksonville, but she doesn't need to, because life isn't boring anymore. She doesn't know exactly where she's headed, but at least she's not stuck running in place. This is the beginning of a new season for her, and she's ready to take on whatever life throws her way.

※ ※ ※

Last Friday night, I attended a night of worship at my church in Southlake. From the moment I entered the room, it felt like God was right there with us. I froze, as a sense of awe washed over me. I couldn't move—not because I was afraid, but because I didn't want to. In that moment, the storms of life seemed to vanish.

Several minutes passed before I gained my composure. I glanced around the room and realized I knew almost everyone present; the room was filled with friends ranging in age from seventeen to seventy. We huddled in that small room and sang to Jesus for over three hours. It was raw and messy and beautiful, and I think Jesus healed a lot of hearts that night.

I think when we pray, we often see it as more of something we have to do than something we get to do. But what if God simply wants us to walk into the room, lay our burdens on the floor, and pause for a moment as He washes us with His love? I don't think He wants us to walk up and down the shoreline, reading things off our list without ever stepping into the water. I think He would much rather us run into the ocean and let the waves slap us in the face, perhaps even knock us over.

※ ※ ※

My two favorite seasons are autumn and spring.

Autumn, because there is so much beauty in death. I can't get over the reality that a hillside of trees reach the peak of beauty right before their death. The colors explode in one final display, before giving way to the bleak nothingness that winter brings.

Spring, because that's when new life begins. The trees will bud, the birds will sing, the flowers will dance; winter never lasts forever. The trees die and come alive again year after year.

As the air grows warmer, we become aware that new life will soon break in all around us. We hope, wait, trust, and pray. We anticipate the end of the long winters that life tends to wrap around us in an attempt to blind us from seeing the truth. The dawn of a new day is coming, yet it is already here, closer than the very air we breathe.

Seasons always change, sometimes rather quickly. The moments we wish we could hold onto forever tend to slip out of our hands in the blink of an eye. Life has a way of sneaking up on us, sometimes getting the best of us, no matter how hard we strive to script everything perfectly.

I often find myself wishing I could fast forward through the boring parts of my life and press pause on the moments that matter the most. I've been through seasons where I worked all the time and longed for spare moments to write and have lengthy conversations over coffee. And I've been through other seasons where I was free to write as much as I wanted, but I found myself aching for a full-time job. When I tried to change one season, I typically wound up in the other, and I didn't catch on until I'd gone around the block a few times. We'll always find something wrong with the season we're in if we try hard enough, which is why we have to be content with wherever we are in life. This idea is incredibly simple, but it's a lot harder to work out in the real world.

Be free. Live unscripted. Embrace the adventure that lurks around every corner. Take a few risks. Don't be afraid to fall. Nearly every failure is fixable, except a life that was never lived.

CHAPTER 10

HALLWAYS

I used to think life was about arriving,
but now I know it's more about the journey.

Hallways. Some are warm and inviting. Others are dark and lonely. Life is kind of like a hallway sometimes, like a hallway inside of a hospital—cold, lonely, and poorly decorated.

It works like this: you have a dream, crunch some numbers, find out what form of action is needed to obtain it, and get to work. You're standing in front of a door, one you've never seen before, and your mind is running wild with anticipation. You open the door, and are more than disappointed when you find a cold, seemingly endless hallway on the other side. You step through the door as it slams shut behind you. Suddenly, you're not quite as excited about the dream as you were before.

Sound familiar?

At this point, most people turn around and run back through the door, and they don't stop running until they see something familiar and life makes sense again. It takes courage to stare the hallway in the face and take that first step forward. But if you turn and run, you end up becoming another person caught in the fallout of fear. I think I would rather sink while walking on water than miss the opportunity altogether.

I've been in a few hallways before. We could spend a weekend discussing them at a coffee house somewhere in the Pacific Northwest, but for the sake of time I'll focus in on one in particular.

I wrote very briefly about losing my job a few chapters back. You might have brushed past it, as I summed up the story rather quickly. It was a good job; the pay was above average for that of a typical barista. But after a few months, it just wasn't enough for me. This wasn't a hallway I stopped and lived in for awhile, it was one for me to walk straight through, and I fought the tension of living in the "now" and the "not yet" most of the time I was there. While I will always be a drinker of coffee, making it is not my ultimate career path, so it felt like there was no point in going to work every day.

There was one month where I didn't go to work at all; I went to California instead. I traveled with a team of fifteen young adults, and after stops in El Paso and Las Vegas, we journeyed up and down the Golden State—from Los Angeles to San Francisco to Sacramento, and a few other places in between. It was the journey of a lifetime, but I came home with the mentality that I had to work extra hard to make up for all the time I had taken off. [1] Six weeks later, I found myself caught in the lowest point of the hallway. Unsure of what to do, I did the only thing I knew to do. I escaped—again.

My family went to Colorado for a few weeks. As I sat on the deck of our condo, overlooking a peaceful tree-lined lake in the mountains, I was able to let go of everything I'd been holding onto so tightly and embrace what God was doing inside of me. It shifted my perspective, so that I was able to continue on toward the end of the hallway when I returned to Texas.

As it turned out, this particular hallway had a curve at the end. I never saw the door that I ended up being pushed through. I was completely blindsided, and thought I would free fall for weeks before finally hitting rock bottom, but that didn't happen. Instead, I fell about five feet before God caught me. It hurt a bit, but it didn't send me into a spiral of depression or anything.

Now that it's all said and done, I suppose I'm glad I was let go from my job. We probably wouldn't be having this conversation right now had things unfolded differently. I didn't commit a major coffee sin or anything; the decision that I should no longer work at the coffee shop was actually quite mutual. But it had to happen this way, because I wouldn't have quit my job on my own and waited for God to show me what was next. Instead, I would have lined up another job, jumped ship, and repeated many of the same unhealthy patterns. Sometimes God has to interrupt our day-to-day routine so He can get us to see what we need to see.

I learned a thing or two through the experience; most notably that I shouldn't let a silly job define me, and if I'm unhappy in a position (not just momentarily, but ongoingly unhappy), I should keep my mouth shut and find another job I enjoy. I'm not sure if "ongoingly" is a word or not, but it works so I'll leave it.

I soon realized that my short free fall hadn't landed me in a lush, green, wide-open pasture. Instead, I found myself in another hallway. It was really awkward at first, falling from one hallway through the ceiling of another, instead of using the door like a normal person. Now that I've picked myself up and begun walking, I've decided that I like this hallway. The uncertainty of what lies ahead remains, but this hallway isn't as cold and lonely as the last one was. The walls are painted a soothing color. It's not extravagant, just a simple hallway, but at least my soul is at rest. I know I won't be in this place forever, but I'm putting down some roots and opening up my heart to receive everything good this hallway has to offer.

We don't always get to choose our hallways, but we do choose how we walk through them. I don't always get this right; some days simply getting out of bed is an act of faith. But even though I do have my off days, I never let myself stay in that place for too long. God's mercies are new every morning, which means I can go to bed and try again the next day.

※ ※ ※

Henry, my pastor friend in Kansas, is an artist who paints a lot of abstract paintings, most of which make little or no sense to me. I've been told this is because I don't appreciate art, which might be true. But it's not that I don't like Henry's paintings; I just don't get them. I like concrete art better than abstract art because it makes sense to me and I don't have to think about it as much.

I've found that life is much more abstract than it is concrete. If life were concrete, we would all see the world the same way and believe the same things. This would get pretty boring after awhile, because there would only be one way to look at everything.

Michell can see things in a painting that Henry can't see, even though he is the artist. There are also things that only he can see, because he is the one who created them. And then there are things that she can see, point out to him, and watch as the curtain drops from in front of his eyes, as he begins to see them too. This is the beauty of the abstract.

Henry can look at an abstract painting and see a lot of beauty in it, when all I see is a jumbled mess of colors and shapes. I wish I could look past messes and see beauty, because I know that's the way Jesus sees things, and I want to be like Jesus. The value of something is determined by how you look at it. If you see things that no one else can see, you will probably be willing to pay more than they would pay. I'm grateful that Jesus saw value in me and was willing to pay a high price so that we could be friends.

The other day, Henry was staring at one of his paintings. Something about it just wasn't quite right. He took the painting, turned it on its side, and found it changed dramatically (even though it actually didn't). It wasn't just different; it was right— all because he looked at it differently. I think a lot of the things that keep us awake at night wouldn't bother us nearly as much if we would just look at them from a different angle.

※ ※ ※

I've recently become very aware that I'm not a "normal" person. But what if that's nothing more than a relative term? None of us are really "normal."

If you grew up in a home with two parents who had a healthy marriage, you probably think it's abnormal when your friend tells you that his dad has been divorced four times and his mom just got married for the seventh time. You think it's abnormal when he tells you about all the sexual abuse he endured, how he lived in thirty different places before graduating high school. But for him, it's all he knows; he has no concept of what it's like to have two parents who love each other and don't fight all the time.

My parents have a healthy marriage. My friend, Kyle, comes from a broken home. What's normal to me isn't normal to him.

After Kyle graduated from high school, he moved out of his broken home and into a long hallway. He got a full-time job delivering bottled water and married his high school sweetheart. He made up his mind that even though he came from a broken home, he didn't have to live a broken life. The hallway was long and difficult, but he kept moving forward. It was all new to him, as his only experience up to that point had been several short, pain-filled hallways. Eventually, he reached the end of the hallway. Now, he's in a different one.

Today, Kyle works in youth ministry. He has been married to Janelle for more than twelve years and they have two adorable children. His story has inspired thousands. He broke free from his past and built a stable world for his children to grow up in. While their lives won't be perfect, they won't have to deal with the same struggles and hardships that were part of Kyle's day-to-day life growing up.

※ ※ ※

It's funny how when we're going through something, we think we're all alone. We buy into the lie that no one else could possibly understand what's going on inside of us, so we carry our pain ourselves. I know I'm guilty of this. But when I pause and reflect, I see several of my friends living in similar hallways as myself. Some are young, some are old, but we all have one thing in common: none of us know what our futures hold. This scares us, perhaps more than we realize.

I wish I could just slow down and enjoy life and not try so hard to make things happen before it's time for them to happen.

I've spent the last year navigating this hallway with my friend, Elise, who I met when she was hired at the coffee shop a few months after I was. She didn't like me at first, so we didn't talk for five or six months, until one day, when we became friends. We've grown pretty close over the past year, as we've shared our hurts, disappointments, and fears in between making drinks for customers. Suffering has a way of bringing people together. I'm gone now, but she's still there, although she'd like to be somewhere else. She has big dreams, like we all do, bigger than her present circumstances can contain. We haven't really talked specifics, and I'm beginning to think perhaps she's afraid to. You can't fail if you never unleash your dreams from the confines of your mind, but you can't succeed, either. It takes guts to get your dreams out there, to bear your soul for the world to see. It might be easier if we weren't so quick to rip one another apart. For some reason, it somehow makes us feel better to kill the dreams of another; it helps take our mind off how deeply buried our own dreams are.

While I'm not sure exactly what Elise wants to do with her life, I'm sure she wants to find her niche, become who she was created and redeemed to be, and perhaps change the world. Until then, she's stuck making coffee. At least, that's how it feels to her. We're never really "stuck" unless we choose to be.

Neither of us have adjusted to the whole system of living in the hallways, between the "now" and the "not yet." Elise says our lives are but a breath, so we better breathe it, and I think she's right. We might as well get used to living in the hallways, because life is happening now. As Andrew Shearman would say, "Man of God, show up for your life!"

⌘ ⌘ ⌘

My friends, Jeremiah and Nicole, are also living in the hallways right now. I mentioned them briefly a while back, when they were in a much darker place than they are now. Their circumstances haven't changed much, but the way they view life has changed dramatically.

They still live in the 300-square-foot shack behind her parent's house. They still owe tens of thousands of dollars in student loans. They still don't have the jobs they want. They still don't have much money. They still don't know what the future holds. Yet, in their own words, they couldn't be happier. They have each other, and the world is wide open before them. They're blessed, and they have been all along. Now that their eyes have been opened, they realize it.

Jeremiah and Nicole have found something that many people chase after their entire lives, yet fail to obtain. Life is not about houses, cars, or money; life is about the people we share it with. We were created for deep, meaningful relationships—with God and each other. My friends have discovered that. As a result, all is right in their world.

I've never heard a story about someone who changed the world by chasing after houses, cars, or all the things we think we need to impress people we've never sat down and shared a meal with. The people who have made a difference in this world are the people who discovered that people are more important than things. You can put a price tag on a Mercedes-Benz or an apartment in the city, but you can't put a price tag on a human life.

I love the way Donald Miller puts it: *If you watched a movie about a guy who wanted a Volvo and worked for years to get it, you wouldn't cry at the end when he drove off the lot, testing the windshield wipers. ... Nobody cries at the end of a movie about a guy who wants a Volvo. But we spend years actually living those stories, and expect our lives to feel meaningful. The truth is, if what we choose to do with our lives won't make a story meaningful, it won't make life meaningful either.* [2]

※ ※ ※

I was reading the second most famous verse in the Bible the other day, when I realized how much we take it out of context when we print it out and plaster it on our refrigerators.

Many of us feel like our lives are stalled; we don't have a clue what's going on or where we're going. We know we're continually moving toward things, but it feels like we're running in place. So we pray that our lives will end up being about the right things and not the wrong things, because we believe that if we finally get things right, God will love us more and life won't be so hard. We'll chase after anything that gives us a shimmer of hope, even if it's only for a moment.

I think that's why we like Jeremiah 29:11 so much, because it gives us the hope we desperately long for. The only problem is, when we take a single Bible verse (particularly a "famous" verse), and put all our marbles on it without reading the verses around it, we often end up in trouble. You can make a verse of Scripture mean pretty much whatever you want it to mean if you take it out of the context of the verses around it and the larger story the Bible is telling. In theological circles, this is referred to as hermeneutics.

If we look at the larger context of Jeremiah 29:11, we see that God is talking to a people that He is punishing for repeated disobedience. This gives this verse far more meaning than it does when we take it out of context and make it all about us.

Of course, God does have plans for each one of us—plans for good and not evil, so we can look toward the future with hope. But that is not the primary message we are to receive when we read this Scripture. Instead, we are to catch a glimpse of the heart of God. Even though things were going to get really bad for the people in this story, this was not God's plan for their lives. This is not how He intended things to be. He intended their lives to be full of good things that produce hope. When we read Jeremiah 29:11, we should see that no matter how much we screw things up, God wants to give us hope that a beautiful life is still attainable.

Bob the Freedom Guy says we all ache to feel alive, to the point where we will chase after anything that makes us feel alive, even if it's false. He also says human beings are the only creatures who can lie to themselves and believe their own lies.

The people in the story Jeremiah tells did this. They chased after all sorts of things that they thought would make them feel alive. Ironically, these things ended up having the opposite affect, leaving them feeling more empty than before. God sent Jeremiah to warn them that they were moving toward something that would not only not make them alive, it would ultimately destroy them. They wouldn't listen, so God finally resorted to Plan B.

Gathering everyone together, God laid it out there without any fluff.

I've tried and tried to get through to you, but you refuse to listen. Because of this, I'm sending you into exile. You will find yourself in a very long hallway. Things are going to get hard. My desire is that you will stop moving toward destruction and turn back to Me. I want you to make Me the center of your life, because I am better than everything else you think you want. And you will find Me and the life I give when you abandon the things you think will bring you life, but cannot. Then, I will restore you and life will be better than anything you could possibly imagine. [3]

There are certain things that we know are best in our hearts, but we still find ourselves moving away from. It's a ruthless cycle. I think sometimes we're just curious about what else is out there. Nearly every parent has experienced this dynamic with their children at one time or another. Sometimes, you have to go after the wrong thing before you realize that the right thing is what you really want after all. I guess that's why we have to examine all of our options, count the cost, and decide that Jesus is the one we really want. We won't risk everything until we know that what He offers is better than everything else out there.

I like that even though God sent the people into exile for seven long decades, He didn't leave it at that. He told them to build houses and plant gardens and enjoy the fruits of their labor. He told them to get married and have children and pray for their enemies and get used to life in the hallways (Jeremiah 29:5-7). It's almost as if He looked them square in the eyes and said, *You're going to be here for awhile, but I want you to make the most of it.*

Some hallways are short and temporary—the kind that are to be walked straight through—while others are more long term. If you find yourself in a long hallway, it's okay to let your roots go down deep. Even if you're in a short hallway, allow yourself to be fully present in it.

No matter what sort of hallway you are in right now, you are not alone. No hallway will last forever. You will never fully "arrive" in this present life. When you see God face-to-face, you won't be in the hallways anymore, but you don't have to wait until then to be fully alive. Invite God to fill every inch of your hallway with the life and hope that only He can give.

Life is more about the journey than the destination. It's a journey from one hallway to another, until the day you find yourself on the wide-open shores of eternity. Even when you reach the place you thought would be your destination in this present life, you'll find that it's really just another hallway.

Man (or woman) of God, show up for your life!

ACT II

Break

Here is the world.
Beautiful and terrible
things will happen.
Don't be afraid.

~ Frederick Buechner

CHAPTER 11

RIPPED OUT AND TORN APART

I used to think I knew what romantic love
was like, but now ... I still don't.

I have a five-year-old cousin named Danica, who is quite possibly the cutest kid in the universe. I remember when she was five days old, smaller than my arm, and I would hold her until she fell asleep in my arms. She's growing up way too fast, of course, and it's awfully bittersweet. I don't have any brothers or sisters, so this is the first time I've watched a child grow up and move through the various stages of life.

It's beautiful, how unaffected Danica is. She lives in the same broken world I do, but she hasn't figured it out yet. We all start out this way, until life comes and rips us apart. Eventually, we reach the point where we realize just how broken we are, so we set out trying to find something or someone to fix us. It doesn't seem to end, does it? Life has a way of breaking us over and over again. We spend most of our lives searching for a savior, whether we're aware of it or not.

I once heard a pastor say that we all experience pain, but unless we turn it over to God it keeps building up until it changes us into someone we were never intended to become. [1] I guess this explains all the angry people in the world. They aren't angry because they like being angry; they're angry because they don't know how to deal with their pain. Most of us were never taught how to deal with our pain, so when we experience it, we do the only thing we know to do: bury it and hope that it never resurfaces.

⌘ ⌘ ⌘

I met a girl at church a year ago. Let's call her "Ashley." We were friends for about nine months, until she ripped my heart out.

I'm not really sure how it all began. She was dating this guy when we met, so I kept my feelings for her under lock and key. But then they broke up, and it had been a couple of weeks since we'd last talked, and we saw each other in the hallway at church one Friday night. That's when it happened—or so I thought.

We texted each other over the weekend, and spent Sunday evening together at church. It was almost as though we were in high school—which makes sense, because she was.

Monday came, and I sensed that things had changed. Something was different between us; that spark wasn't there anymore. Our interactions grew worse as the week progressed. By the weekend, we were barely talking at all. I went to church on Saturday night, hoping to run into her. We saw each other briefly in the hallway, but it just wasn't the same, you know?

After church, I went to a nearby coffee house. After ordering my favorite comfort drink, I saw one of my friends behind the counter, so I grabbed her by the shoulder and told her we needed to talk, because she was a girl. She just stared at me.

I sat down with my barista friend (who on this particular evening had her short hair dyed blue) and told her the whole story. She sat there for over an hour, listening intently. When I was finally finished, she told me that Ashley was probably ignoring me because she was frustrated that I didn't have the courage to move forward and ask her out. I nodded in agreement, like an idiot who was beginning to see what had been right in front of his face the whole time.

"But I just want to be friends," I said. "I don't want to bring in this whole dating thing right away. It's too soon." (Of course, what I actually meant was I was afraid. Just friends? A likely story.)

"But girls don't see it that way," she said. "We're different."

"So you really think she likes me?" I inquired, after a long pause.

"Oh yeah," she replied with a smile. "That's why she's playing hard to get."

I nodded. It all made sense now.

Ashley and I didn't talk much the next day, mainly because she wouldn't respond to any of the text messages I sent to her mobile device. Monday came, and sometime in the afternoon I told her we needed to talk (or at least, I needed to talk). She responded rather quickly, and said we could talk later that night, after she was finished with her homework.

I went to church again that night, and prayed the whole way home. When I arrived, I immediately went upstairs, to the closet of the room I used to sleep in before I moved into the guest room. There, I made the call.

Ten minutes later, I found out that it had all been a mirage.

After I told Ashley that I had feelings for her, a dead silence hung in the air for a moment that felt like eternity.

Finally, she spoke. "Thanks for being honest, but ..."

I didn't hear anything after that, but I remember exactly how I felt—as if my heart had been ripped out of my chest. And then another silence came, a lasting silence, a silence where the best escape is to just hang up the phone and pretend the whole conversation never happened.

"Well, this is awkward," I said bluntly.

"Awe, I'm sorry. I didn't mean to make things awkward," she replied.

She never came right out and said she didn't like me, but she did tell me she was enjoying being single since she had broken up with her boyfriend, and she didn't want to lose her freedom. I didn't know you could lose your freedom by being in a relationship, but from the way she described it, I could tell it was right up there with losing your virginity.

I confessed my love for her that night—or at least what I thought was love—and she shot me down hard. I had liked her for so long that I convinced myself she was Jesus, and she wasn't. I was looking for her to save me, but she did not possess the power to do so, and she didn't even want to. She wasn't looking for anything more than someone to flirt with, someone to look at her like she was the most beautiful girl in the world, which I thought she was.

And me ... well, I was looking for someone to rescue me, someone to show me I was worthy of love. I was terrified of being rejected, because I thought that this was it; I thought that she was the best I was ever going to get, as if she were the only girl left in the world. I put way too much pressure on her, and she cracked under the weight of it. Neither of us were ready for a real commitment, so we settled for messing with each other's hearts. It didn't turn out so well.

On a related note, isn't it ironic how the things we do because we're afraid of being rejected end up being the very things that cause people to reject us?

Ashley closed out our brief conversation by telling me she was going to go watch television. She might as well have said something along the lines of, "Sorry to break your heart, but I'm going to go watch the latest episode of *Gossip Girl* now." She didn't say that, of course, but she might as well have.

I hung up the phone and leaned against the wall of the closet. I sat there for twenty minutes before calling Elise.

I told her what had happened with Ashley, that I hadn't cried this much in months. At least the pain reminded me that I was still alive and capable of experiencing emotion. And there was so much beauty in the breakdown, as there usually is. Things were falling apart, but that didn't start when Ashley rejected me. I had not been okay for quite some time, but I was just now beginning to grow weary of propping up the facade. It's hard to walk around pretending that all is well when you really want to stand in the middle of a crowd and scream at the top of your lungs.

Elise was quiet for a moment. When she spoke, there was a weight to her words. She told me that sometimes it takes more strength to be real, to cry and face the pain. It's easy to pretend your heart is intact when it's not; it's hard to admit you don't have it all together.

That's really all you can do when your facade has fallen—face the pain. When things are crashing down you turn away, so you don't get hurt in the fallout. But at some point, you have to turn around and look at what your life has become now that your facade is a pile of rubble. Because if you walk away, it won't be long until you find you're walking in circles; you'll bump into the pain somewhere down the line. Burying it is only a temporary fix. It's still there, locked inside of you, even if you think you've gotten away from it.

Bob the Freedom Guy says God's view of pain and rejection is different from ours, that He finds beauty in it because He sees things we can't see. He sees where we're headed and who we can be. In His eyes, I hadn't just experienced rejection. Rather, I had been given the opportunity to experience unconditional love, from Him and from those around me. I didn't realize it at first, but as my heart was being broken, it was being healed at the same time.

Elise and I said goodnight two hours later. The moment I hung up the phone, silence began to invade the room, a silence I couldn't bear to face alone. Phone still in hand, I called another friend. Jordan and I talked for another two hours, and I was finally able to drift off to sleep after that.

I woke up the next day far too early and way too angry, but I was thankful for a busy day to help take my mind off things. We like to drown ourselves in busyness if it helps us forget the things that are slowly and painfully destroying our hearts.

I finished up my first meeting of the day and was walking through the field behind my church in Southlake, when I noticed the sky was growing rather dark. Within the hour, the tornado sirens went off and I was escorted into the sanctuary with eighty other people who happened to be in the building at the time. We were stuck in there for over an hour, while twelve separate tornadoes tore through Dallas. There was a lot of damage—most notably empty semis being thrown into the air over the freeway—but remarkably, no lives were lost that day.

As I was sitting on the steps of the altar, I thought back to the day after I first re-connected with Ashley. My family had gotten up early to go for a bluebonnet drive.[2] Everyone around here knows you're not a real Texan unless you have pictures of your kids, dog, and guinea pig in a blue sea composed of our state flower.

As we drove the back roads with everyone and their mother-in-law in toe, I noticed several patches of bluebonnets that had been crushed into the ground. I guess because there were so many flowers, people didn't care if they had to trample some of them to get to the ones that looked better. As long as there were some left to take pictures with, they were happy.

Far too often, we treat each other like these flowers. *There are so many out there, so it doesn't matter how many you trample to get to the one you really want.* We have the tendency to be quite selfish, and when power is placed in our hands, we can become very dangerous. But that is the risk you take when you love someone, or even when you only "like" someone. You don't have to be "in love" to get your heart broken.

Love—or whatever you want to call it—requires risk. When you tell someone how you feel about them, you place a measure of power in their hands. You may end up happily ever after, or you may get your heart ripped out and torn apart. But your heart can heal, and a life without love and risk is dull and unexciting. The truth is, we've all rejected people, and we've all experienced rejection—so we might as well stop pretending that we've never experienced this type of pain.

The seemingly endless sea of bluebonnets was breathtaking, even the ones that had been trampled into the ground. We drove the day away, deeper into the heart of Texas. We would stop the car every five minutes or so, take a few pictures, and then move along. The views kept getting better and better, and since we didn't know which field of bluebonnets would be the best, we stopped to photograph them all.

As the day was winding down, we reached the field that was the pinnacle of beauty. As I sat on top of a fence post and gazed out across the rolling green hills, I realized we had saved the best for last. Bluebonnets covered the landscape, like something that you would see on a postcard. If you looked closely, you could make out the faint skylines of both Dallas and Fort Worth on the golden horizon.

In the course of our journeys, we sometimes get distracted by what we see. Something beautiful turns our heads, and we think we'll never find anything more beautiful than what is right in front of us. But the best is still ahead, at the end of the road. If we keep moving, we'll make it there before the sun sets on our lives. We'll take in the view from that vista, and wonder how we ever ended up in place so beautiful.

※ ※ ※

The storms eventually passed and we were let out of the sanctuary, but I wasn't able to think straight for the rest of the day. I had so much on my mind, and was still reeling from the events of the previous day. I felt a lot like that blind guy in the Bible, Bartimaeus, crying out, *Jesus, Son of David, have mercy on me!* (Mark 10:47).

Of course, my situation wasn't that bad, but the pain was real, and I didn't know what to do about it. I ran into my friend, Alana (pronounced *uh-lan-uh*), and she told me that one day I wouldn't feel the pain anymore, that it would just become part of my story.

Alana was right. I was really hurt and angry for a day, but I was fine after that, and I think the reason why I was able to heal so quickly is because I turned my pain over to Jesus before it had a chance to set in and screw everything up.

Drugs. Alcohol. Sex. Money. Power. Fame. We will always find ourselves searching for something to save us when we don't take our hurts, struggles, and fears to Jesus. People who wrestle with addictive behavior aren't necessarily bad people, they just don't know what to do with their pain. In their attempt to find something to numb it, they reach for anything—sometimes another person.

Have you ever wondered why some people run from one relationship to another in the blink of an eye? None of their relationships last because the other person can never handle the pressure of being forced to play the role of a savior. There is only one Savior, and you don't have to work up the courage to ask Him out, because He promised He would never leave your side.

I remember asking Ashley if we were still friends before I hung up the phone, on the night she broke my heart. She said we were, but we haven't talked since.

In the end, Ashley couldn't save me. Your Ashley won't save you either. You have to let go. There's a better way, a better Savior. Get hungry. Get desperate. Bring whatever is holding you back to the feet of Jesus.

CHAPTER 12

WRECKAGE

I used to think failure was forever,
but now I'm learning to see beauty in brokenness.

I was enjoying a cup of coffee in my living room one Saturday morning when I heard the news that a plane had crashed in Kansas the day before. There were five people onboard the twin-engine Cessna when it went down. Four guys and a girl—all in their twenties—the rest of their lives still ahead of them. These things happen nearly every day, but this time was different.

The five twenty-somethings were on their way from Tulsa to a youth rally in Iowa when the plane went down in a field and caught on fire. Garrett, Stephen, and Luke died instantly, while Austin and Hannah survived the initial impact. Having previously served in the Marines, Austin knew exactly what to do in emergency situations, but nothing could prepare him for this. With burns on nearly every part of his body, he somehow managed to pull Hannah out of the plane. The two made it to a nearby road where two women found them shortly thereafter.

When the rescue crews arrived, helicopters carried Austin and Hannah in opposite directions. He was taken to a hospital in Wichita, while she was flown to Kansas City. They both made it through the night, but Austin passed away the next morning, about the time I got word of the crash.

Hannah's parents—Ron and Katie—arrived in Kansas to find their daughter with burns on one-third of her body. I can't imagine the pain they must have been going through as they looked at their daughter, lying unconscious in a hospital bed, knowing everyone else on the plane had perished. They remained at her side for weeks, until it was time to bring her home to Texas.

This story stuck with me all day as I went about my weekend activities. My dad and I were driving to the store to buy mulch for our flower beds when I told him what had happened. He didn't say anything at first. I glanced over, and saw tears in his eyes. And I think the most beautiful part was that neither of us had ever met Hannah, her parents, or any of the others who were involved.

Death. Despair. Wreckage. But somewhere, in the midst of it all, a miracle. There aren't any answers for that, are there? It's so bittersweet, the joy that comes in the midst of unspeakable pain. Redemption doesn't always happen in the ways we expect.

As funerals were being held in the wake of the tragedy, Ron was asked to describe Luke, the pilot of the plane, in one word. Passionate was what came to mind. It's one of those words that says it all, you know. Luke was the kind of guy who lived life passionately—not halfway, like many of us do. He loved Jesus, and wanted to spend his life making Him famous. And that's exactly what he was on his way to Council Bluffs to do, until life got the best of him. He fell asleep amidst the wreckage in that Kansas field, and woke up to see Jesus face-to-face. If he were writing this, I don't think he would say life got the best of him. I think he would say that he finished his race and kept the faith (2 Timothy 4:7); the ending just came sooner than he thought it would.

For Hannah's parents, their world shrunk from the busyness of ministry life to the size of their daughter's hospital room. They cherished the little things, like the joy on their daughter's face when she would wake up and see them gazing at her with love in their eyes.

Hannah was dumbfounded by the stacks of cards and letters she received in the weeks that followed. She was in a continual state of awe at the large number of people that were praying for her, that so many had been inspired by her story. She kept asking how so many people found out about her. She was even more amazed when the phone rang one day; it was the Governor of Kansas, and he had called just to talk to her! He asked how she was doing, listened to her story, and prayed with her.

Hannah began walking a few days after the governor called. Her family began making arrangements for the flight that would take her home to Texas to continue her recovery. I think at that point, she knew that everything was going to be alright. She had survived and she knew she was loved, and that was really all that she needed.

Just before the trip home, Ron and his son traveled a few hours south to gain some insight into the events that had unfolded three weeks before. Not long after arriving in the sleepy town of Chanute, they ran into one of the girls who had been first on the scene. She and her friend had been driving down the back road when they saw the smoke. At first, they thought it was a farmer burning trash, but they quickly realized it was more than that. Driving toward the smoke, they found Hannah and Austin walking down the middle of the road a mile later.

A few miles outside of town, Ron and his son parked their car on their side of a back road and walked a few hundred yards, where they found a small memorial in the midst of the charred landscape. The mood was surreal as they tried to come to terms with what had taken place there. That otherwise forgettable plot of land had become the focal point of their lives—and the lives of four other families as well.

That's what wreckage does, it changes everything. But then we emerge from the middle of it stronger than we've ever been, and more focused on the things that truly matter in life. Wreckage tears us apart, but it has a way of bringing us together at the same time.

I had driven through Chanute a few months before the crash on my way to Henry and Michell's house in Great Bend. It was still dark as I approached town, but the fully-lit grain elevator could be seen for miles across the level landscape. I still remember how picturesque the town was. Inviting and beckoning. Like a city on a hill. Like a prelude to redemption.

Editor's Note: At the time of this writing, Hannah is undergoing therapy at a hospital in Dallas, where she is expected to make a full recovery.

CHAPTER 13

ANSWERS

*I used to think I had to be God's PR agent, but now
I know I'm called to weep with those who weep.*

I've reached the point where I've been without a job for four months now. Well, that's not completely true. It's been four months since I was let go from my job at the coffee shop, but I still have my job with the youth outreach ministry, which is actually going quite well. It's a contract job—not full-time, or even part-time—but things are moving along, and it looks as though my career as a writer will begin to take off over the next few years. On the other hand, there is the possibility that it will not happen like that at all, and I am just wasting my life. I suppose time will tell.

Some days, I'm excited to be doing what I love, while other days, I barely feel alive. My life still seems to be wrapped up in uncertainty. It's often a struggle to keep my head above water, and the answers seem to have gotten lost somewhere along the way. I feel as though God is doing something that I haven't caught onto yet.

There's this place in the Bible that talks about Jesus doing things that His disciples did not fully understand at first—until the time came when they saw the fullness of His glory. All of a sudden, everything fell into place. [1] But in the meantime, they had to trust. My friend, Amber, says trust requires unanswered questions, and we have to believe in our hearts for what we can't see with our eyes. I don't like it, because I would rather see things with my eyes and then trust, but at the end of the day, I know she is right.

I went through a dark time in my life recently, when I didn't feel like contributing anything to society. So for a couple of weeks, I sat on the couch all day, watching reruns of *Law & Order*. I longed for light to break in on the darkened stage that my life was being acted out on, but just when I thought it was approaching, it seemed to turn and go in the opposite direction. There were times when I would crawl into bed in the middle of the day and bury myself under the covers for hours, trying to dull the pain. I couldn't move. I couldn't feel. I couldn't dream.

Christina told me that she's been fighting a similar battle lately. She's found herself running from her fears instead of facing them, and her vision has faded in the process. She's lost sight of the big picture of who God is and who she is in Him. She described it as a huge fog that blinds you to everything around you, so that you keep hitting the same wall over and over, even though there's an open door nearby the entire time.

One day, I got up off the couch and went running in the middle of the day, which was pretty stupid since it was over one hundred degrees outside. I came home dripping with sweat and nearly collapsed on my kitchen floor. It was worth it though, because after that I was able to push past the resistance and actually get a few things accomplished. When you're struggling through life, sometimes the simple action of getting out of bed (or off the couch) is an act of faith. But if you're able to bring yourself to do so, good things will follow.

I remember one weekend when I was at my friend's house on the other side of town. Seth and I stayed up and talked until we couldn't keep our eyes open any longer. When I woke up the next morning, I didn't have a clue where I was. I had never experienced anything like that before; it was such a strange and alarming feeling. I panicked for a moment, and then I remembered that I was in Waxahachie and I was safe.

There was another time when I was sitting in my studio reading a book, and then I just couldn't anymore. I fell out of the chair and onto the floor. I laid there for an hour, until Jesus came and got down in the dirt with me. He held me until all was right in my world.

When we encounter suffering on any level, we typically look for an explanation from God, but that's usually not what we receive. It's far better to receive a revelation *of* God than an explanation *from* God when we suffer. It even sounds catchy, so it must be true.

Sometimes, it feels like the healing we long for will never come. But when we give up, when we let go, when we fall out of our chairs, that's when the healing comes. My friend, Josh from Tulsa, says Jesus already knows that He's needed, and He's just waiting to be wanted. He's waiting for us to realize that we have no other options. He's waiting for us to stare Him in the face and cry out, "You're all I have left!"

※ ※ ※

I was lying awake in bed the other night, my mind racing. I finally got up and wandered around my house aimlessly for a little while, and then went outside and stared at the stars. There weren't any, so I went back inside and crawled into bed. I cracked open my Bible to the book of Job, not because I needed one, but because I was suffering, and I knew that Job was a man who went through a lot of crap without ever calling God a jerk.

I immersed myself into Job's world, right in the middle of the story where his friends were trying to help him cope with his losses, even though they were actually driving him off the edge of a cliff. I don't fully understand the story of Job, but I like it, because it's raw and honest and real; it talks about people's failures, not just their successes.

As I was reading, a verse jumped off the page at me, and for a moment, it felt like I was reading my own story. Job was talking about how his life was dark and he felt as though God was blocking his path so he couldn't move forward (Job 19:8). I kept reading, and the story just got darker and more miserable, until things suddenly changed. It was as though the veil was coming undone and scales were hitting the floor, as Job's perspective was restored in a moment.

He affirmed that his Redeemer was alive, and that after everything else had passed away, they would see each other face-to-face. In that moment, it wouldn't just be theory anymore. He would stare God in the face with his own two eyes, reach out and touch Him with his own two hands, and fall in love with Him all over again (Job 19:25-27). The anticipation of that day was enough to erase the pain of everything that Job was going through, even though his circumstances had yet to change. I think we can all learn something from that story.

※ ※ ※

I was watching a church podcast the other night where a few people shared their stories. One man talked about how he almost ended his life a few years ago. He had written the notes, left them around his house, and was driving aimlessly around Birmingham when he got stuck in traffic. The reason for the traffic jam? It was Sunday morning, and hundreds of people were descending upon a satellite campus of the largest church in town.

The man tried to make his way around the traffic, but a police officer waved him into the church parking lot. Driving onto the grounds, he found himself pulling into a parking space. He sat there for a moment, then found himself exiting his vehicle and walking toward the building. He entered the church and found his legs moving him toward the auditorium, which was quite crowded.

After worship concluded, the woman next to him put her hand on his shoulder, looked him in the eyes, and told him that everything was going to be okay. She had no idea what she was doing at the time; she just felt it was something she needed to do.

When the service dismissed, the man made his way back into the lobby. On one hand, he felt as though he was alone in a crowded room, but on the other hand, he was beginning to think that perhaps he wasn't. I'm sure he was wrestling with whether or not he should still carry out the plan to end his life. Then, without warning, a pastor whom he had never met approached him. That pastor gave the man a big hug , as he always does, and told him he was glad to see him. What he didn't know was this stranger had never been hugged by another man in his entire life.

On the podcast, the man began to weep as he talked about how his life has improved in the years since that day. He feels at home in the story that God is writing and has this unexplainable joy and zeal for life that rises up from within him.

It makes me wonder … What would have happened if the policeman had not waved him into the church parking lot? What would have happened if the man had turned around and driven straight out? What would have happened if the woman hadn't paused to talk to the stranger next to her during the service, perhaps following a prompting from the Lord to tell him that everything would be okay? What would have happened if the pastor had not hugged him, opting for a handshake instead because he didn't want to come across as creepy or awkward?

Tears began to fill my eyes as I pondered these things. I turned on an old Michael W. Smith song,[2] put my head down on my desk, and it felt like it was 1999 again. Almost as if I were there, in the suburbs of Denver.

The earliest tragedy I remember witnessing was 9/11. That was in 2001. I wasn't aware of the events of Columbine as they were happening on that April day before the turn of the century, when thirteen lives abruptly stopped short in an hour-long shooting.

There was a lot of information floating around in the aftermath. We know about the girl that was eating lunch on the grassy knoll outside the school entrance. We know she was shot four times and died immediately. We know about the girl who hid under the table in the upstairs library. We know she was shot in the face, point blank, after affirming her belief in God. We know about the boy who was shot three times, twice in the head and once in the foot. We know he used the last of his strength to drag himself across the library floor. We know he fell through the broken window into the arms of rescue workers below, an image that would make headlines the next day.

We know about Rachel. We know about Cassie. We know about Patrick. But there are other stories we don't know about, stories that didn't make as big of a scene.

We don't know about Rachel's brother, who survived the shootings in the library by lying on his face in the blood of his dying friends.

We don't know about the student who hung himself in his garage a year after the shootings. A recent break-up, coupled with the pain of losing a close friend and watching his coach bleed to death in the science room the year before, had become too much for him to bear.

We don't know about the student who was with a friend in the library when they were both shot. He survived, but his friend did not. He has never set foot in a library since, and still struggles to make sense of the events that unfolded on that terrible day.

We don't know about Cassie's mom, who couldn't fall asleep that night, unsure of whether her daughter was dead or alive. She would later quit her job in order to homeschool her son, who was able to escape the massacre. It must have been strange for him, living directly behind the high school where his sister was murdered, yet never entering it again as a student. He's married now, and has moved on with his life—what's left of it, at least.

We don't know that the FBI reports have shown that it is highly unlikely that Cassie was asked anything before she was shot. The student hiding next to her, who survived the attack, claims the Do you believe in God? exchange never took place, and several others confirmed this story, but we don't talk about this because it ruins a perfectly good (marketable) story. I guess that means the song I'm listening to right now is a lie, which is a shame because it's such a beautiful song.

We don't know about the family of one of the shooters. Can you imagine the tension that entered the room when the mom received a call at work from her husband, informing her that a bloody massacre was taking place at their son's school? There was nothing for her to do but make the half-hour drive home from downtown Denver, completely in the dark as to whether her son was dead or alive—and she didn't even know that he was one of the shooters.

Her husband met her at the house, and they paced up and down the brick sidewalk in front of their home, waiting. When the news finally broke, helicopters circled overhead and neighbors came out of their houses and stared at them, as if to say, "Look what you've done."

It was all over, but in many ways, it was just getting started. The pain was real; it stalked her day and night. She longed to speak to her son one last time. In the weeks that followed, she would burst into tears without warning, and get lost while driving the familiar streets of her suburban community. She avoided eye contact with strangers and was afraid to use her last name in public. There were days when she just wished she could die. Everyone thought she was a monster, because she had raised one. At least, that's what the media said, and the general public seemed to agree with them. People who had never met her made harsh judgments of her parenting skills, ignorant of the fact that she had done the best she could to raise her son in a loving home.

She would read his writings months later, giving her some insight into his world. He talked about his longing for love, his feelings for a girl that barely knew he existed. He talked about the pain he was experiencing, and often wondered if the world would be a better place without him. I think many of us can relate to feeling like this. When we don't have love, everything else falls apart.

It snowed the day after the shootings, a bit unusual for April on Colorado's Front Range. The community awoke to find the makeshift memorials in the school parking lot blanketed in white; it was almost as though God couldn't bear to look at the blood stained ground anymore, either.

Much has happened over the last decade. Lawsuits have been filed. Damages have been awarded. Books have been written. Movies have been made. The truth has been revealed. Lies have been spread. We know things now that we didn't know then, but many have chosen to remain ignorant. We tend to believe what we want to believe, ignoring the truth even when it's right in front of us. [3]

I don't remember Columbine. I only know what I've read. But I do remember Virginia Tech. Omaha. Colorado Springs. Fort Hood. Thirty-two people died at the University in Blacksburg. Eight in the upscale Omaha mall. Two in the church parking lot in Colorado Springs. Thirteen at the Texas military base.

I remember standing speechless in front of the television. The stories, the pictures, the faces; I can see them when I close my eyes. Where are the answers? Sometimes, there aren't any.

But we don't just need answers; we need someone to tell us we're okay. We need someone to tell us that humanity is mostly good, that evil is something we only read about. It makes us uneasy to think that a teenager could walk into his school and start killing people, when he was raised in a good home with parents who loved him.

We crave answers, because we're wired for justice; we were made in the image of a God who is just. But God doesn't answer our cries for justice by wiping out our enemies in one fatal swoop. Instead, He instructs us to love them (Matthew 5:44), and He answers our questions with Himself, in the person of Christ. God became human—not kind of human, fully human—the only son of God, eternally begotten of the Father, God from God, Light from Light, true God from true God ... For us and for our salvation he came down from heaven: by the power of the Holy Spirit he became incarnate from the Virgin Mary, and was made man. [4] He inserted Himself into our world without answers, lived mostly in obscurity, and went on a three-year ministry tour before He suffered the ultimate injustice, fully defeated evil, and then ...

left. Where are the answers there?

Ironically, it was the unjust crucifixion of Christ that defeated the power of evil, but then He left, leaving us in a world where evil has been fully defeated, yet still operates. He has promised to come back and deal with it once and for all, and has left the Holy Spirit among us and inside of us in the meantime. We sense His presence, but we also feel His absence.

Is it possible that senseless violence happens, not because the devil is out to get us (though he is), but because humanity is disconnected from God? How can we defeat evil when we default to it so easily ourselves? How do we protect our identity as sons and daughters of God when things seem out of our control? How do we keep our footing when life is fragile and messy?

These questions likely have multiple correct answers, but that is not the point. Our natural minds grasp for answers, but what if Jesus just wants to draw near to us through the pain? I think sometimes we have to stop searching for answers and simply let Jesus pull us close.

We often forget that Jesus was a man of suffering, One who was familiar with pain (Isaiah 53:3), and He is waiting for us to open our arms, expose our wounds, and let Him take the pain, so we don't have to carry it anymore. When we place our wounds upon the wounds of Christ, it doesn't multiply woundedness. Instead, His wounds become a source of healing for our wounds. This is what we mean when we say by his wounds we are healed (Isaiah 53:5).

When we attempt to live a life without pain, we attempt to be something other than human. [5] Pain is inevitable; healing is optional. God may not give you answers, but He will always give you Himself, if you draw near to Him. And when you find Him, you'll likely realize that the answers to the questions that keep you awake at night are found in the One who is making all things new. (Revelation 21:5).

ACT III

Settle

All of creation is finger
pointing to the Lord of
creation, in whom life can
be found. Creation was made
to introduce us to Him over
and over again.

~ Paul David Tripp

CHAPTER 14

SILENCE

I used to fill my life with a lot of noise, but now
I've learned that God speaks loudest in the silence.

My life is much quieter now. I've stopped asking so many questions and let God become my answer. The silence is peaceful, yet terrifying at the same time. Bob the Freedom Guy says people constantly surround themselves with noise because they're afraid of facing the silence. They're afraid of slowing down, because they know that when they do, the voices will show up and begin talking to them about their past, about all of their mistakes and failures. They'll realize how powerless and empty they are. It's unsettling at best, terrifying at worst.

No matter where we go or what we achieve, we'll always feel empty inside until we let Jesus come and show us who we really are. Bob says there are a lot of people who have been around church for awhile, and are even walking with Jesus, but still don't know who they are. They're afraid to slow down and let Him talk to them about their lives because it's far too painful. And they're right—facing the past is painful.

I think many people view Jesus as harsh and condemning, that He just wants to bring up their past and make them feel guilty. But Jesus isn't like that, and God isn't like that, either. My pastor says many people view God as the mean one, Jesus as the nice one, and the Holy Spirit as the weird one. But Jesus said that if we've seen Him, we've seen the Father (John 14:9), and Paul echoes that Jesus is the visible image of the invisible God (Colossians 1:15). In short, God is as nice as Jesus, Jesus reveals

God, and the Holy Spirit—far from being weird—reveals Jesus. In this way, we cannot interact with one member of the Trinity without interacting with the others.

If you want to know how God feels about you, I invite you to look into the face of Jesus. His loving eyes are already on you, and there is no hint of anger in His voice. But in order to draw near to Him, you must truly believe—in the deepest part of your heart—that you are loved, valued, and welcome in His presence. [1]

Bob the Freedom Guy says when Jesus was on earth, He hung out with ordinary, common people who were hurting, afraid, and screwed up a lot. He was willing to get down in the dirt with those who couldn't find the bottom rung of the social ladder. In short, Jesus likes us a lot more than we think.

※ ※ ※

I'm on another adventure now, a journey into the unknown. It's like the one I took this spring, but things are different this time. Back then, I felt like I had to get out of town and go somewhere unfamiliar in order to escape my circumstances. I was running—and I didn't even know what I was running from—but things are different now.

I drove the first hour in silence, kind of like those guys who live in castles, wear robes with hoods, and pray in their heads all the time. It was really beautiful at first, until I got tired of it. I wanted to turn on some music, perhaps mutter a few words aloud—anything, really.

"Hello, Oklahoma." Those were the words that broke the silence as I crossed the state line. I had faced the silence, and I had won. Now it was time to move on.

I used to work really hard to try to prove myself. Now, I feel like I have nothing to prove. I'm learning to dream again, to not try so hard, to just enjoy life and take things one day at a time. I'm learning to plan for the future without worrying about it. And above all else, I'm learning to stay planted when times get tough, to settle in and not be so afraid of the silence.

I'm sitting in a coffee shop in the suburbs of St. Louis. I was born in Missouri, but I've only been to St. Louis once—when I was a baby—so I don't remember it. It's nice here, and I think I might like it, but I haven't seen the Gateway Arch yet, and I think I need to see it before I make an official endorsement of St. Louis.

I was driving through the Ozark mountains a couple of hours ago when my phone rang. It was an important business call related to a project I've been working on for the youth outreach ministry, so of course, the call was dropped twice in five minutes. I finally decided to pull over alongside the freeway, so I could call the guy back without getting disconnected a third time. As I exited my lane of traffic onto the shoulder, I noticed the car behind me doing the same. I rolled to a stop, and the other car stopped in front of me. A young guy, not much older than me, got out and began walking toward my car. I canceled the call and hid my wallet, forgetting for a moment that I was in rural Missouri, not East Los Angeles. As I rolled my window a third of the way down, I silently prayed I wouldn't be robbed or murdered. I held my breath as the stranger grew closer to my car.

"You alright, man?" he asked, bending down to look at me through the window. I was silent.

"Do you need to call someone? You can borrow my phone if you don't have one."

I exhaled, a sense of relief flooding in. I looked up at him, smiled, and told him I had just pulled over to make a phone call.

"Alright, man. Glad you're okay," he said with a smile before turning back toward his car. I was blown away. In a world that is becoming more and more self-focused, this guy was willing to go out of his way to help a complete stranger. This encounter restored my faith in humanity. If only all of us lived our lives this way—myself included—then maybe the issues we spend a lot of time and money attempting to solve would take care of themselves. There is goodness that exists somewhere inside each one of us, because we are made in the image of God. I know that seems hypocritical of me to say, since I spent the last essay talking about how we're not good. In reality, both answers are correct—it's a tension to manage. We were made in God's image, but because that image has become distorted by sin and a broken world, we don't always look like our True Father.

Have you ever considered that Adolf Hitler was made in the image of God? People do terrible things when they aren't connected to their Creator. But even if one is disconnected from their Creator, it is possible for His characteristics to shine through the darkness every now and then. And while I think it's important to recognize we are sinners, I think we should call out the greatness in people. We can tell them that greatness came from their Father—their True Father—and then introduce them to Him. Once they meet Him and He changes their hearts, they won't want to sin anymore. This is a far more effective evangelism strategy than criticizing people for their sin when they've never experienced true Life.

I remember reading somewhere that Hitler wanted to be an artist at first, back before the world domination thing. He pursued that career path for five or six years, but people said he wasn't good enough to make a living from it, so he gave up. I wonder what would have happened if someone had called out the greatness in Hitler? Because he was told that he wasn't good enough to pursue his dream, he became a psychotic politician, resulting in the deaths of millions of innocent people. [2]

I long to see a generation that is encouraged to dream and follow their dreams, no matter how crazy they may seem. A generation that walks with Jesus and isn't afraid to talk to Him about their mistakes. A generation that isn't afraid of the silence, that knows how to face the past and look forward toward the future. A generation that discovers who they really are.

This generation receives their value, affirmation, and identity from the reality that they were made in the image of the God who invites them to become His children again. Because of this reality, they don't need the drugs, sex, hot cars, big houses, and all of those things that tell them they're valuable if they sell themselves to obtain them.

For far too long, we've been content with just getting people "saved," and have neglected to tell them that Jesus wants to do far more than just save them. The Gospel is about so much more than not going to hell when you die, but we sometimes forget the parts about God making all things new.

May His voice cut through the static and the silence and
all the crap you've filled your life with.
May His grace wash you and cleanse you and make all things new.
May His love chase you and catch you and surround you for all of your days.
May He hold you close and never let you go.
May He show you who you really are—who you were all along.

CHAPTER 15

NINE HUNDRED MILES

I used to be afraid to step outside of my comfort zone, but now
I'm learning that the spontaneous scenes of my story are often the best.

After leaving the coffee shop in the suburbs of St. Louis, I drove east until the Gateway Arch came into view, with the Mississippi River and Illinois beyond it. The next thing I knew, I had crossed over the river and descended into the ghetto. I had heard that East St. Louis was a rough place, but it was a lot worse than I expected. I had never been to Illinois before, and my high expectations for the state were quickly shattered. There wasn't much of anything alongside the highway for several miles, so I guess I wasn't the only one who wasn't a big fan of the area. All I saw were a bunch of strip clubs and billboards that said "Repent!" in big letters. I wonder how many people have actually repented and gone back to Missouri after seeing one of those billboards?

As I drove deeper and deeper into the Land of Lincoln, I felt so grown up, being in a strange state all by myself. After making my way across Southern Illinois, I crossed another river into Indiana, the second unfamiliar state of the day. The sun had already sunk low on the horizon, and it was dark by the time I arrived at a small house in a small town on the plains of the Hoosier State. I glanced down at the odometer. Nine hundred miles. I was nine hundred miles from home; nine hundred miles from the safety and security of my life in the suburbs of North Texas.

The screen door opened as I exited my car. Sarah walked briskly down the steps, greeting me halfway. I carried my things inside and placed them in the only free corner of the living room before shaking hands with her father and sitting down on the couch. It wasn't exactly normal, because I had never met either of them before this moment, but I would be sleeping on their couch for two nights and attending her high school graduation the next day.

I'm not sure exactly how Sarah and I met, perhaps because we never really did. Three years prior, an email showed up in my inbox from a girl who was barely hanging on to life. I had just decided that it was time to get serious about following Jesus, and even though I didn't really know how to at the time, I knew I could not turn away a girl who had just gotten out of rehab and was contemplating suicide, so I hit "reply" to her cry for help. To this day, I have no idea how she found me. I don't know anyone in Indiana at all, except I recently found out from Grandma Stump that Rick and Marilyn—whom I talked about earlier—used to live in the same town as Sarah.

Washington is a quaint town in the southwestern corner of Indiana, where high school basketball is king and churches dot the corners like sprinkles on an ice cream cone. But when you look past the facade, it's an awfully depressing place, which is no secret to the locals. I've heard stories of numerous students in Sarah's class that never lived to walk across the stage on that Saturday in May. There were two brothers who passed away ten weeks before graduation, and another student committed suicide a few days before Christmas. It was as if the senior class was growing smaller and smaller—one tragedy at a time.

The morning of the graduation, we went to breakfast with a guy named John, who is a teacher at the high school. His wife, Nancy, was there too, and the four of us ate pancakes and drank coffee. We told jokes and shared stories; the conversation ranged from casual and lighthearted to dark and serious. We talked about three years ago, when Sarah tried to end her life. John had found her at the last minute and had gotten her connected to some people who could help. And he stayed by her side over the years—checking in on her and investing in her life as much as he could.

As I sat in the bleachers of the massive basketball arena later that afternoon, I couldn't help but think of the students who hadn't made it. They never got to walk across that stage—and Sarah was almost one of them.

I remember the times when she would argue with me about whether or not life was worth living. I remember one night, in particular, when she came dangerously close. I couldn't take the pressure of trying to save her life, so I turned to my friend, Matt, who was my youth pastor at the time. My phone call woke him up, but he crawled out of bed and called her, this girl in Indiana that neither of us had ever met. It wasn't exactly normal, and I know some may think it was an "inappropriate" form of ministry—right up there with Jesus talking to the woman at the well without his accountability partners within earshot (John 4).

I realize now that if that phone call had not taken place, Sarah would have ended her life that night. But she made it, and while she still has a long journey ahead of her, she's come a long ways from the place she was three years ago. Sometimes, we get so focused on the ground we have yet to take that we forget about the ground we have already gained.

My time in Indiana was somewhat of an emotional roller coaster. Initially, I was going to stay with someone else in town, but when that fell through, and Sarah's family offered me their couch, something in me wanted to accept, because I wanted to fully immerse myself in her world and gain insight into her struggle. By the time Sunday rolled around, I had gotten far more than I bargained for. Sarah's family is quite dysfunctional, a mirror image of the dysfunctional town she lives in. Being thrown into the middle of it made me feel so powerless. Everything inside of me wanted to jump in and fix her life and make everything better, but I knew it wasn't that simple. You can't just apply a formula to someone's life and make all of their problems go away; that only works in the self-help books, and real life is not like that.

Most families are dysfunctional to some extent, and the ones that seem like they aren't are just good at creating a mirage. From my time with Sarah's family, I observed that they wanted to love and support one another, they just didn't know how. Perhaps the reason why they have trouble distributing love and affection is because it's something they haven't received very much of themselves. This dynamic is true in many families, a never-ending cycle for some.

I still have no idea how Sarah and I crossed paths three years ago, and I've never thought to ask. I suppose you could say God set it up, that He knew I wanted to make a difference in someone's life. Of course, I wanted it in a much more glamorous, socially acceptable package, but God is more concerned about His will being done than us looking really cool and spiritual.

Regardless of how Sarah found me, I'm glad she did. If you had told me when she first contacted me that the story would include a scene where I would drive nine hundred miles across the Midwest to witness a display of redemption, I would have laughed. But now that the scene has actually taken place, I'm beginning to believe that the stories of our lives have the capacity to take us places we never thought we could go.

CHAPTER 16

MIDDLE AMERICA

I used to wish things would always stay the same,
but now I know that everything must change.

I left Indiana after church on Sunday. By late afternoon, I was driving aimlessly through the suburbs of St. Louis, searching for coffee, when Christina called. We didn't talk about anything in particular aside from the hurricane that was bearing down on her coastal Florida town. She told me she was afraid, because her town was quickly flooding. I could hear the rain in the background, pounding against the side of her house.

Our conversation about nothing carried on for a few hours as I drove across the Northern Missouri countryside. True friends can spend hours talking about nothing, yet somehow manage to talk about everything. That's what we did as the sun sank past the horizon and another warm, summer night swept across the landscape. Our conversation eventually came to an end, and I arrived in the small town where my mom's parents live an hour later.

My great-grandparents' health began to slide downhill several years ago, so Grandma Darlene put her life on hold. She left behind the house she and Grandpa Joe had built—the house my mom grew up in—and moved twenty miles away to their retirement community in the next county over. With this move, she could now brag that she had lived her entire life in two adjacent Missouri counties (it was only one previously). For the past eight years, she has lived in their four-room apartment. (That's four rooms total, not four bedrooms.) It's a huge sacrifice, the kind that doesn't come with photo ops, a pat on the back, or a tax receipt at the end of the year.

My great-grandfather slipped into eternity four years ago. For the next year, it was just Grandma Darlene and her mom. Three years ago, Grandpa Joe was forced into an early retirement after being laid off from the residential construction job he had held for decades, when the Great Recession hit. He moved in too, leaving the house he had built on Bobcat Avenue vacant. They drop in a few times a week when an aid comes by to stay with my great-grandma, who can't be left alone due to her health condition.

I remember visiting the big house on Bobcat Avenue several times as a kid. One year, my cousin and I used Grandpa Joe's scrap wood to build a tree house in one of the towering maple trees that he had planted when he first built the house. I use the term "tree house" very loosely; what we constructed was an eyesore, but we loved it. When the week came to an end, my uncle made us take it down, which was quite frustrating. We responded by re-building it the following year, and he let us leave it up this time. We added to it every year, making it more and more of an eyesore as the years went by. We didn't care—we were professional contractors in our own minds.

My mom and Aunt Machelle grew up in that house. Their rooms are still pretty much as they were when they left for college. When I was younger, I visited so often that the house itself became a part of my story, but that life has come and gone. The house seems much smaller now, and has fallen into disrepair. It's almost as if time stopped eight years ago.

I remember back when when my great-grandpa was still alive. We called him Pappa (pronounced pap-paw). It sounded a lot better than his real name, which was Azzle. Azzle Charles Miller is the kind of name you would think belonged to a writer with a cool mustache who lived more than a hundred years ago, the kind of guy who wrote about the evils of slavery, or perhaps went on an expedition with Lewis & Clark.

There are a lot of odd names on Mom's side of the family, which is probably why many of her relatives go by their middle names. I would blame our German heritage, except for the fact that Dad's side of the family is German as well, without the odd names that seem to have been pulled out of a vault that should have never been opened.

Though his health was declining, Pappa Miller remained calm and steady through his final days. He wanted to stay strong for his wife and family, but in the end, he just couldn't keep up.

I still remember the last time I spoke to him. The year was 2007, the same year Grandpa Stump narrowly made it through the night in the ICU over Thanksgiving weekend. This time it was between Christmas and New Year's. We had been in Kansas City, and drove an hour north to Chillicothe for lunch. After the meal, Pappa was having trouble getting back to his recliner from the kitchen table, which was about five feet away. I can still remember his exact words when he finally made it.

"I just feel so weak!" he exclaimed, exhaling deeply as he sank into the recliner.

Sitting down on the floor next to the recliner, I took his wrinkled hand in mine and held on with everything I had. I gazed into his eyes, past his dated, thick-rimmed glasses. I saw so much love, but also a lot of sorrow. It was all blended together into a mess of emotion. As we sat there in silence, his hand in mine, I felt the presence of the Spirit there with us.

As we were preparing to leave, I gently wrapped my arms around his bony neck. Drawing my mouth to his ear, I whispered my love, assuring him that I would see him again. I kissed his wrinkled cheek before slowly pulling away, unaware that this was our final good-bye.

We drove toward Kansas City in silence. With every passing mile, I was slowly waking to the reality that this moment together might have been our last. Up to that point, few people close to me had died. In fact, there had only been one. I suppose this was due in part to the fact that I had never been close to many people in my former life, but things are different now.

※ ※ ※

The call came six weeks later. At fifteen, I was about to attend my first funeral. Uncle Gregg rented a van big enough to hold all of us, and drove with Aunt Machelle and my cousins from Austin to our house in Dallas late one night. Originally, the plan was to leave first thing in the morning, but that was soon overturned. We ended up driving through the night across Oklahoma, reaching our destination in Missouri by mid-morning.

My two cousins are Caleb and Rebekah. Caleb is the one I used to build the treehouse with and Bekah is Danica's mom. Like me, Danica was about to attend her first funeral; the only difference was she wasn't even a year old.

A few years ago, back before Bekah was anywhere near pregnant, I was sitting on the couch with Pappa, and I mentioned that it would be cool if one of the three of us had a kid while he was still with us, so that he would have the chance to become a great-great-grandpa. He just stared at me, as if I were from Mars, before chuckling like Abraham's wife Sarah did when a messenger from God told her she was going to have a son (Genesis 18:10-12). Pappa spent his last Christmas holding Danica—his great-great-granddaughter—in his arms. Sometimes God catches us by surprise.

There were twelve of us crammed inside that tiny apartment. The close proximity of so many loved ones eased the pain, until it all but vanished. Visitation was held the night before the funeral. Danica took the liberty of crawling all over the dimly-lit room of the funeral home. As I watched her, I couldn't help but ponder the great paradox of life and death—one life comes to a close, while another is just beginning.

Nearly everyone commented on how precious Danica was, as if it were some great revelation that we had yet to stumble upon. I think when we look at children, we see something we've been longing for all our lives. We see someone who isn't innocent, yet lives as though they are. We see the way they approach life—how carefree they are—and realize it's because they have yet to discover how broken and messed up our world is. It causes us to ache somewhere deep inside, longing to rediscover who we once were. We're pushed with desire to express this longing, but fear often keeps us at bay.

Why is this? I think it's because we think we're the only one who feels this way. We're afraid of being judged, made fun of. If only we realized that we're all thirsty for redemption. We settle for a nice, yet overdone comment about how cute the child is, and the parent responds with a "thank you," followed by a tight-lipped smile, as if to say, "I understand your ache. I feel it too."

I think we have more in common with the rest of humanity than we realize. Each of us realize that life is not all it could be. We all ache. We're all afraid. We're all thirsty for redemption. And each of us thinks we're the only one that feels this way, so we remain quiet and shove down our desire. We go through the motions of life, and reach for things that will numb our pain—even if it's only temporary—so that we'll make it through another day without having to confront the ache that we were made for so much more than the lives we've been living. Until our heads hit the pillow, and everything we've been trying to suppress comes rushing back, causing us to realize how empty we are. We tell ourselves tomorrow will be different, and then we drift off to sleep and wake up the next day and do it all over again, like rats in a maze.

※ ※ ※

We awoke the morning of the funeral to discover it had snowed overnight. We ate breakfast and got dressed for the day, mostly in silence. I spent half an hour clearing the sidewalk in my slacks, dress shirt, and tie. We then loaded into Grandma Darlene's black Suburban, and headed to the church for the ceremony.

I don't remember how many people attended the funeral. All I remember is sitting in the first pew with my family, including some relatives I had never met. We tried to be strong at first, but this only lasted about two minutes before our charades hit the floor. I most vividly remember Aunt Machelle breaking down, burying herself in Uncle Gregg's chest. I wish I had been more aware of the surroundings of the room, though I now realize it was nearly impossible to see past the pain that so thickly encompassed the place where we stood.

A plot had been prepared for Pappa two counties over, in a cemetery located along a back road. It was set amongst rolling hills a few miles north of the Missouri River. The hearse couldn't make it in the snow, so we watched as the casket was loaded into the back of a crimson red Suburban. There was no funeral procession, just two Suburbans and a rented van driving forty miles down the highway, from four lanes, to two, to one—a gravel road that ran parallel to the railroad tracks.

There were only a handful of us at the cemetery. I remember helping unload the casket out of the Suburban with Grandpa Joe, Uncle Gregg, Caleb, and the funeral home director. The pastor kept the service brief, as the cemetery sat exposed on top of a hill, offering little shelter from the wind. That was it. Another life had come to a close and was laid to rest. That was four years ago. Things are much different now.

My great-grandma, Mamma (pronounced mam-maw), is ninety-seven, and her health has fallen apart more than once. She has trouble remembering things, and doesn't know who I am anymore. None of us are really sure how she has survived this long, but we treasure every moment we have with her, and when we close our eyes, we find ourselves drifting back to a happier time.

One day while I was visiting, Mamma got into a fight with her daughter. It lasted close to an hour, and was difficult to watch. Grandma Darlene was just trying to take care of her, but Mamma didn't realize that. She didn't realize that her health was failing and she couldn't take care of herself anymore. She kept yelling and screaming and swatting at Grandma, desperately begging her to "take her home." Grandma kept explaining to her that she *was* home, but Mamma didn't seem to get it.

As I was watching this take place, I couldn't help but wonder if maybe Mamma was referring to a different home. Perhaps she was ready to see Jesus face-to-face, to dance with Him like she was young again. In His eyes, she is—even while caught in the fallout of a broken world full of sin, sickness, and death. It's hard to comprehend that when Jesus looks at her, He sees an innocent child who has yet to grow old and weak, who has yet to experience sorrow and pain.

I can't help but wonder just how much of reality Mamma is aware of. She doesn't know who I am, but does she know who she is? I guess I won't know on this side of eternity.

※ ※ ※

By the way, I've driven past the Gateway Arch twice now, and have decided I love St. Louis. I could see myself living there someday, but I say that about a lot of cities I visit.

Chapter 17

Community

I used to think just me and God was enough,
but now I know I was created for community.

After a week in Missouri, I headed south. Driving across the plains of Kansas and Oklahoma, I arrived in Shawnee by dusk. After grabbing a java from the local coffeehouse, I headed to the missions base that my friends run—a converted storefront that now houses a ministry internship.

I was surrounded by friends from the moment I entered the building. Three of the interns traveled with me to California for three weeks last summer. I remember how we used to sit around late into the night and talk about how we were going to change the world someday. We haven't yet, but I know it's only a matter of time.

My friend, Dave, grew up in Oklahoma and spent some time on the East Coast before returning to his hometown of Shawnee. He was a youth pastor for awhile, before the internship began to take off. Dave told me they had no clue what they were doing the first two years. All they knew was that they wanted to create a place for the square pegs who didn't fit into the round holes of the local Bible Belt culture to come and figure out life together.

In recent years, a large community has developed in the little college town. It's an eccentric group of people who love God and each other, and their ministry is centered around helping people discover who they were created and redeemed to be, so they can display the Kingdom of God in their everyday lives.

I've never lived in Shawnee or been a part of the internship before, but the community has welcomed me anyway. We all stayed up late that night—talking, laughing, and wrestling with the bittersweet reality that the third class would be graduating the next day. They had spent a year of their lives together, but in a moment, it was all coming to an end.

Sometime after midnight, a guy named Cristian arrived from South Texas. He was a part of the second class, and hasn't quite gotten over the difference it made in his life. He told Dave that he had been considering packing up everything and surprising everyone by moving to Shawnee. He said things weren't the same once he arrived back home. He missed the community, the late nights of worship, the conversations, and everything in-between.

We eventually grew tired and drove to a farm outside of town where the interns lived. I collapsed on the couch just inside the door. When I woke up later that morning, I could hear Cristian playing his guitar and singing to Jesus on the front porch. It brought back memories of last summer when I went to California on a ministry trip with Dave, Roger the Nazarite, Josh from Tulsa, and ten others. I had never been to the West Coast before, but had heard from several people that it was full of liberals, environmentalists, and sinners.

We met at a McDonald's along the Interstate, and drove into the Oklahoma countryside. We then spent a couple of days preparing for the trip at an undisclosed location.[1] We were itching to get on the road by the time training was finished, so we spontaneously decided to leave Oklahoma a day early, under the cover of darkness. We drove through the night into Texas. Dawn broke somewhere west of Abilene, illuminating the bushes and shrubs that dotted the landscape. (Trees don't exist in West Texas.) We made it to El Paso by evening and arrived at a church called Nuevo Pacto,[2] which was a fun name for us white kids to attempt to say.

We camped out at that church for four days. The girls slept in one classroom, the guys in another. There were a few prayer meetings, services, and evangelistic outreaches at malls and laundromats, but the majority of our time was spent just hanging out. This was mostly because the transmission in our van had given out, stranding us for a few extra days. I would disappear in the afternoons for hours at a time. I spent a lot of time on the roof of the church talking to God under the blazing Texas sun. You could see into Mexico from there, and I vividly recall the way I felt when we went to the border one afternoon. We took a guitar and djembe and worshiped Jesus on the edge of U.S. soil—Mexico before us; the Border Patrol behind us in their American SUV's, which were more than likely manufactured in Mexico. As I gazed across the Rio Grande into Juarez, I wept for the Christians that were being persecuted there while I stood safely across the river, free to worship and pray in public.

I felt so alive when I stood on top of a mountain, looking down on the cities of El Paso and Juarez. I quickly forgot they were in two separate countries—one significantly more developed and safer than the other—because from my vantage point, they were one. In the Kingdom of God, the lines we draw to protect ourselves from whatever we fear don't seem to matter much.

I remember the wind slapping against my face as the sun sank in the distance. From the ground-level, it would have appeared that the sun was setting over the States, but from atop the mountain, it was clear that the sun was setting over Mexico. It's easy to think we're God's favorite country sometimes, until we realize that the sun, moon, and stars shine the same wherever you are.

Josh led us in worship, and the presence of God descended, nearly sweeping me off my feet. We stayed up there for hours, until the dark of night set in and the park rangers told us it was time to leave. I rode the tram down the mountain with Dave, Roger, and the park ranger. She had been watching us worship from a distance, and asked if we were a church group.

"Yeah, kind of ..." Dave replied.

"What denomination?" she inquired as we exchanged glances.

"Jesus," I replied before the three of us had a chance to agree on a response.

"I like that." She smiled. "My mom is Baptist and my dad is Catholic, so I grew up pretty confused," she said quietly, trailing off toward the end.

I nodded, understanding exactly how she felt. We talked a bit more, and when we reached the bottom of the mountain, I asked if we could pray for her.

"You want to pray for me?" she asked. "About what?"

"I don't know." I paused as I hadn't thought ahead this far. "Would it be okay if we just prayed a blessing over you?"

"Sure," she replied.

I proceeded to pray the most anointed prayer I have ever prayed in my life. Not because I was good, but because Jesus showed up. Even Dave and Roger, who have been around the block a few more times than me, were taken aback.

We parted ways with the park ranger and rejoined our group, which had taken the tram ahead of us and were waiting at the van. I stumbled along, still reeling from the encounter. To someone looking on, it may have seemed like nothing more than a simple prayer, but it was so much more than that.

It's funny how we call these trips "ministry trips" as if we are the ones ministering to others. We were, but during encounters like this one, I felt like God did far more for me than I did for Him. In other circles, we call them "mission trips," because we are on mission to do great things for God, but at the end of the trip, I can honestly say the mission wasn't what we thought it was. We thought we were going to bring the Kingdom of God to earth—which we did—but most of the time, it just showed up and we went along with whatever God wanted to do in the moment. That's what you have to do when you're ministering on the streets, because the homeless and rejects of society aren't impressed by our fancy plans or religious formulas.

At the beginning of the trip, Roger told us our real mission was building relationships with one another and seeing God move in our own lives. It didn't make sense to me then, but after three weeks, I realized he was right—not because he convinced me of it, but because I experienced it firsthand.

When you live out of a van with fourteen people, sleeping an average of four hours a night, sometimes being forced to go for days without showering, you notice things you wouldn't normally notice in the context of everyday life. You quickly see everyone's bad side; you become familiar with their blind spots. You see the crap in their lives that they are oblivious to. To go through all of that and still love each other ... well, that's the challenge.

When our van was finally fixed, we left El Paso for our next ministry stop in Las Vegas. It was late in the afternoon when we left, so we didn't make it to Arizona until a few hours before midnight. I was excited, because I had never been to Arizona; it was all new from this point forward. I didn't see a whole lot in the dark, just the faint reflections of mountains pressed up against the moonlit sky. We drove for several more hours before reaching Roger's in-law's house in the suburbs of Phoenix, where we crashed for the night.

The next morning, one of the guys discovered he had been stung by a scorpion while sleeping on the couch, which made me glad that I had decided to sleep in a corner on the floor. It was still early when we rolled out of town, and already 108 degrees. It was so hot in the van, with little room to move around or get anywhere close to comfortable. We drove through miles of suburbia, and then there was nothing but mountains and cactus for several hours. I managed to fall asleep for awhile, and when I woke up, someone told me we were in Nevada. I knew we couldn't possibly be in Nevada, but I fell for it anyway. I was kind of upset that we had entered Nevada and no one had told me, even though we actually hadn't.

An hour or so later, we crossed into Nevada—for real, this time. We drove on the new Interstate bypass across a rocky gorge with the Colorado River flowing freely below. If you looked out the window, over the concrete median, you could make out the top of Hoover Dam with Lake Mead being held back behind it.

After federal agents searched our van and trailer to ensure they were free of firearms and alcoholic beverages, we were able to park in this big parking lot and walk up several flights of steps, until we were on the same bridge we had crossed over before. This time, we were on the other side of the concrete median. It was truly a breathtaking sight as we took in the dam and the river flowing out of it hundreds of feet below the bridge that seemed to be suspended in midair.

After leaving the dam, we drove for about half an hour, still in the desert. But then we started to see houses, cars, and other signs of life, so I thought perhaps we were nearly out of the desert by now. And then we went down a hill, and there was a massive city stretched across the horizon, with a line of tall buildings outlined in the distance. And past that, there was more city, and then nothing, and then mountains again. It was like this place had fallen out of the sky and landed in the middle of the desert. They called it *Las Vegas*, and I had heard there was a lot of sex and sin there. I didn't see any sin the first day, but that's probably because our first stop was a missions base a few miles north of the strip.

The first person I encountered at the base was Joanna, whom I knew from back home. I distinctly remembered the last conversation I had with her a few months earlier at a coffee house in Dallas. She was home on break to help plan her sister's wedding, and she came over to my table and asked if I wanted to come spend the summer in Vegas telling people about Jesus. I politely declined, not knowing that our next conversation would take place outside of a missions base in the middle of the Nevada desert.

We spent two nights at the base, conveniently located in one of the most violent neighborhoods in the United States. Jesus was there too, I think, and the thought of that made me happy. I remember lying awake the first night in my bunk, unable to sleep. I got up and crept down the hall to the prayer room. It was a small, dimly lit room that apparently didn't have air conditioning. I sprawled out on one of the beanbags and tried to think cold thoughts. The room had entire walls covered in colorful sticky notes where people had written their prayers and other things. I sat there for an hour or so, staring at the ceiling and crying my eyes out. I think maybe Jesus was healing me as I lay in that dark, strange room in a strange city, so I stayed there until I got kicked out by one of the guys on our team because he wanted to have a private conversation with his girlfriend. I didn't think that the prayer room was a good place to do this—unless they were going to be conversing with Jesus at the same time—but I didn't say anything. Maybe they just wanted to be close to Him as they worked through their issues. They were in there for a long time, so I went back to my room and lay awake in my bunk. After awhile, I wasn't awake anymore, so I assume I finally drifted off to sleep.

The next morning, we had breakfast, and then spent some time in worship and prayed for one another. We gave all of the junk that was weighing us down to Jesus and let Him deal with it. He's pretty good at that, taking our messes and making something new out of them. We spent a lot of time on that, dealing with our junk and what not. I think it's good that we did it that way. I think sometimes we go out and try to heal other people when we haven't let Jesus heal our own hearts yet, and it can get us into trouble. Not that we can't heal others when we're in the process of being healed ourselves, but more along the lines of the idea that it's kind of hard to give something to someone else when you've never received it yourself. If our lives are about receiving the love of God and giving it away, we have to first receive the love of God; otherwise, we have nothing to give away.

After we got our junk out of the way, we gathered in a big circle, and the director of the missions base briefed us on what we were about to experience on the strip. He also told us not to look at naked people. I had no idea there would be naked people when I signed up for this trip. We then loaded the team into two unmarked vans and rolled out. Twenty minutes later, we were standing at the intersection of Tropicana Avenue and Las Vegas Boulevard. On one corner was the Tropicana; on another was New York, New York. Excalibur was across the street, with the MGM Grand occupying the final corner. We were right there in the middle of it all, hemmed in on every side by the city of sin. I still hadn't seen much sin at this point, but I guess that's because I wasn't looking in the right places.

We split up into groups for a prayer walk and set out feet to the pavement. My group took on the MGM Grand, walking the never-ending halls for upwards of an hour. It was the middle of the afternoon, so the casino was just waking up for the night. Most everyone I saw looked surprisingly sad, like their very reason for living had been ripped out from under them. A song about breaking hearts played in the background. I think this city has broken a lot of hearts in its time. It was so odd to me that more people weren't smiling. They were on vacation, after all. A few days of freedom to go anywhere their budget allows, and they pick a town that winds up breaking their hearts.

After our scouting trip, we headed back to the missions base to discuss the things we had seen and the people some of us had ministered to. We went back to the strip with guitars later that night, where we ended up leading worship on a street corner across from the Bellagio. It wasn't long before a guy approached and began mocking us. I turned away, and when I glanced in his direction a few minutes later, I was shocked to see him weeping in the arms of the missions base director. He was reintroduced to Jesus that night, and enrolled in a rehab program at a local church after expressing his desire to quit using drugs.

Throughout our journey, we prayed for hundreds of random people on the streets, from El Paso to Hollywood to San Francisco. Many of them needed physical healing; for others, it was emotional. Most were healed, but not everyone. I didn't understand this at first, until I remembered that not all of the people that Jesus encountered were healed either. Often, He would walk through a crowd of sick people and only heal one.

I can't find any place in the Gospels where Jesus turned down someone who came to Him directly for help, though He often utilized unorthodox methods to solve their problems. But when Jesus walked through crowds of needy people, He didn't just begin healing them left and right. Bill Johnson, a pastor in California, says this is because Jesus doesn't respond to need, He responds to faith. [3] But what if I don't have faith? We all have faith, it's just most of it is rooted in the wrong things. It's usually not a good idea to put your faith in something that is incapable of being faithful in return. I do this a lot, and I really wish Jesus would fix me, so I wouldn't anymore.

I don't see Dave very often, and I see Roger even less, because he lives in Northern California. But when we're together, we skip the small talk and dive straight into the deep waters of our souls. Depth of relationship has nothing to do with how often you see a person. (Unless you're married to them, of course; then you should probably spend time with them more than once a year.) Dave and Roger know me far better than most of the people I see at church every Sunday, most likely because we spent three weeks on the road together. We've laughed and cried together, although there has been far more laughter than tears. Since returning from that trip, I've made an effort to be intentional about connecting with people on a deeper level—even the people I only see on Sundays. [4]

Editor's Note: The ministry trip that Jared took to California is called the Burn Wagon. They take trips to different regions of the States every year for the purpose of evangelism and discipleship. To learn more, visit www.burnwagon.com.

※ ※ ※

Ross Parsley, who pastors a church in Austin, says there are a lot of people out there who love God, but don't like His family very much. It's easy to love a perfect God, but hard to love imperfect people, [5] which is kind of ironic, since we are all imperfect. But the reality is, as the Church, we have not fully stepped into being the people we were created and redeemed to be.

We are not people who risk, love, pray, create, serve, proclaim, and sacrifice very well. Church is a very unattractive place for most people. And while countless churches are changing and adapting to become all that they are called to be in the

Kingdom, countless more are not. [6]

I think if we are going to give our lives to God, we have to make a commitment to His family as well. The whole family, not just a specific church. While we are already part of the larger Body of Christ, I think it is important that we participate in regular community as well, which could mean becoming involved in a local church.

Jesus gave us a vision for a diverse community of people who never would have gravitated toward each other on their own, but there they are. They are loving and devoting themselves to one another, because they have Jesus in common. [7]

This is the beauty of joining a local church. If you choose to fellowship regularly with a hand-picked group of believers, you'll end up with a bunch of people just like you who believe all of the same things you believe. Being a part of a local church forces us to connect with people we would have never chosen to connect with, aside from the common denominator of the cross.

Donald Miller's pastor, a guy named Rick, says that our diversity automatically brings about a tension. We don't all get along and we don't all like each other. But we don't get to choose our family, they are chosen for us. [8]

I think Rick is right. Sometimes living in community is awkward. We have to say "hello" and have conversations with people we would never be friends with if we did not both attend the same local church, but I think we need to embrace the awkwardness of it. It's not a problem we need to solve; it's something we must work through as we do life together. And we must do life together, because that is the way God wired us from the beginning of time.

Rick says it is impossible to be a follower of Jesus independently of other followers of Jesus, because we are all united through our confession of Jesus as King. It is only possible to be someone who is not participating in the life of Christian community. When we choose not to participate in community, it is harmful to the community as a whole, because God gifted us for the common good of the Body of Christ. We are the Church if we follow Jesus. We hurt the Church when we choose to leave her. [9]

I know a lot of people like the ones Ross and Rick talk about, people who love Jesus, but don't like the Church. But if we are to say "yes" to Jesus, we must say "yes" to His family as well. We must embrace His bride, no matter how ugly she may appear at first glance.

When we are part of a family, there will be times when we get hurt, and even betrayed, but we can't let that stop us from being part of the family. If we're going to love, we must be willing to get hurt, and we must be willing to bring our hurts to God and let Him heal them, so we can go out and love again.

My friend, Beth, who is above average and serves as a freedom pastor at my church, says she is sick of the masks people put on when they come to church on the weekends. When asked how they're doing, they reply "Great!"—just like they're supposed to. When asked if they have any prayer requests, they just smile until something generic comes to mind, such as "wisdom at work." It's vague and safe, but quite ridiculous.

Somewhere along the line, we've created a place where we can't be real with one another. Our modern-day church culture is a far cry from the early church, where the greatest spiritual leader bragged about his weaknesses and shortcomings (2 Corinthians 12:9). My pastor says church should be a place where people can talk about their deepest, darkest secrets. If they can't talk about that stuff at church, where else are they going to find hope and healing?

I long for the day when church is less of a social club where we fight to maintain our status and position, and more of a community where we can come and fall apart in the arms of a stranger during our hour of greatest need. A place where we don't have to pretend like we have it all together; a place where we can let down our facades and admit that our lives are jacked up, and we can't seem to fix them. Maybe then we could help each other get our lives un-jacked. I think that's what Jesus would want

We need each other. We need people. We need community. We need relationship. We need God. They are all interconnected, and it flows in both directions.

I've heard some people say if all you have is God, that is enough. And it sounds true, it sounds right, until we open up the Bible and find that when Adam and God were in the garden together, God said it wasn't good for Adam to be alone; he needed another human companion (Genesis 2:18), which is crazy if you think about it, because this was before sin entered the world. If Adam—in perfect relationship with God—needed community, how much more do we?

CHAPTER 18

CONFESSION

I used to think I was the only Christian with issues,
but now I know we all struggle.

I've noticed many of us live under the illusion that everyone else has a perfect life, and we are the only ones with crap to work through. This is simply not true. Everyone has issues; no one is perfect—no, not one. Even on our best days, we fail in so many ways. The fact that we get tired and need sleep every night proves just how weak and frail we are. We're not capable of much on our own, yet we're somehow able to do a lot of damage when left alone for too long. Even after we've been redeemed and made right with God, we're still able to get ourselves into trouble and cause a lot of pain, especially to those closest to us.

Life gets easier when we realize we all have bad days, insecurities, and imperfections. The pressure to be perfect disappears when we realize perfection is something none of us will obtain on this side of eternity.

Why are we told to confess our sins to one another? Because the things that hold us back lose their power when we realize that other people struggle with the same things we do. We're all broken; we all stand in need of redemption. [1]

When I was in California on the ministry trip, we would get together in a circle every night before we did a service, and Dave would ask whoever was feeling insecure to raise their hand. Josh from Tulsa was usually the first to raise his hand. After that, everyone who had been waiting for someone else to be the first to raise their hand would raise their hands as well. As it turned out, most of us were insecure about admitting we were insecure. After the hand raising, we would pray, but we never prayed for the insecurities to go away. We didn't need to, because they had already lost their power. All it took was looking around the circle and seeing everyone else had their hands raised too. Sometimes, when we own our crap, that's all it takes for it to go away.

I was in a meeting once that turned into a mass confessional, as all of the leaders in the room got their issues out on the table. Since it was my first time at the meeting, I sat in silence, trying to convince myself that my issues weren't that big of a deal.

I remember this one girl named Michelle who told everyone she was planning on quitting her job that week. She didn't have another job to fall back on, but she was tired of coming home in tears every day. She said she knew God would take care of her, and that made her unafraid to do what she needed to do to take care of herself.

I was in Austin on another occasion when I ran into a young woman who knew me back when I was in elementary school. I was a little devil child back then, so she was shocked to find out I now worked for a youth outreach ministry. She first came into my life at a time when she was young in her faith, dealing with a lot of crap from her past that seemed to wait for her around every corner.

She caught me up on her life, telling me about her husband and kids. I asked how many kids she had, and she told me she had two. I looked at her for a moment, my eyebrows raised. "Are you sure you don't have four?" I asked. I didn't know why I was asking her that; it just popped into my head and I found myself saying it.

She began to weep. I pulled her into a close embrace as tears streamed down her face. When the tears finally stopped, she told me I was right. She *did* have four kids. Two of them were at home with her husband; the other two were in heaven with Jesus. She had aborted her first child, miscarried her second, and the two kids she has now are three and four years old, respectively.

She had carried the shame for most of her life, unable to open up her heart to receive grace, healing, and redemption, but things were beginning to change. Jesus was chasing her down and overwhelming her with His love. He was starting to bring the past to the surface, which was uncomfortable at best, and terrifying at worst, but it was all part of the healing process.

She told me she usually kept her past in the dark when people asked about her kids, but lately she had been feeling as though she was supposed to begin talking about it. She looked me in the eye, tears still forming in hers, and told me that she was going to begin telling people she had four kids—two on earth and two in heaven. She didn't know why she felt like she was supposed to do this, but she knew she could only run from her past for so long.

Perhaps Jesus wanted to use her story to heal others while He was healing her. We can't wait until we're completely healed to start sharing our story, because the majority of our healing often comes as we open up and begin sharing the gritty details, especially the ones we'd rather keep in the dark. It's kinda like that confession thing we've been talking about.

I once heard a pastor say God treasures the parts of our stories we don't treasure. I think perhaps she is right. We simply don't see things the way God does. We look at ourselves and see little more than stains and dirt, while God sees us as clean and spotless. We see ashes, but He sees beauty. We wrap ourselves in shame, but He wants to clothe us in His righteousness.

It's hard to train ourselves to be honest about our weaknesses when we've become so good at glossing over them. It's hard to open up the door and let the light shine into our lives. I don't think it ever becomes second nature for us. I think it's something we constantly have to make a conscious effort to do, because it's so much easier to bury things than it is to dig them up.

※ ※ ※

I was driving through some of the wealthiest neighborhoods in town one morning with my friend, DJ, who is old enough to be my grandpa. I'd seen these houses dozens of times, but this time I took in the sprawling estates as if for the first time.

"Look at these houses," I said. "Who even needs a house that big?"

"You know," DJ replied. "A lot of the people in these big houses are some of the loneliest people you'll ever meet."

I knew he was right, because I'd met some of the people in those houses. They may have everything they ever wanted, but many of them are starved for intimate relationships and community. The saddest part is, they often don't even realize it—and the cycle of going to the mall to see if one can find happiness on sale continues. I suppose if your house is big enough, you'll be able to go about your life and forget your problems, or perhaps hide them away in one of your five spare bedrooms.

Of course, people who live in small houses are capable of burying their problems too. We all are. But when you lead a simple life in a small house and live paycheck to paycheck, it's a lot harder to bury your problems, and if you do manage to do so, they'll probably dig themselves up, and you'll find them waiting for you on your front porch when you get home from work.

I suppose this is why Jeremiah and Nicole find it so easy to admit that they have issues and need help. When you live in a one-room shack behind your parent's house, it's pretty hard to pretend you don't have your life together, because the evidence is right in front of you.

Christina says being strong means facing our problems, rather than burying them. I know she's right, but it's just so hard to put into practice. Most of the time, I find myself unable to find the courage to lay my problems out on the table, so that the people I love can work through them with me. So I bury them, and they stay hidden for awhile, until one day when they blow up in my face. Then I'm forced to talk about them. I don't know why I'm so afraid to do something that I know is better for me in the long run. I wish I could find the courage to be real and honest with people, to not care so much about my reputation.

Bob the Freedom Guy once told me the opposite of fear is not courage. This struck me as a bit odd, but he went on to tell me the true opposite of fear is love, which is why perfect love drives out fear (1 John 4:18). So, next time you find yourself afraid, don't bother with trying to act cool and tough and courageous. Instead, simply remind yourself of how God feels about you—how perfectly you are loved—and after that, you'll probably find that you aren't as afraid as you thought you were.

CHAPTER 19

FITTING IN

I used to think I would never fit in
anywhere, but that was a lie.

My dad's boss invited my family to play golf with him and his family recently. So, for the first time in my life, I swung a golf club. I didn't hit the ball on the first swing—or the second swing, for that matter. I wasn't trying to get a hole-in-one or win the game by any means; I just wanted to actually hit the ball, and perhaps not look like an idiot. Interestingly enough, the harder I tried not to look like an idiot, the more I ended up looking like an idiot.

While all of this was taking place, I recalled a sermon I had listened to a few months prior. I remembered the preacher talking about grace, and how it's there for us in moments such as this, moments where you suddenly become acutely aware of everything you're not. Because when you realize you can't do something as simple as swing a golf club, the message that plays in your mind typically isn't, "I guess I'm not good at golf. I should try something else." Often, it's more along the lines of, "I'm a total failure. Is there anything I don't mess up?"

Grace meets you when you're in a crowded room with a bunch of important people—becoming more and more aware of how not-important you are—and you're stricken with the fear that you'll be exposed for who you really are, that the spotlight will suddenly turn to you, and everyone will see that you don't belong.[1]

When you lean into grace and confront this fear, something remarkable happens. Nine times out of ten, it loses its power. Grace rushes in and meets you in that moment as you own everything that you're not and move forward to embrace everything that you are. You're no longer concerned about what others think of you, which frees you to be yourself. When you catch a glimpse of who you really are—even if it's only a small glimpse—it makes it awfully difficult to go back to being someone you're not.

When I confronted my fear that others would see I wasn't any good at golf and reject me because of it, I was able to relax and enjoy the evening. The funny thing was, they could already see I wasn't good, and they hadn't rejected me. But when we don't confront our fears, they often become self-fulfilling prophecies. Because we think others are going to reject us, we begin relating to them in a way that is different than how we would normally relate to people. We begin treating them like they have already rejected us, and this makes them feel uncomfortable. Instead of asking us what's wrong and getting to the bottom of things, they often walk away, confused. We then tell ourselves, "I knew they would reject me; they always do." But in reality, they are probably thinking, "I wonder why Jared was pushing me away tonight?" And then they think it is actually you that is rejecting them! Do you see how ridiculous this can be?

※ ※ ※

I remember how I spent the better half of my life struggling to fit in. I didn't know who I was or where I belonged. I often wondered if there even was a place where I belonged. I used to lie on the floor of my closet late at night and cry, and I would get in my car and turn the music up and scream at the top of my lungs. If I screamed loud enough, the pain would go away for a moment, and things would make sense again.

In my desperate attempt to fit in, I changed the very core of who I was. I started talking differently, dressing differently, and the deeply held core values I had grown up with became of less and less importance. I went a lot of places I wish I had never gone and did a lot of things I thought I would never do, all because I wanted to be loved and accepted for who I was. The only problem was, people weren't accepting me for who I truly was; they were accepting who I had become to make them accept me, and even that didn't last for long. I had reached the point where it didn't matter what values a person held; I was desperate for anyone to accept me, so I chose friends with no concept of loyalty.

I did a lot of damage in the world and caused a lot of pain, but none of it eclipsed

126

the pain I felt inside. I always had to put on a front and be who I thought others wanted me to be, because the pain would never let me be myself. I believe now, more than ever, that most of the pain we experience in this life comes from our failed attempts to find out who we really are.

There came a point in the middle of this where I gave my life to Jesus, where I abandoned my life to receive His life. But not everything changed overnight. I still struggled with who I was for awhile—and I still do sometimes.

Fitting in is not just about finding a place where you belong; it's about becoming so aware of who God created and redeemed you to be that you feel a sense of belonging anywhere you are, no matter how many times you hear a voice in your head telling you that you don't fit in.

The other day, I went to the quick lube to get a headlight replaced on my car. An older man with graying hair met me behind the garage and guided me into the bay. He was probably one of the nicest mechanics I've ever met—above average, at least.

"What can I do for you today, son?"

"I have a headlight burnt out, but I'm not sure which one," I replied.

"Okay, turn on your headlights for me real quick," he said.

I nearly had a heart attack. It took me about twenty seconds of fumbling around to find the switch for the headlights, and that was more than enough time for the memories to come flooding in.

This past winter, a friend was having me follow him in his car while we moved some things around in preparation for an event. My car has automatic lights that come on and go off on their own, so I never really pay much attention to them. My friend, however, didn't have automatic lights in his car, but he didn't tell me that.

As I was driving, I didn't even notice that the road ahead of me was darker than it should be—not until my friend, who was driving in front of me, called to tell me my lights weren't on.

I asked him how to turn them on, and he was quiet for a moment.

"You mean you don't know how to turn on headlights?"

"My car has automatic lights," I replied as the shame flooded in.

Another awkward pause ensued. He then told me how to turn on the lights, but I couldn't seem to find the correct knob. He had to call me two separate times before

I finally managed to get the lights on. On top of that, I forgot to turn them off when we stopped for dinner, and back on again when we resumed driving. This story was re-told time and time again amongst our mutual friends.

Here I was at the quick lube, pretending I knew the basics of operating the car I'd been driving for more than three years, but it was quickly becoming apparent I had no clue what I was doing, and I'm sure I looked like an idiot. At that point, I decided to drop the facade.

"I don't know much about cars," I admitted as I stepped out of my vehicle.

He laughed, but not in a condescending sort of way. The smile on his face was so warm and friendly that I couldn't help but feel that he genuinely cared for me.

"That's alright, man. I'll get you taken care of. Just go have a seat inside, and I'll have her out for you in fifteen."

I stepped inside, sat down in an open chair, and waited. When my name was called, I walked to the counter and paid the receptionist. After everything was taken care of, she looked at me, smiled and said, "Thanks; we'll let you drive your car out."

As I entered the garage, I wondered why they hadn't driven my car out into the parking lot for me, like they normally do. I then looked down and saw that I was holding my keys. I had been the entire time. I got in my car, flustered that on top of everything else, I had forgotten to leave my keys in the ignition. A man guided me out of the bay and waved as I drove past. The smile on his face? Almost as big as the man from earlier.

As I was waiting to turn onto the busy highway toward to my house, I began calculating in my mind all the things I had done to make myself look foolish in the span of less than half an hour. But then I stopped, and just sat there for a moment, until grace invaded, and none of it mattered anymore.

✵ ✵ ✵

I know a guy named Tommy, who is the oldest pastor at my church. He's tall, almost eighty years old, and absolutely hilarious. I once heard him talk about growing up on a farm in Alabama where his parents were sharecroppers. His dad worked hard to provide for their family, but at the end of the day, they didn't have much more than one another.

Though he loved him deeply, Tommy's dad never told him it was okay for him to be tall and not play sports like the other boys. As a result, Tommy never really felt like he fit in, especially after his dad died while he was still in high school.

Tommy says each of us need to develop a "sense of being," which essentially means being comfortable in your own skin wherever you are. It means having the capacity to live in the present moment with the awareness that you are one with Christ and fully accepted by Him. Because when you're fully accepted by the Creator of the Universe, it really doesn't matter if people reject you.

If you have a sense of being, you can walk into a room full of strangers and feel as though you belong, even though you don't know anyone in the room. If you don't have a sense of being, you can walk into a room and feel like you don't belong—even if you're among people you've known all your life. I've experienced this before; I know what it's like to walk into a crowded room and feel completely alone—even when everyone there loves and cares for me. It's a terrible feeling, one I never want you to experience, although you probably already have at one time or another.

I remember this one time when I was at my church in Southlake for an event. I was a few hours early, so I walked into the kitchen where several of our hospitality volunteers were getting things set up. As I stepped through the door, I boldly announced, "I'm Jared, and I'm here to harass you!"

Everyone laughed, and two ladies I had never met before stopped what they were doing and each gave me a big hug. I guess they liked that I had the courage to just walk into the room and be my eccentric self.

※ ※ ※

I volunteer with the youth ministry at my church in Frisco on Wednesday nights. It's a lot of fun, especially since I work on the outside team with Bob, Shauna, and Kristine. (Bob the Architect, not Bob the Freedom Guy. Some refer to him as a "builder," but I think using that term is some sort of copyright infringement, so I will stick with "architect" instead.)

I love the outside team because we never really do anything. We just stand outside the church and talk,while the kids play dodgeball. Occasionally, we will yell awkward greetings at students as they exit their parents' cars. I am especially good at this.

There's a guy named Jackson in our youth group who is a junior in high school. He used to have a job at a fast food restaurant where he served chicken to our upper-middle-class community. But then one day, he realized it just wasn't worth it. So he quit that job, and currently works two days a week in our children's ministry. He doesn't get paid nearly as much as he did before, but he's okay with that, because he's doing something that he actually enjoys. He once told me Wednesday is his best day of the week, because he gets to hang out with people who love God and one another.

There's another guy in our youth group named Sean who is also a junior. Sean is a bit unlike some of the other kids, because he never wears shoes. I ran into him in the church parking lot this past Sunday, and he was wearing shorts and a tank top. I didn't think anything of this, until I looked down at his tan, dirty feet.

"Did you not wear shoes today?" I asked.

"Yep!" he replied.

"Not at all?"

"Well ... I have a pair of flip flops in my car in case I want to go somewhere that makes you wear shoes."

"Oh," I said. "That's cool."

Of course, by saying, "that's cool," I really meant, "you're weird," but that's a story for another time.

As Sean and I walked through the parking lot toward the building, I realized how special my church is. It's the type of place where a person can show up on a Sunday morning wearing anything from a suit and tie to shorts and a t-shirt, and they'll be equally accepted either way. It's the type of place where no one judges you for dressing up too fancy or not fancy enough. Basically, you can wear whatever you want and no one will care, even if you decide you want to worship barefoot.

I don't know why I like this so much, but I do. Perhaps because it reminds me of Jesus, who invites us to pull up a chair at His table, without giving a second thought to what we look like or where we've been.

We need churches that welcome everyone, without demanding they change before they can belong to the family. Jesus is a lot better than we are at changing hearts, and I think sometimes we just need to get out of the way and let Him do His work. We need to throw aside our prejudices and welcome the rebels, misfits, rejects, and outcasts of society with open arms. Don't you remember when *you* didn't fit in? I know I do.

※ ※ ※

Bob the Freedom Guy and his wife, Jackee, have four kids. One lives at home, one lives on a missions base in Hawaii, one is married, and the oldest has Down's Syndrome. Bob says each of his kids have their own unique purpose and mark to leave on the world, and his primary role as a parent is helping them discover who they were created and redeemed to be.

Ian, Bob's oldest son, sees the world so much differently than I do. He sees the beauty I often miss because he looks for things I don't look for. He doesn't lay awake at night wondering if he'll ever fit in, he just assumes that he does. He lives with a reckless confidence that I have yet to obtain.

This one woman, who serves on the altar ministry team at my church in Southlake, says Ian comes by often after service to tell the team that he loves praying for people. Another lady says she loves watching him worship. He usually sits on the front row and gives it everything he has, not caring what anyone around him thinks. I wish I could be more like Ian sometimes.

One day, Bob and Ian were raking leaves outside of their house in a Fort Worth suburb when Ian suddenly dropped his rake and laid down in the middle of the giant leaf pile. Bob stopped raking and stood still for a moment, watching him.

"What are you doing, son?"

Ian was silent at first as he moved from side to side, leaves crunching beneath his feet.

"Hey Dad, remember when we were kids and we would jump in the leaves?"

"Yeah ..." he paused as the word rolled smoothly off his tongue and quickly faded into the static. "I do." Bob could feel tears forming behind his eyes as vivid memories of his early years as a father began to flood forth from his subconscious.

I think we all need to be more like Ian. I think we all need to get back to that place where no matter what has happened to us, we know who we were created and redeemed to be—sons and daughters of the God of the Universe who aren't afraid to jump into the leaves.

※ ※ ※

I was sitting in the back of a coffee house once when I heard the girl sitting on the couch across from me tell her friend that she's wanted to be a stripper ever since seeing the movie *The Girl Next Door*.

This caught me by surprise, because she didn't look to be more than sixteen, perhaps seventeen years old—not even out of high school. I wonder if she knows who she was created to be. Perhaps she did at one point, and just forgot for awhile.

ACT IV

Shift

You will burn and you will
burn out; you will be healed
and come back again.

~ Fyodor Dostoyevsky

CHAPTER 20

THE TIME OF OUR LIVES

I used to let fear stop me from taking risks,
but now I take risks in spite of fear (most of the time).

I was sitting on the third row of my church in Frisco one Sunday morning. My pastor was teaching on the Holy Spirit, a topic that is often avoided or abused. I've been on both sides of this, but this time, I really liked the way my pastor presented it: from a balanced and biblical perspective. [1]

As he was talking, I felt something stirring inside of me, and it built throughout the message, which ended with a call for those who wanted a fresh encounter with the Spirit to come forward. I did not hesitate for a moment, which is a bit out of character for me in moments like these. I found myself standing and I was painfully aware that I was the only person doing so. I walked down the center aisle, to the dead center of the altar. Standing a few feet from the stage, I closed my eyes as my pastor began to pray. He didn't yell or scream or jump around the room, but there was an authority in his voice that made me feel safe.

I could feel something happening inside of me as I stood at the front of the sanctuary, my arms outstretched. It felt as if something was coming up through the floor and into my feet. This sensation flowed throughout my entire body, and then I felt something equally powerful, yet completely different—I felt something flowing out of me, down through my legs, to my feet, and out into the floor. The only way I know to describe it is my death flowing into Jesus as His life flowed into me.

Jesus came to bring things that were dead back to life. He did it two thousand

135

years ago in the Middle East and He did it again on a Sunday morning in North Texas.

After church, several of us went to a party at a nearby lake house. The family that owned the lakefront property had a blob and several jet skis, and Bob the Architect brought his boat, so we could go tubing on the lake. I had never been tubing before, and the last time I had been out on a boat was four years ago when I went wakeboarding on Lake Brownwood in West Texas.

My two biggest fears in life are rejection and being dragged behind a speedboat on an inflatable tube—especially in the middle of a lake that is infested with alligators.[2] I like adventure, but not too much adventure. I like to take risks, just don't ask me to face my fears.

Bob didn't pressure me one way or the other. His reassuring voice was strong, yet gentle. In the end, I made the decision to get out of the boat—literally. I climbed onto the tube and lay flat on my stomach, my feet dangling off the edge. I could feel my toes dipping into the cool lake water; the late afternoon sun was warm on my back. It was so peaceful out there in the middle of the lake, which seemed like it was a world away from the urban landscape that surrounded us on three sides.

All of a sudden, the boat began to speed across the lake. I was dragged along in its wake, bouncing from side to side in the choppy surf. It seemed as though I was moving through the water much faster than when I had been reclining in the captain's chair moments earlier. I couldn't help but laugh, because the experience did little to align with my expectations; it wasn't scary at all! In fact, it was far less intimidating than wakeboarding, which I had successfully done once (which was enough).

Sometimes, you just have to push your fears aside and get out in the water. You may find yourself able to walk on it with ease, or you may end up being dragged along on top of it, but either way, you'll make it to the other side without going under. Just keep your eyes fixed on the One who helped you find the courage to get out of the boat in the first place.

Bob the Freedom Guy says whenever we feel afraid, we should simply take a moment and ask God how He feels about us. Often, all it takes is one word from God—an encounter with His perfect love—to get rid of the fear that's been holding us back.

⋇ ⋇ ⋇

One random day in June, a few friends and I decided to go dancing at a club in the old part of Fort Worth, near the stockyards. I remember it was a Thursday—not a Friday, because that would be cliché.

Evening came, and we all met together after work to begin our structured adventure. It was then that we realized most of our group did not really want to go dancing after all. An air of sorrow quickly made its way through the group as our plans fell apart. We were disappointed, but only for a moment, as far better ideas began to take shape in our minds. Before long, we had planned to be spontaneous.

We began in Grapevine, an upper-middle-class city next to the DFW airport. It's one of those places where people who commute to the glass towers of Dallas or Fort Worth reside, in nice houses with manicured lawns, pools, and hardwood floors. Of course, not everyone in the town is affluent—some don't even have pools. Regardless, it's a community that thrives on family, culture, and good coffee. There are even a couple of vineyards within the city limits, right next to the bustling freeways and never-ending road construction.

We immediately headed downtown, thinking it would be alive, and perhaps its life would somehow make us feel alive. When we got there, all that was open were a few restaurants, a biker bar, and an old-school dance hall—complete with a disco ball. A couple of girls in our group still wanted to go dancing, but we managed to talk them out of it.

Disappointed, we left our cars parked in various locations along the downtown strip, cramming everyone into Kyle's beat-up Suburban.[3] We drove to the next town over, a little closer to the Dallas city center. The demographics changed quickly, as if the income level was cut in half the moment we crossed from one town to the next. I guess you could say this town was more like the real world, though that's kind of a lie since eighty-five percent of the world makes less than two hundred dollars a month.[4]

There we were in the ghetto with the whole night ahead of us. It wasn't really the ghetto, but we told ourselves it was enough times that we actually started to believe it. We went to In-N-Out, and another friend met up with us there. We ate burgers and drank sodas and gave our hearts to Jesus at the sight of John 3:16 on the bottom of our cups.

After In-N-Out, we headed to a nearby Walmart, but we didn't buy anything. We just walked the aisles, tried on hats, and looked for crazy people. We didn't see any, so it was kind of a waste of a trip. At least we were all there, together, living life outside of the ordinary. We were no longer coloring inside the lines of perfectly planned escapades; we were free to embrace whatever came our way. In that moment, on that night, all was right in our world.

Our next destination was the lake. Returning to Grapevine, we found the streets had long since emptied. It was after midnight as we came to a stop at the top of a large, empty parking lot. We quietly exited the Suburban and walked a few hundred yards to the shoreline. Darkness prohibited us from seeing the opposite shoreline, which was no more than a mile away. We walked out onto a floating dock, which bounced up and down with every step. It seemed desperate to break free from the shore and make its way across the lake on an adventure of its own.

A couple of the guys stripped down to their underwear and jumped into the murky water. They teased the girls with talk of pulling them in—fully clothed—which caused the girls to shriek every time an arm came near one of their legs. None of them actually got pulled in, though Jordan came awfully close. Aside from the girls' shrieking, there wasn't much talk. It was a sacred moment—the way the still of the night met the gentle lapping of the water—and no one wanted to disturb it. The suburbs usually slow down by 10:00 or 11:00—aside from the occasional SUV transporting adolescents to the nearest taco stand—and we were not far from staring 1:00 square in the face.

I find it a bit strange that our Christian subculture is constantly telling girls to put more clothes on, but at the same time, has no problem with guys taking off their clothes and jumping into the lake. One of the girls did point out it was "disgusting" and "borderline repulsive," but the word "inappropriate" was never brought up. Of course, I can't speak for the entire subculture, just my portion of it. Isn't it funny how we think when just a handful of people around us agree on something, we somehow make up the majority? We forget that we are all individuals, with individual thoughts and opinions. Of course, we agree on core values, like the virgin birth and resurrection of Christ—you know, the important things. But if you were to ask one hundred Christians how they felt about a couple of guys jumping into the lake in their underwear, you'd probably get a wide variety of answers, and that's okay. We can maintain our unity and still disagree with one another on non-essentials. And if that doesn't work, we'll just say *what happens at the lake, stays at the lake.*

It wasn't long before 1:00 came and went. Several other kids our age began to show up, causing the sacredness of the moment to fade as we hiked back through the empty parking lot. I had taken Kyle's keys from him, and we really had no clue where he was. We piled into the Suburban, thinking we could play a prank on him by parking it around the corner.

You see, sometimes us college-aged kids like to act as if we're still in middle school. If nothing else, it momentarily covers up the reality that we're growing up far too fast. We've got our whole lives ahead of us, but we can only act stupid for so long before it becomes sad and pathetic, until we make it to our mid-life crisis, of course, when we get to do it all over again. When you jump into a lake half-naked at twenty-one, it means you're cool, but when you do it at fifty-one, it means you're a creeper, or perhaps something worse.

I put the key in the ignition and attempted to start the Suburban, but the key would not turn. I tried again, but after several attempts, it still failed to start. I began to scan the dashboard for some sort of secret lever that needed to be tripped before the vehicle would start, but didn't find anything.

After ten minutes of failed attempts, I was glad to trade places with Thomas, but his luck wasn't any better. It felt a lot like a horror movie, even though I don't watch horror movies. Except for one time, when I did. I was staying with my friend, Cary, and his family in a little town outside of Oklahoma City. They have the type of home where nearly every teenager in town comes and goes at their leisure. When I arrived, there were a dozen or so people crammed into their living room watching the latest slasher flick, *Scream IV.*

I didn't want to watch the movie, but I didn't want to look like a loser, either. And it turned out I liked it, so much so that I watched it again the next day. But then, in the months that followed, I began to have nightmares. I found myself looking over my shoulder as I walked around my house at night, so now I'm back to not watching horror movies. But if I did watch them, this is what they would feel like: several friends trapped in a vehicle that won't start, in the middle of a darkened parking lot. It was only a matter of time before someone would emerge from the woods and pick us off one-by-one, probably with an axe or a chainsaw because that's a completely realistic way to kill a bunch of twenty-somethings without waking up the neighborhood.

After Thomas failed to start the Suburban, I came to the conclusion that I should head back to the dock and look for Kyle. I got out of the passenger seat and quickly made my way to the shoreline, knowing that in a matter of minutes, Thomas would likely be taking the ignition apart, which would really get us in trouble.

As I approached the lake, I walked past a group of wanna-be hipsters who were sitting on the back of a car. One of them was strumming a guitar in an attempt to add some texture to the stillness of the night. I walked to the end of the dock where a couple of guys were sitting with their feet in the water, but Kyle wasn't one of them. Frustrated, I walked back to the parking lot. I had just passed the hipsters-in-training when a voice called out to me, a voice I recognized. I turned to see Kyle in the group, standing next to the guy who was playing the guitar.

"You looking for me?" he asked.

As I drew closer, I recognized the sounds of worship flowing from the lips of the guy with the guitar. I didn't recognize the song, but I knew immediately it was being sung to the King this stranger and I both shared. They weren't hipsters at all; they were just a bunch of kids from one of the mega-churches on the other side of the lake. Dallas has tons of these cutting-edge cathedrals, especially in the suburbs.

"Hey," I said, nodding at the non-hipsters before turning to Kyle. "How do you start your car?"

I felt terrible interrupting such a holy moment. At least in theory. The truth is, I didn't stop long enough to feel terrible. It was late, I was tired, and the humidity was causing the heat index to rise slightly higher with every passing minute.

"You put the key in—" He paused, as if I were a five-year-old. "And you turn it."

"Yeah, well, we've been trying that for like the past twenty minutes," I replied.

The last traces of mellowness vanished from Kyle's face as he snapped out of the hipster trance and followed me across the parking lot toward his Suburban.

"Those guys were pretty cool," he said as we walked. "They're from The Village."

"Awesome," I replied. "I love Matt Chandler."

Truth be told, I don't really know much about Matt Chandler. I know he pastors a large church in Flower Mound and everyone under thirty loves him. I have also heard rumors that he's a Calvinist, which was disconcerting to some of my friends. I listened to a few of his podcasts awhile back, and I think I liked him.

Kyle and I walked briskly up the asphalt hill to the Suburban. We arrived to find Thomas still attempting to get the starter to turn over, but he gladly slid over to the passenger seat in order to give Kyle a go at it.

Kyle put his foot on the brake and gave the key a turn. Nothing. Pressing down a little harder, he tried again. Still nothing. Frustrated, he exited the vehicle, paced a few yards away, and took out his mobile device. He returned moments later with an update on our predicament.

"Derek's going to come pick us up and take everyone back to their cars."

"From Keller?" I asked. "That'll take what, half an hour?"

"You know, we could probably just walk back to our cars," Thomas piped in.

"Just you and I could go," I said to Thomas. "We could jog it in twenty minutes."

"If you're going to do that, we might as well all go," Jordan chimed in.

"Alright. I'll call Derek and tell him he doesn't need to come," Kyle said.

That settled it. We left the parking lot and began walking, quieting our voices as we passed a row of darkened houses that hugged the edge of the park. We made our way to the beginning of a concrete trail that wound through a heavily wooded area. It reminded me of Austin, the city I grew up in, before my family moved to Dallas. I had never known there were woods like this in Grapevine. Sometimes, in the process of being inconvenienced, we discover little things like this that have been present the entire time, hidden by our busy schedules and fast-paced lives.

The woods were still. A bit eerie, even. Thomas was at the front of our group; Kyle at the rear. We were pretty strung out in between, so if something did jump out of the woods and attack us, the others would have plenty of time to make a clean getaway.

I started out at the front, but lingered toward the back as we journeyed so I could talk to Kyle. He was wielding a baseball bat and kept talking about the zombie apocalypse, which is apparently a big deal. Everyone believes in the spiritual realm, regardless of whether or not they realize it. Some believe it is made up of angels, demons, and those that compose the Trinity; others, zombies, ghosts, and the like. And then there are the ones like Kyle who believe in all of the above.

Kyle is an interesting character, but a good guy overall. He works with Jeremiah, emptying trash at the big corporation, and he loves his job with a passion I have never seen a janitor possess. I'm not sure it's what he wants to do for the rest of his life, but he's pretty good at embracing the moment.

I wish I could be more like Kyle and live in the moment without worrying about the future so much. We are alike, however, in the fact that we both want to grow up and get married and become husbands and fathers and everything that those roles entail. We're both painfully discontent with the lives we've been living—trapped between adolescence and adulthood—and we're in a hurry to grow up, so our real lives will begin.

Maybe Kyle isn't so great at embracing the moment, after all. I suppose it's possible to be fully content and "in the moment" in one area of your life, while at the same time, discontent and yearning for the future in another. Ashley—the girl who broke my heart a few months back—says that after her father died, she learned the time she has now—what is right in front of her—is time she will never be able to get back. She does her best to fully embrace every waking moment, regardless of the struggles that the current hallway may bring.

After a mile or so, the trail emerged from the woods and began to run alongside a four-lane road. I had driven this road at least once a week when I worked in Southlake, but tonight, it looked totally different. It felt odd, to see it so empty and lifeless. It was after 2:00 at this point, and I was really hoping the cops would show up and make the night a bit more interesting. I told Kyle that he better have a plan to quickly dispose of the baseball bat in the event that a police cruiser passed by.

The cops never showed, but I wasn't too disappointed. My adrenaline level was already plenty high on the sheer adventure of the night alone. What made it so great was the spontaneity of the events that unfolded. The night was raw and unforced; nothing was mapped out from beginning to end.

The numbers on the digital clock in my car were just shy of 4:00 when I pulled into my driveway. It had been some time since I had last stayed out so late. I quietly entered my house, tip-toed upstairs, and collapsed into bed. When I awoke a few hours later, I was still in awe of the beauty that had unfolded the night before. The night had proven to the world that you can stay out late with friends and have a lot of fun without drugs, alcohol, or getting into trouble. We did get into a bit of mischief, I suppose, but it was more of the innocent kind, the kind most teenagers abandon in middle school.

Kyle managed to get the Suburban up and running by afternoon. I got online, mapped out our route, and discovered we had walked just under three miles. Who would have thought car trouble could produce so much joy?

※ ※ ※

I returned to the lake the following week. The light of day made everything look different. It was nearly as captivating as it had been on that summer night, but in a different way. I walked out on the dock and lay flat on my back. Turning my head to one side, I gazed out across the lake and watched as water and sky collided and danced across the horizon.

It's always the simple things in life that take us by surprise. We never expect to find ourselves living a rich, fulfilling life in the middle of the ordinary. Most of us are unaware that one can live on the edge of the universe without straying too far from home. I think while adventure is certainly something you get out and do, it's also a state of mind. It's more difficult to take the familiar and find something wonderful in it than it is to get out there in pursuit of something we think will fill our hearts with awe and wonder. The thing is, getting out there and chasing down adventure all the time is not responsible or rational. But then again, I do many things in my own life that I've been told are not responsible or rational. I know, however, that a time will come for me to settle down, to embrace a greater level of responsibility, and spend a little more time calculating my risks. But even then, I don't want to settle into a boring life and forget to embrace the little blessings that are so easy to write off as inconveniences.

We all need to get out there and partake of the beauty of creation more often. It's all around us, just waiting to be discovered. Our familiar lives don't have to be bland and boring canvases of nothingness. God spoke the world into existence from nothing. We are made in His image. We can live furiously in a place where there once was nothing. This is what it means to find adventure in the familiar. I think God is pleased when we give it a try, even if we aren't very good at it at first.

I know I will someday see God face to face; I'll look into His eyes, life will make sense, and I won't be afraid anymore. We'll go for long walks and talk, and it will all carry on uninterrupted. In eternity, I won't have to get out of bed and go to work anymore. Until then, I must make sure my work does not possess me to the point that I forget to stop and fix my eyes upon the beauty that is all around me.

As I was lying on the dock, I noticed a duck standing on the edge of the shore where the water met a concrete boat ramp. He had his feet in the water, but when the gentle waves would roll in, he would lift his body up to keep from getting wet, as if he had forgotten he was a duck. He stood there—half-in, half-out—contemplating whether or not the big, blue lake was safe for a small, brown duck. Another duck came up behind him and dove into the lake like he had just found water in the middle of the desert. After witnessing this, the duck on the shore wasn't so afraid anymore. He dove right into the lake and swam after his friend, quacking like he'd just won the duck lottery.

I've always wanted a duck. I'd like to have one live with me in my house, like a pet or something. I would name him *Charles*, because *Puddles* is a stupid name. Charles would swim in my bathtub. I would have guests over, and they would see him swimming in my poor excuse for a lake, run downstairs, and ask me if I was aware that there was a duck in my bathtub, and I would look at them like they were from Mars, as if to say, "Of course. Doesn't everyone?"

CHAPTER 21

MAYPEARL

I used to think I was really good at following Jesus,
but then I realized I was just acting like a Pharisee.

I spent the second half of the summer working at a youth camp just outside of Dallas. It was on the other side of town, a little over an hour from my house. Not close, but not far, either.

The students would arrive on Monday and leave on Friday. This would happen five times. Five weeks of camp. Easy enough, right? Little did I know, it would be much more difficult than I initially thought. You never really find out how selfish you are until you're thrown into a world where you work eighteen hours a day, sleep on a hard mattress at night, shower in slimy well water, and eat cafeteria food for a month.

I packed my car full of all the things I thought I would need for the month, said good-bye to my mom, and left the confines of my master-planned community. I drove to Lewisville where I met my friend, Luke, at the Chick-fil-A near his office. Luke and I have a standing lunch appointment at this location every month, but it really only happens once a quarter. His work schedule is a bit hectic, and I'm a bit more reluctant to drive across town now that I work from home. We used to hang out a lot more, back before he got married and had to get a real job. I enjoy our lunches, even though they always make me feel as though my life is moving along at the pace of a snail.

I wish things would fall into place for me like they did for Luke, and I suppose they will someday, when I'm his age. He's five years older than I am, so he's farther along in his journey, though neither of us have it all figured out yet. Luke has an associates degree in youth ministry and wants to be a pastor. He worked for the same ministry I work for now up until his engagement, when he realized he would need a more stable income to support himself and Maritza, the girl from Laredo whom he would marry in a few months. He got a job working in the media department of a large ministry, making slightly more than enough to get by. He did that for a few months, until the door opened for his current job. He now works for a multi-millionaire who sells nutritional products, and while I don't know what he does exactly, I know he makes a lot of money doing it. And I also know he still really wants to be a pastor, and it bothers him that he's not in ministry.

We sat in a booth by the window eating our chicken sandwiches, while the soccer moms around us tried to make their kids eat their food instead of throwing it on the ground (which is far more fun). Luke told me that he had worked at the same camp the year before. He told me it was exhausting, yet rewarding at the same time.

Within the hour, we parted ways. Luke headed back to work, and I headed south—through miles and miles of endless suburbia—until I broke free from the sprawl on the other side of Arlington, where the freeway finally dead-ended at the intersection of a country road. Turning left, I drove across the countryside until the flat landscape of small towns, cement plants, and steel mills gave way to gentle, rolling hills. Maypearl came into view on the horizon, a tiny community of less than a thousand. I turned left at the dollar store, and saw a church sign that read Your goodness is insufficient. You need a Savior.

I thought it interesting that someone would plaster this message on a sign outside their church, thinking perhaps it would draw people in to experience the love and life that Jesus offers. I've never been to this church, and I don't think I ever will go. Just driving by, I get the feeling that I wouldn't fit in, that they wouldn't like me.

I don't think people need to be reminded they are insufficient and need a Savior. I think most of them already know, and are actively looking for a savior of some sort—they just don't call it that.

Most people cannot put what they feel into words, but they all feel the same ache on the inside. They ache to know that their lives have meaning, that they are valuable, that they are loved. They know something is missing in their lives. What they reach for in an attempt to fill the void varies, but they are all desperately searching for the same thing—for something or someone to save them. We know we need to be rescued from this world, but we're not always conscious of this reality. It's a scary thing to know the world is a mess and there's nothing we can do about it, that we need something outside of us to save us. So, for the most part, we ignore what is happening inside of us and all around us; we ignore the inward angst by living faster, falling harder, and working our lives away to obtain things we think will make us happy. Perhaps then, when we've made it to the next "level" in life, we'll be happy enough to forget our deep spiritual poverty.

I believe the greatest need of humanity is to allow Jesus to re-connect us to the life He offers. We need Him to remind us who we are and that our lives are going to turn out okay, as long as we stick with Him. Once Jesus tells us who we are and what our purpose in life is, we find we no longer need all the other things we've filled our lives with, all the things we sold our souls to obtain.

I continued driving past the church sign, knowing I was not far from the campground. It appeared out of nowhere a few minutes later, a series of brick buildings in the middle of a clearing. I turned into the parking lot of a large office building, which seemed out of place across the street from the campground. Parking my car in one of the narrow spots, I walked across the hot asphalt to the main entrance. As I walked through the front door, I found my boss [1] waiting for me in the lobby.

"Stump! You're early."

I was early, by a few hours, actually. A girl from East Texas had beat me there, which was okay, since I wasn't trying [too hard] to impress anyone. The others staggered in throughout the afternoon and into the evening, until all of us had gathered in a conference room on the second floor where we would be briefed on the ins and outs of camp.

We spent the next few days doing a lot of manual labor, which I was not a fan of. Not because I'm against working hard, but because I'm not very good at it. All the other guys were in the warehouse building things or out driving stakes into the ground, leaving me to pretend that I was good at working with my hands. I know we're supposed to become like Jesus and everything, but I don't think I'll ever make a very good carpenter.

※ ※ ※

During our time of preparing for camp, we filmed several videos that would be used during chapel services over the course of the five weeks. For one of the videos, we each had to share a brief testimony of how things used to be before grace invaded our lives.

Before God came into my life, things were a mess. Now, my entire outlook on life is different. You could say that everything has changed, though things are still pretty messy. I was a bit intimidated by the whole thing. It's easy to talk about who you used to be, but I haven't met very many people who can easily talk about the crap they still deal with. We ache to find a place where we can be honest and real and talk about our issues, but it seems those places are few and far between, and church is typically not one of them. When people hear "everything has changed" they often confuse it with "I've arrived."

My turn came before I was ready. I was escorted into a makeshift studio, which had been set up in a hallway. It was completely dark, except for the bright studio lights. I sat down in the white leather chair and stared into the camera.

"Then ... I felt like I didn't fit in anywhere." I paused for a moment without breaking eye contact with the lens. I knew exactly what I wanted to say—the words were right there in my gut—I was just struggling to bring them to the surface. They came all at once. Like the opening of a spillway on a dam, I couldn't hold them back any longer. "Now ... I know that I belong."

In a moment, I had spread all my cards across the table; I had just given up my right to be insecure. Because I had stated that I knew I belonged, I now had to live as if I actually believed it was true. The only problem was, I actually didn't. At least, not to the extent I thought I needed to.

I think we sometimes hesitate to share what Jesus has done in our lives because we're afraid our humanity will break in and we'll revert to our old selves, thus negating our testimony and confirming our status as a hypocrite. But really, a hypocrite is someone who says they are someone they are not, and I am not an insecure, fearful person anymore—even though I tend to be insecure and fearful at times. I'm a new creation—a child of the King—even though I forget sometimes.

It's a trap to think we must fully arrive before we can share our stories. It may be awhile before I get over my insecurities, but when I do, I'm sure I'll find new ones waiting for me.

Life seems to be a never ending series of highs and lows, doesn't it? We really do live in the hallways. We finally reach that mountain top—the one we've been climbing for so long. We become overwhelmed with joy in our moment of accomplishment. Finally, our lives have meaning. We throw our hands up in the air and shout aloud that we've arrived, only to find ourselves slipping into the valley again moments later.

I suppose life is not about arriving. It's more about the journey, and I know God places people in our lives to help us through the rough patches. We need each other. We need to receive love from others and then give it back to them, but we need to receive God's love first; otherwise, we'll have nothing to give away.

I think there are people out there who need my story. I think there are people beside me, in front of me, and behind me who need to hear about my struggle, my fears, my pain. I don't think that's an arrogant statement to make—that there are people out there who need my story—because I know I have needed the stories of others for my own life to make sense. If those people had never shared their stories, I probably wouldn't have the courage to share mine.

Ashley and I don't talk anymore, but I read her blog the other day, and she wrote about how each of us was created for things far greater than we could ever imagine, and that we should run to Jesus, give Him the broken parts of our hearts, and let Him make them beautiful again. I couldn't help but smile slightly at the irony of this, that a person who contributed to my hurt would also contribute to my healing. Often, the very things that bring us pain turn around and end up bringing us peace as well.

I'm beginning to think God designed us to need one another, to learn from one another, to speak courage into one another, to help one another grow. We just have to learn to balance the tension between needing people and becoming needy people. Because when we become needy people, we end up driving away the people we need the most. It's taken me awhile to learn this, but co-dependency is not a fruit of the Spirit.

I don't think God is waiting for us to get to the point where we have it all together and can stand on our own without any help. As Tullian Tchividjian puts it, when we think we're getting better, we're actually getting worse. When we get to that point where we start to think, "Well, I needed God's grace a lot when I first got saved, but now I've gotten to the point where I don't need grace as much anymore," we've actually become sicker than we were before, and are more in need of God's grace than we were when He first found us. [2]

It's interesting to think that the religious people—the ones who thought they were getting better—were the ones Jesus was mad at most of the time, whereas the sinners—the ones who knew they couldn't get better—were the ones He embraced when they came and kneeled at His feet. The posture of the religious person is folded arms and a closed heart, while the posture of the sinner is arms and heart wide open, longing for the unconditional embrace of the Father. *Satan's masterpiece is the Pharisee, not the prostitute* [3] This is because they have the outward appearance of being righteous, while their hearts are filled with all kinds of darkness (Matthew 23:25).

When God comes into our lives, things do tend to get better. This is because He changes our hearts from hearts of stone to hearts of flesh (Ezekiel 36:26). But the reality is, we're still sinners in need of a Savior, even though we're also the righteousness of God in Christ. This is a tension we have to work through. It's not one or the other, because even though there is evidence in our lives that we are children of God, there is also evidence to the contrary. I am not saying that the work of the Cross is invalid or somehow insufficient, but simply that we need Jesus more than just once; we need Him every single day of our lives. I've heard people advocate for one side or another, and I think this is toxic, no matter which side we fall on. Either we end up wallowing in shame, unable to fully accept the love of God, or we end up arrogant, and forget how much we still need Jesus.

I think Tim Keller sums up the middle ground quite well when he says, *The Gospel of justifying faith means that while Christians are, in themselves still sinful and sinning, yet in Christ, in God's sight, they are accepted and righteous. So we can say that we are more wicked than we ever dared believe, but more loved and accepted in Christ than we ever dared hope—at the very same time.* [4]

In a way, I suppose the church sign in Maypearl is accurate—our goodness *isn't* sufficient, and we *do* need a Savior. But just because something is factually correct, doesn't mean it's *right*. A statement like this comes across as harsh and forceful, and I think the Gospel is supposed to sound a bit more like good news.

When the angel appeared to the shepherds to announce the birth of Jesus, their natural response was to be terrified, which is a pretty natural response to an angel showing up while you're standing guard over your sheep through the night. The angel responded to their fears by telling them they had no reason to fear, but that the news of Jesus' birth was *good news that will bring great joy to all people.* [5]

When we are presenting the Gospel to people, I think we should ask ourselves if it comes across as good news that will bring people great joy. This isn't to say that everyone will accept our message as one of great joy. We are not responsible for how people respond to our message, but we are responsible for how we present it. We have been given the task of telling the world that God is good, not that He's mad at them. This is why I try to avoid reducing the Gospel to cute one-liners. They may tell a portion of the story, but it is impossible to tell the whole story in 140 characters or less. Perhaps people are rejecting the story of Jesus because they have only heard a partial telling of it. Perhaps they were only told they need to go to church on Sunday, when God is making all things new seven days a week.

When we live as humble, broken people—aware of, but not bound by our shortcomings—we lean on God when all is right, and trust Him to pick us up when we fall. This is the divine paradox of grace: we can be broken and empty, yet whole and complete at the same time. Even though we may get to the point where we overcome destructive patterns of behavior—such as excessive drinking or sexual addictions—I don't think we'll ever get to the place where we'll be 100% flawless on this side of eternity. I think that's why God gives us His righteousness through Jesus, because He knows we'll never be able to obtain it on our own.

Be perfect, therefore, as your heavenly Father is perfect. ~ Matthew 5:48

This is the standard that God requires, and there's no getting around it. But I think He set the bar high on purpose, so high that we'd never be able to get over it on our own. This way, we would recognize our need for a Savior; we would recognize our need for the righteousness of God in Christ, that we might say as Paul said, *For*

151

it is by grace you have been saved, through faith—and this is not from yourselves, it is the gift of God—not by works, so that no one can boast (Ephesians 2:8-9).

Be merciful, just as your Father is merciful. ~ Luke 6:36

This verse from Luke sounds a lot like the verse in Matthew. This is because both statements were taken from the Sermon on the Mount—more specifically, the part where Jesus talks about loving our enemies. They are talking about the same thing, but what Matthew calls *perfection*, Luke calls *merciful*. The Greek [6] word Matthew uses for *perfect* is *teleioi*, from which the word *telos* is derived. This word speaks of an end purpose or goal. *Teleioi* is used four more times [7] in the New Testament, and each time it is translated as *mature*.

From this, it is reasonable to conclude that the end goal of our faith is to become mature, so we are like our Father in Heaven. If this is the case, we must ask ourselves, "What is our Father like?" Matthew and Luke seem to be telling us that our Father is perfect in showing mercy to those who do not deserve it, which is what Jesus means when He tells us to love our enemies.

Brian Zahnd says it like this: *You can't be 'perfect' (in the literal, moralistic, or "sinless perfection" sense)—but you can be merciful.* [8]

Micah (the Old Testament prophet) says it like this: *And what does the Lord require of you? To act justly and to love mercy and to walk humbly with your God.* [9]

James (the brother of Jesus) says it like this: *Mercy triumphs over judgment.* [10]

And Jesus says it like this: *Go and learn what this means: 'I desire mercy, not sacrifice.' For I have not come to call the righteous, but sinners.* [11]

What if the Gospel is not about being moral, but being merciful?

What if the Gospel is not for those who think they are righteous, but those who know they are sinners?

I have not come to call the righteous, but sinners to repentance. ~ Jesus [12]

What if repentance is about choosing to trust in God's righteousness over our own?

What if morality is not about avoiding sin so that God will be happy with us?

What if the reason why God tells us to avoid certain behaviors is because He knows they will harm us and the people around us?

What if God isn't trying to keep us from enjoying life, but live life to our fullest capacity as humans?

I have noticed that the Church often misses the point when it comes to these things, as is our custom quite often. We tend to water the Gospel down to the point where it becomes nothing more than behavior modification, instead of the scandalous story where God came to us and clothed us in His righteousness while we were still covered in the shame of our sin. We read about how we shouldn't lie, cheat, steal, or have sex before marriage, so we quickly clean up our lives (the parts everyone sees), so we can then go around thumping people on the heads with our Bibles when they fail to live up to the impossible standards we set for them. The problem with this is it looks nothing like being merciful.

Sure, the judgement of God is talked about in Scripture, but those same Scriptures also tell us that mercy is greater than judgment.

Mercy > Judgment.

Let that sink in for a moment.

Mercy triumphs over judgment.

Perhaps we should spend less time judging others and more time thinking of ways we can show them the mercy of God. As G.K. Chesterton said of Saint Francis of Assisi: *He walked the world like the pardon of God.* [13] There's no point in yelling at someone to get their act together, because the whole reason Jesus came was because we *couldn't* get our act together! God didn't shout at us from far away; He came and dwelt among us. [14]

The Word became flesh and blood, and moved into the neighborhood (John 1:14a, The Message).

I realize some may not like that I quoted from *The Message*, because it isn't a "real Bible," but, to be perfectly honest, I don't care. Here, Eugene Peterson takes an already beautiful verse and makes it even more beautiful, and he is more of a biblical scholar than you or me.

If someone has truly given their heart to Jesus, they are already righteous, regardless of whether or not we see it manifest on the outside. Give them some space, some time, and some grace; if Jesus has changed their heart, you will begin to see it reflect in their outward life over time. And if you don't—love, serve, and support them until you do; it often takes time to grow into the new life that Jesus gives. Sanctification doesn't happens all at once—not for you, not for me, and not for the "big sinner" you are thinking of right now.

※ ※ ※

If you think about it, we all have addictions. Some are addicted to sex, drugs, or alcohol—the "big sins." You know, the ones that "separate you from God." But there are also those of us who are addicted to food, shopping, appearance, popularity, and the approval of others. We all have something that we retreat to when we feel pressure; we all have something that we cling to when we feel helpless and out of control, something that makes us feel safe and in control again.

I know a guy who is in his late 40's who has never consumed a drop of alcohol in his life. But as we talked, he told me that he can't sit down at a restaurant and eat a meal without having his drink refilled four or five times. He drinks and drinks and drinks—and then he drinks some more. He knows it's not good for him, but he can't control himself; he can't seem to make himself stop. But at least it's soda, instead of alcohol. It's an addiction—he will admit—albeit a socially acceptable one.

So, I have this problem ... I buy books and never read them. I have other problems too, but this is the easiest one to talk about, because it's so ridiculous. I'm not just talking about one or two books here and there; I will literally walk into a bookstore and walk out with dozens of books I will never read. It's not that I don't *want* to; I just don't have time, and it's hard for me to sit still for too long. I love reading, yes, but it's something I have to make myself do.

I think the root cause of my addiction is a desire to obtain knowledge. This is not a bad thing, of course, but I tend to desire knowledge because I think it will save me. Somewhere, in the depths of my soul, I actually believe that if I obtain all of the right information, God will be happy with me. It's no different than trying to obtain the righteousness that Christ freely offers through works, and we've already discussed how we are saved by grace through faith—not by works.

It may seem like a stretch for some, but my addiction to knowledge is no different than the alcoholic's dependence on alcohol. We're both dependent on something other than Jesus to tell us who we are and quiet the angst in our souls. Like the alcoholic who must avoid alcohol to keep from getting drunk, I must avoid bookstores to keep from feeding my pursuit of knowledge over Jesus. [15]

Problem solved, right? Not quite. You see, I have the Amazon app on my mobile device, and I use it several times a week to browse for books I don't have time to read. Fortunately, there is a "wish list" option, so I rarely ever buy the books. I just read the descriptions and reviews and imagine ordering and receiving them in the mail, even though I know I would merely glance at the covers before burying them on the "to-read" shelf in my studio. I get caught in the ecstasy of the experience, and have been known to waste hours browsing through books to feed my addiction. It's really no different than thinking about sex all the time without ever actually having it.

My addiction will do far less damage than the addiction of the alcoholic—especially since I buy most of my books on sale—but the underlying cause is essentially the same. In the same way, a craving for illicit sex will probably do more to harm a relationship than a craving for approval, at least on the surface. But if we were to dig a bit deeper, we might find the craving for approval is actually the real problem, and sex is merely the symptom, the thing we use to numb the pain that stems from a lack of approval. Using this theory, we could say cravings for approval and cravings for sex have equal potential to harm our relationships, because they are so connected.

I don't know the solution to our addictions, I just know we all have them. [16] But I also know that God is bigger and stronger and more powerful than anything we crave. I wish that He would change me now, instead of gradually over time, but He doesn't seem to be in as much of a hurry as I am. When I get to the point where I've overcome one addiction, I just find two or three others waiting for me.

We need to stop judging those who have different addictions than we do. We need to learn to be truly merciful toward one another, so that perhaps the outside world will finally see Jesus shining through our lives. If the picture they see at present is distorted by pride, bitterness, judgement, or any other junk that seems to permeate the Church in excess, it's our fault, not theirs. We need to stop trying to fix one another and simply let the love of Jesus flow through us to the world around us. Then, we won't have to beg people to join the family of God, because they won't ever want to leave.

※ ※ ※

My friend, Annie, once told me she was concerned about one of her friends who had adopted a sort of new theology that the Holy Spirit does not convict those who believe in Jesus of sin.

Annie was a bit surprised when she heard this, so she asked her friend to explain the reasoning behind her evolving belief. Her friend told her that as she searched the Scriptures, she found lots of verses about the Holy Spirit comforting us, but not many about Him convicting us—at least, not in regard to sin.

"What do you think?" Annie asked me.

"Of course the Spirit convicts us of sin," I replied.

"I agree. Do you know of a Scripture to back it up."

"I'm not sure where it is in Scripture, but I know that He *does*," I said, after thinking it over for a moment.

It seemed right, and it's what I had been taught most of my life. But when I really thought about it, I had no idea where it was in the Bible—or if it was even in the Bible at all. So, I began searching for a verse about the Holy Spirit convicting believers of sin. The only problem was, I couldn't find one. Well, there was one, but it didn't say what I wanted it to say.

I put these thoughts on the back burner for awhile, pondering them every now and then. Several months passed, and I slowly began to realize I had adopted a way of thinking that was contrary to God's way of thinking. For most of my life, I had thought that the Spirit was given for conviction of sin first, and to comfort second.

Right before Jesus went to the cross, He pulled His friends aside and told them that someone better than Him—the Holy Spirit—would come not long after He left (John 16:7). He then told them the Spirit would convict them of righteousness, rather than sin.

And when he [the Holy Spirit] comes, he will convict the world concerning sin and righteousness and judgment: concerning sin, because they do not believe in me; concerning righteousness, because I go to the Father, and you will see me no longer; concerning judgment, because the ruler of this world is judged (John 16:8-11, ESV, brackets mine).

This is the one Scripture I was talking about—the one that didn't say what I wanted it to say. Unfortunately, for my preconceived notions, this is the only Scripture that comes close to talking about the Spirit convicting believers of sin.

From the text above, you'll find the Spirit convicts of three things: sin, righteousness, and judgment. It's very easy to breeze through this and think that the Spirit's role is to convict *us* of these three things. In reality, John goes on to talk about the three unique groups that the Spirit's conviction is aimed toward. If you slow down and simply *read* the text, you'll catch it—no knowledge of the Greek language required!

Concerning Sin

... concerning sin, because <u>they do not believe in me</u> (John 16:9, ESV).

Who does the Spirit convict of sin?

Well, Jesus is the one speaking here, so the text tells us that those who do not believe in Jesus are the ones the Spirit convicts of sin. This is consistent with numerous Scriptures that talk about us not being able to come to Jesus without the Spirit first revealing our need for Him.

We know that this verse does not refer to believers, because Jesus was speaking to the disciples, and He said "because *they* do not believe in me," not "because *you* do not believe in me."

Concerning Righteousness

... concerning righteousness, because <u>I go to the Father, and you will see me no longer</u> (John 16:10, ESV).

Once again, the text points to a specific group of people. It's quite clear that the second work of the Spirit is targeted at the group Jesus was speaking to. We've already established that Jesus was speaking to the disciples, to "those who believe in Him," which means that the conviction of the Spirit concerning righteousness is directed at those who already believe.

When the Spirit reveals our need for a Savior and we come to Jesus, He exchanges the death in us for the life in Him. The theological term for this is *righteousness*, which is given to us freely. [17] But we don't always feel or even believe we are righteous, do we? We know, as Christians, our truest identity is not that of a sinner, but of one who is righteous. God chooses to call us righteous when we believe in His Son, not when we finally get our act together and live righteously.

We all have conflicting evidence in our lives—that we are fallen humans who sin and that we have been made new, making us just as righteous as Jesus. If an outsider were to examine our lives and the secret parts of our hearts, they would see evidence both for and against the claim that we are God's righteous children. No one is an exception to this. There has only been—and only will be—one perfect human that walked this earth, and it isn't you!

The word *convict* used in John 16 simply means to *fully convince*. Jesus said the Spirit would fully convince believers that they are righteous *because I go to the Father, and you will see me no longer.*

I don't think the disciples needed to be convinced they were righteous when Jesus was right there with them. But what about when He hung naked on the cross? That's when they got scared, when they wondered if everything they had believed in was really just a fairy tale. They didn't know Jesus would rise from the dead, even though He had told them He would. In their minds, the crucifixion was a picture that Jesus had failed in His mission—and it was, apart from the resurrection.

If only the disciples had had the Spirit at that point. Not only were they not fully convinced of their righteousness, they weren't even fully convinced that the person they had been following really was the Savior of the world.

We know what happens next. Jesus was taken off the cross and put in the grave. On the third day, the Father raised Him from the dead, proving that He was not just another failed revolutionary who claimed to be the Savior of the world. He then appeared to the disciples, and they hung out together for a few weeks before He ascended to the Father's side, which is where He remains today.

Because we walk by faith rather than by sight, because we believe in Someone we cannot see or feel or touch, because Jesus isn't physically present with us to remind us that we're righteous; we need the Spirit to fully convince us of our righteousness.

There you have it—the only group of people that the Spirit convicts of sin are those who are not in relationship with Jesus.

Bob the Freedom Guy says that sin is a condition before it becomes a behavior. Sin is more about the absence of God from your soul than it is the bad things you do. Your behavior—good or bad—flows out of whether or not God is present at the core of your soul.

Once we've realized there is no remedy for our sinful condition apart from Jesus, the Spirit doesn't keep reminding us. He doesn't need to—we are good enough at that on our own.

Because we live in a fallen world, we're still capable of sinning even after the Spirit has convicted us of our sin and we've turned to Jesus. It's possible for Jesus to have your heart, but there still be wounded areas of your soul that you haven't fully opened up to Him. Yet, it's important to note that Jesus' focus is not on the parts of us that aren't healed, but the work that He has done through the cross, which enables Him to see us for who we will become, both now (in part) and in eternity (in full).

Instead of trying really hard not to sin, we should recognize that we have been set free from the power of sin (Romans 6:18). When we do mess up, God isn't standing by waiting to yell at us; He wants to help us get on the right track again. If you are hearing a condemning or accusing voice, it's not the voice of the Spirit, because the Spirit is kind and gentle. The Spirit is merciful, just as God is merciful. He reminds us who we are, that we belong to a King who has a better way for us. He comforts us when we fail, and deposits the truth in our hearts that we are no longer defined by our failures. The Spirit does not point out our faults so we can work hard to become better people. Rather, He's trying to get us to wake up to the reality of who we already are because of Jesus. This is what it means to be *convicted of righteousness*.

Concerning Judgment

... concerning judgment, because <u>the ruler of this world is judged</u> (John 16:11, ESV).

Here we see God's judgment is aimed not at believers, but at the *ruler of this world*. This leaves us with another question: Who is the ruler of this world?

Let me tell you a story. When God first created mankind, He created us in His likeness, and gave us dominion over the earth. In other words, He created us to look like Him and reproduce who He is throughout the earth. Adam and Eve had dominion over everything—we could call them the *rulers of this world,* in a sense.

God gave them dominion, yes, but He also gave them free will. God did not create evil, but in creating free will, He allowed for the possibility of evil.

The tree God told Adam and Eve not to eat from was the tree of the *knowledge of good and evil.* Initially, Adam and Eve didn't know there was a difference between good and evil. They didn't know that evil existed, that evil was a possibility—all they knew was good. All they knew was the image of God, which they reflected perfectly and completely.

All of that quickly changed when Adam and Eve ate from the tree. In breaking their connection with God, they forfeited their dominion of creation to satan, who became the *new ruler of this world*. Ownership of the world never changed (as God owns everything and always has), but at this point, the world received a new general manager. The only problem was, he refused to run the world the way the owner intended, which is why redemption was planned.

Adam and Eve had dominion. Adam and Eve lost dominion. Jesus came and reclaimed dominion. This is redemption.

Now is the judgment of this world; now will the ruler of this world be cast out (John 12:31, ESV).

Through the death and resurrection of Jesus, God fired the world's general manager and replaced him with His Son. This is what we mean when we say *the ruler of this world was cast out.*

It is important to note that this is *past* tense, which makes me wonder ... If the *evil* general manager was fired and replaced with a *good* general manager, why is the world still broken?

The answer is simple, yet quite complex. To put it simply, the evil general manager was fired from his position as ruler of the world, but he didn't leave the world—kind of like the guy who keeps texting the girl who broke up with him last month. Unless the girl changes her phone number (which is what we attempt to do when we live with the mentality that God's primary method of restoring creation to its original design is taking us to heaven, rather than bringing heaven to earth), the guy can still text her. Even though she receives and is likely frustrated by these texts, she doesn't have to text back. Because the moment she does, she gives him an "in."

What I am trying to say is, satan has lost his authority and his position. While there is no hope of getting his position back, he can still manipulate us into giving him authority. And while we can't give him authority over the whole world (because we are not the owner), we can give him authority over our own lives. Get enough people doing this, and his sphere of authority can grow quite large, though it can never eclipse the authority of the sons and daughters of God.

There will come a day when Jesus will return to earth, eradicate evil, and take care of the failed general manager of the world once and for all. Until then, we live in the midst of the struggle, in the hallways, in the tension between creation and redemption.

Now that we know that the Spirit's judgment is aimed at the ruler of this world, we must ask ourselves, "Who needs to be fully convinced of this reality?"

First, I think the Spirit convicts satan that he has been fired from his position, and that his time here on earth to manipulate people into giving him authority is limited. This is necessary, because with so many people giving him authority, he probably finds himself thinking that he never got fired in the first place, and he needs to be "fully convinced" of this reality.

Second, I think the Spirit convicts us that satan has already been judged and cast out, and a new general manager is in charge of the world—even though we don't see that playing out when we turn on the news. This is definitely something we need to become fully convinced of, because free will is still in the equation, which means people are free to give satan authority to carry out his evil schemes through them, allowing him to pretend he still rules the world.

Conclusion

The Holy Spirit is an essential member of the Trinity, carrying the role of conviction concerning sin, righteousness, and judgment. We just need to understand what that actually means. [18]

CHAPTER 22

A SMALL ROLE IN A LARGE PROCESS

I used to think God needed me,
but now I know He wants me.

The first week of camp passed rather quickly. The weather was unusually cool for July in Texas, which made the long days a bit more tolerable. We would start with prayer at 8:00 in the morning, play games between breakfast and lunch, have a three-hour service in the afternoon, break for free time before and after dinner (which actually meant work for us), play more games, and then hold an end-of-day event that lasted until around midnight. The students would then head off to bed while we debriefed and set up for the next day. Because I was on the media team, I was the last person in bed nearly every night—no earlier than 2:00; sometimes as late as 3:30. The next morning, I would literally wake up minutes before prayer was scheduled to begin. I showered at least every other day, but it was always at the most random times.

This daily schedule was repeated three times, and then it was Friday. After a half-day of camp, the students would get back on their yellow buses and white church vans, and head back to whatever cities and towns they were from. The campground would get eerily silent after the final vehicle pulled out of the parking lot. We would gather in the cafeteria for lunch, and then go back to our rooms to sleep.

It was a strange feeling, as the fast-paced life I had been living suddenly came to a screeching halt. All of the noise that had filled my life that week was gone in a moment, and I was left alone with my thoughts.

That was when the voices started. I began to wonder where my life was headed, what I was doing there, and if any of it was really worth it. It's funny how we can be full of confidence one moment, but completely void of it the next.

The next thing I knew, I was in my car, headed north. Eighty miles later, I pulled into my driveway. Exhaling deeply, I entered the house with my duffel bag. I didn't even bother to unpack; I just collapsed on the couch in the loft, where I slept until early evening. When I woke up, I thought back to one of the high points of the week, during the Thursday afternoon service. I don't remember what the speaker talked about; I just remember that after his message, he had the worship team come back up to play in the background as he led the students in prayer for their schools— not a boring, monotone sort of prayer, but a deep intercession that comes only from the core of the soul. One by one, the students began to cry out for their friends who were in need of encounters with the Father. Their voices filled the room, penetrating the silence and the static.

God, I will fight for Vanessa!

God, I will fight for Emily!

God, I will fight for Jonathan!

It was a holy moment, almost surreal.

Was there an element of hype?

Probably.

But was it real?

Without a doubt.

Was it beautiful?

Definitely.

As I reflected on this moment, I began to wonder what happened as each of those students returned to their familiar corners of the state and came down off the mountaintop. I wondered if they would still be fighting for those they loved when life returned to its normal, mundane pace. I wondered if they would still be full of passion when school started again in the fall, when the anxiety and pressure of growing up returned.

It's hard to wake up the world when you're still struggling to wake up yourself, and it often feels like I've been asleep for most of my life.

※ ※ ※

The weekend progressed quickly. I spent much of it "resting" on the couch, which is the politically correct way of saying I was a lazy bum. I didn't really feel like going to church when Sunday rolled around, so I didn't; I just stayed on the couch. A feeling of dread came over me when noon hit, as I knew that in a few hours, I would have to leave in order to be back at the campground by dinnertime. I had some work I needed to do to prepare for the week ahead, but instead, I picked up the remote.

I told myself it was okay that I spent most of the weekend in front of the television (i.e., losing touch with reality), since I worked so hard the week before. I feel as though I'm not alone, that most of us spend our weekends this way. We convince ourselves it's okay, since we're such workaholics the other five days. And it's not that it's wrong, per se, I just think there's more to life than going to work five days a week and spending the other two on the couch.

As I made my way through the maze of suburbia to the campground, I couldn't help but ask myself what I was doing. I felt like I didn't fit in with this group, like I didn't belong. I also felt like a loser, because I couldn't even live up to my own testimony—that whole *I know I belong* thing.

I have found when I let my walls down and get vulnerable, I'm almost immediately challenged in that same area of life. It's almost as if the enemy of my soul challenges my identity the moment I speak it out loud. Perhaps he realizes that when I verbalize it, I'm beginning to believe it. Ever since I told the world (or at least, North Texas) I knew I belonged, I felt like I didn't belong. Go figure. But as I was driving down the freeway into Waxahachie, I saw a billboard that read, You Belong Here. It didn't matter that it was for a bank, because I knew it was there just for me. I saw two more billboards with the same message later in the week, and by that time, I got the message that God was trying to communicate to me. I knew I belonged, even though I didn't always feel like it.

※ ※ ※

The second week of camp was fun and fast-paced, a carbon copy of the first. For many of the students, it was the best week of their lives, but for me, it was just another thing I did. When you're down in the dirt making everything happen, it's pretty easy to lose sight of what is actually being accomplished. I don't think the full weight of everything that happened at camp will ever hit me. I heard testimony after testimony after testimony of God doing what He does best, but even though I was playing a small role to help facilitate it, it didn't feel like I was really a part of it.

There were a few people on the team who were mobbed out, because God wasn't "using" them as much as they had thought He would or in the ways they thought He would. Perhaps they were just looking for a spotlight, and were disappointed when they got shoved into a dark corner.

I kind of chuckled to myself as I heard these stories. The first week, I only prayed for three or four students while everyone else prayed for dozens, even hundreds. It kind of bothered me for a day or two, but then I got over myself.

When we get caught up in ourselves, we ultimately end up feeling insignificant, because all we see is the small role we are playing. But when we get outside of ourselves, when we step back and look at the larger process that God is unfolding, we'll feel significant, and even honored, to play our small role. While it is nice to play a key role in the story, even that is just a small role in a large process.

I'm not too concerned about whether or not God "uses" me. I would rather us just hang out, like friends. You know, the way Jesus did with the disciples. They just lived life together in close-knit community. They didn't go out looking for people to heal or witness to; they simply lived life and helped people along the way.

I think we get caught up in wanting God to use us because we secretly believe we have to impress Him, while He is simply looking for relationship with us. God wants our hearts more than He wants our ministries.

I'm not advocating passivity, because there is no worse feeling than falling into the "blah-ness" of not doing anything with your life. I'm just saying God is more concerned about what happens *in* us than what happens *through* us. He wants our works to be done from a place of passion, not mere duty. He wants us to have a deep assurance of who we are before we go out and try to change the world. This is why the disciples spent time training in dark places before being thrust into the spotlight of Pentecost (Acts 2:14-41).

God is perfectly capable of accomplishing everything He wants to accomplish on earth without our help or intervention. The Apostle Paul says He doesn't need anything, because He is the one who gives life and breath to all things (Acts 17:25). He can save everyone who needs to be saved and heal everyone who needs to be healed simply by speaking salvation and healing into existence. You've heard the stories of Muslims overseas having encounters with Jesus in their sleep and waking up radically changed, haven't you? In most cases, God did that without any human help. But I have found that He wants to involve us in the process. I guess doing the impossible alone gets a bit boring after awhile.

CHAPTER 23

AMAZING GRACE

I used to think following Jesus meant being immune from pain,
but now I know He holds me closest when I'm hurting.

From the moment I rolled out of bed Tuesday morning—the first full day of week three—I knew I was late. I hurriedly dressed, ran downstairs, and jumped into my golf cart. Half a mile later, I arrived at the open-air pavilion just in time to catch the tail end of early morning prayer. This was different than our required staff prayer each morning at 8:00, and it began even earlier. I wasn't there to pray, though. I was in charge of all of the still photography for camp, and I needed to photograph the outdoor prayer meeting, which took place on Tuesdays and Thursdays.

After I got the shots I needed, I drifted to the edge of the pavilion. I pulled out my phone as Coach Abrams said the closing prayer, and immediately noticed a text message from my mom. My heart began to sink as I slid my finger across the lock screen. I read her message a second time. It didn't seem real, but there it was, in plain English. My great-grandma, whom I wrote about in *Middle America*, had slipped into eternity in her sleep the night before. Grandma Darlene had gone in to check on her sometime after midnight. She heard her breathing quietly, so she went back to bed. But when she got up again an hour later, she realized she was gone.

I had known this moment would come, and had been preparing myself for it for several years. But after so much time elapsed, I tricked myself into thinking this day would never come. And then it did, catching me by surprise. It's so odd, you know, because I just saw her a few months ago. I knew she wasn't doing well then, but she's been that way for years. Even when I was writing about her earlier in this book, I never expected she would be gone this soon.

I called my mom, and we talked for a few minutes. She told me Grandma Darlene was taking it pretty hard, but in the back of our minds, we knew Mamma was in a better place—though neither of us would acknowledge it. In a way, we were grateful that her decade-long struggle had finally come to a quiet and peaceful end. Mom also told me that Grandma had requested me to be a pallbearer at the funeral. I had never done that before, but I quickly accepted. I wanted to immerse myself in the process as much as possible.

My boss pulled up on his golf cart moments later, and I told him the news. The funeral was that weekend, but I would need a few days off from camp since it was all the way in Northwest Missouri.

"You think Jon will let me off?" I asked, knowing that absences from camp were rarely allowed.

"Of course he'll let you off. Your grandma just died—"

"Great-grandma."

"What?"

"Nothing."

"The no-time-off policy is to keep you guys from jacking around. Of course you can attend your grandma's funeral."

I didn't even try to correct him that time. The moment the words were off his tongue, Jon—the camp director—rolled up in his golf cart.

"Hey, Jared just found out his grandma died," my boss said.

"Great-grandma."

"Oh, wow. I'm so sorry to hear that," Jon told me. The compassion in his voice was evident.

"Is it okay if I take a few days off from camp to attend her funeral?"

"Of course it is. Take as much time as you need."

I left the campground early on Friday, in a bit of a daze. I drove aimlessly up the freeway, through the ghetto, past downtown and uptown, and through three rings of suburbs, until I finally hit the highway on the outskirts of the city. I turned west, toward home. I spent the rest of the day catching up on tasks from the week before, knowing that it was the only chance I would have before the next week of camp started.

There was a night of worship going on that evening at my church in Southlake. I knew it was exactly what I needed, and I would like to say that I went and looked to Jesus in the midst of my circumstances, but I didn't. The full weight of emotion from Mamma's passing had not yet hit me, but I was already exhausted in every sense of the word. I saw some pictures on Facebook later that night, and knew I should have been there, right in the middle of things. Sometimes you need to push yourself to do things you know are right and figure out the details later.

※ ※ ※

The next morning, my aunt, uncle, and cousins drove up from Austin, meeting us at a truck stop not far from our house. These days, we normally see each other every three to five months, but we had all just been in Austin together between weeks two and three of camp, where we spent the weekend talking, laughing, and playing spades. Now, we were together again, though under entirely different circumstances. Our two-car caravan headed north, through Oklahoma, Kansas, and finally into Missouri. We didn't talk much as our tires lessened the distance between Dallas and Kansas City; the joy that was present the previous week had given way to pain.

We had to stop a lot, because Danica was with us, and five-year-olds aren't good at sitting still when you're on a road trip that involves crossing multiple state lines. Aunt Machelle told me Danica was cute and sweet around me and my parents, but around everyone else, she whined and complained and threw tantrums. I think a lot of us do the exact same thing—we smile our best smiles and put on a show for the outside world, but then take out our pain and frustration on those closest to us.

We arrived in the small town of Chillicothe shortly before sunset. As we turned into the retirement community on the outskirts of town, Grandpa Joe met us at the curb outside the tiny apartment and helped us unload our cars. Grandma Darlene had already mapped out our sleeping arrangements, putting my parents in Mamma's room—in the bed she had died in just a few days before.

Mom and Aunt Machelle began whispering amongst themselves, neither of them wanting to sleep in their grandma's old bed, regardless of how long it had been since she was last there. Aunt Machelle gently broke the news to Grandma Darlene, telling her that she couldn't bring herself to sleep in that room, not even on the floor. I watched as Grandma Darlene let out a sigh of relief as she confessed that she couldn't even enter the room herself.

It's reassuring to know you haven't gone mad, that there are others out there who know how you feel, that someone else is experiencing the same pain that you are. When we encounter pain in our lives, we must process it properly. It's not healthy to just "get over it" and move on as if nothing happened. We must take the time to attend to the work of grief, to confront and process our pain rather than shoving it beneath the surface.

That night, we covered every inch of the four-room apartment with air mattresses and sleeping bags—all but one room. We even set up a tent in the backyard for Bekah and Danica to sleep in. In this instance, dealing with our pain meant sleeping shoulder-to-shoulder while an entire room of the tiny apartment sat empty.

✳ ✳ ✳

The next morning, we ate breakfast and dressed for the funeral, giving thanks for the small miracles (such as ten people sharing one bathroom without erupting into madness). We then loaded into our cars and drove downtown to the church where Pappa's funeral was held four and a half years prior. The same family from the local funeral home was performing the ceremony. They greeted us in the parking lot, remembering each of us by name. We entered the fellowship hall at the same time a Sunday school class was exiting; the teachers hushed their students out of respect for our family. It was beautiful that they stopped what they were doing and joined us in silence as our paths crossed, as if they were, for a moment, sharing in our pain. The extended family had already arrived as we entered the church gymnasium. I quickly scanned the room, realizing that I knew very few of the people who were present. A meal had been prepared just for us. The solemness of the occasion quickly gave way to feasting as we came together at the table and laughed in the face of death.

It reminded me of the way we partake of the Eucharist at church, how we take of the bread and the wine—reminders of the death that Jesus suffered, and how in the His death, He triumphed over death itself. In this way, the Eucharist is a sort of laughing in the face of death, though it is many other things as well. Because Jesus suffered and tasted death, those who trust in Him will never die, which is what we proclaim when we eat of the bread and drink of the cup.

I noted that none of us were dressed in black, and I liked that. We all knew Mamma was in a far better place, and life had swallowed up death, so we were free to celebrate more than we mourned. In the words of the great theologian C.S. Lewis: *Has this world been so kind to you that you should leave with regret? There are better things ahead than any we leave behind.* [1]

No matter how much we achieve or how many good things happen to us, this world has a way of chewing us up and spitting us out. However, that is not the end of the story. God is bigger than the systems of this world and the effects of systemic sin that suck the life out of us. The Kingdom of God will outlast each and every kingdom man tries to create.

The cross frees us from the power of death, promising us new life and resurrection. Because there are brighter days ahead, we celebrate. Because a life we loved and cherished has come to an end, we mourn. It's not one or the other; it's both/and, but one demands more of our attention. I cannot mourn my great-grandmother's death to the point where I forget to celebrate her life. Because she knew Jesus, her death is temporary, but her life is forever. This is a beautiful mystery.

For the unbeliever, death is the final word. It's dark and dreary, totally void of beauty. But to the believer, death is not the final word. We believe in life that transcends death. We believe in the resurrection of the dead. Because of this, there is a beauty in death that outlasts its sting. As Brian Zahnd puts it: *Pain is temporary; beauty is eternal.* [2]

Now is the age of faith, not the age of sight (2 Corinthians 5:7). But at the end of the age, the curtain will be pulled back, so we can see what already is. [3] A day will come when the fog lifts, and we will be able to see everything clearly (1 Corinthians 13:12). On that day, everything will be right in our worlds, and we'll turn to Jesus and quietly whisper, "Why did I ever doubt you?" But until that day comes, we must choose to trust.

We entered the sun-soaked sanctuary with its high ceiling, wooden pews, and stained glass windows to see the white casket taking center stage in the middle of the altar. It was open, revealing Mamma lying there in a pink suit, several rings adorning her fingers, pins on her collar, and her leather-bound Bible falling apart in her hands.

She had such a peaceful look on her face, a look I hadn't seen in years. I was unable to shed a tear as I looked at her. I knew she was with Jesus, that they were laughing and dancing and singing together. I knew her memory had been restored, she could speak clearly again, and she wasn't in pain anymore.

I had never seen her read the Bible she held in her hands, as Alzheimer's had not allowed her to do so the entire time I had known her. In that moment, I realized she had been a woman of great faith. Mom told me pink had been her favorite color, and Aunt Machelle added that she had always been so proud of her pins. The way they adorned the collar of her suit made her look so stately, even though she was gone.

Danica tugged on my aunt's sleeve, and proceeded to ask her what was happening. Her answer was beautiful, as she bent down and explained to the youngest member of our family that we were at a funeral, a ceremony where we put Mamma's body in the ground and give her back to God. I remembered the last funeral, when Danica was too young to ask such questions—or even know of the existence of death, for that matter.

Do you remember waking up to the reality that our world is broken—full of sorrow, death, and pain? I don't, but I do remember learning about how God is redeeming and restoring all things. Someday soon, Danica will as well.

Uncle Gregg ascended the platform as the ceremony began. Sitting down at the piano, he began to sing *Amazing Grace*. That was the point when most of us broke. He went on to sing *In the Garden* and *How Great Thou Art*, and then Rev. Larry (the associate pastor of the church), got up and read a few Scriptures.

It was the messiest eulogy I had ever heard. Rev. Larry was visibly emotional and stuttered a lot, before finally putting his glasses on. He told a few stories about my great-grandparents, revealing a side of them I had never known. Isn't it funny how you think you know someone, but then at their funeral you realize you had barely scratched the surface?

Rev. Larry talked about how the three of them had served in the church's prison ministry for decades. One day, while they were visiting a prison, he commented on how he wished he had his pocket knife in order to accomplish a certain task. Pappa then leaned over to him and whispered, "Here, use mine." The tenseness of the room gave way to mild laughter, but quickly turned sober again as the reverend began another story.

He awoke to the phone ringing, just before 7:00 on a Saturday morning. It was Pappa, asking him to come to the house as soon as he could. Rev. Larry hung up the phone and drove to their house on Webster Street, while the rest of the town slept. Entering the house, he found Mamma to be quite distraught. She was pacing back and forth across the living room while Pappa sat in a chair looking on.

"What's wrong?" he asked.

"She's concerned that she's not saved," Pappa replied, almost nonchalantly.

He was a bit taken aback by this. She was a grown woman—a grandmother—who had been a faithful member of the church for decades. Of course she was saved! Or was she?

They sat down together, and she went on to tell him she couldn't remember a time when she had given Jesus her heart, though she spent most of her life attending and serving in the church. She had done all of the right things—such as reading her Bible and avoiding sin—but something was missing; something was not right on the inside.

Rev. Larry began by asking her a few questions. Moments later, he led her to the cross, right there in her living room. In that moment, she told him she felt a deep sense of peace wash over her, unlike anything she had ever experienced before. He suggested that she stand before the congregation the next morning and tell them about what had happened to her, and perhaps even be baptized.

She panicked. How could she tell them she had just gotten saved when she had been a fixture of the church for so long? In the end, she swallowed her pride and walked the aisle. Standing before her friends and family, she admitted she had just recently given her heart to Jesus for the very first time. I'm sure it was the surprise of their lives, to hear a lifelong church member announce her newfound salvation. But there was also something beautiful about it, something honest and real. I suppose it's never too late to make a decision that will alter the course of your life forever, even if everyone around you thinks you've already made that decision.

It's a strange feeling when someone you love slips away and you end up discovering the substance of their life from someone else. It makes you feel as though you never really knew them at all. At the funeral, I caught a glimpse of the life my great-grandparents lived, whereas most of my actual memories involve them being old and unable to care for themselves. I never saw the lives they lived; all I saw was life being taken out of them. The only thing worse than losing someone is losing them while they are still alive.

I'm not entirely sure what happened next, as my memory is a bit hazy. I remember Rev. Larry closing the eulogy by urging us to draw closer to Christ. I remember everyone behind us standing up and coming forward in a single-file line. I remember each one shaking my hand. I tried to look them in the eyes, but it was really hard, you know. I remember them moving on to hug Grandma before briefly glancing into the casket and shuffling out of the sanctuary.

After the final guest had left, we stood in unison—from one end of the row to the other. Taking a few steps forward, we huddled around the casket, held one another, and wept. Tears are necessary, but they are not the end of the story, because Christ will someday wipe every tear from our eyes (Revelation 21:4).[4]

When we had finished our goodbyes, we exited the sanctuary, where I was surprised to find everyone else crammed into the small foyer. I guess I had assumed they had just left after paying their respects, but they were there, waiting for us. I nodded slightly at each person I made eye contact with as if to say, "I have no clue who you are, but I appreciate you being here today. Thanks for sharing the burden of our pain." That's what a funeral is at its most basic level—the sharing of pain.

We made our way to the parking lot where a police cruiser was waiting. The guests began to line their cars behind the cruiser, and the funeral home directors carried the white casket out the front door and down the steps of the church to a white Suburban that was waiting at the curb. Like with Pappa's funeral, a Chevrolet SUV filled in for the traditional hearse. Even though there wasn't snow on the ground this time, the rural cemetery was still best accessible by vehicles with all-wheel drive.

The funeral procession began moments later. The police cruiser was at the helm, followed by the white Suburban/hearse and a black Suburban, which held my grandparents, Mom, and Aunt Machelle. Dad and I were in a red SUV behind the black one, and Uncle Gregg and my cousins were in a silver SUV behind us. I don't know who else was behind them, but there were more than a dozen vehicles in all. The police cruiser led us through a red traffic signal as we exited the church parking lot onto Washington Street—the main highway that ran through town from north to south. The mood was surreal as we slowly made our way through town, proceeding through every intersection regardless of what color the signal was, while every other vehicle on the road pulled to the shoulder. I watched each one as we drove by. They all did the same thing; they all came to a sudden stop on the side of the road when they saw us. I loved how even the cars on the opposite side of the road did this. There wasn't really any need for them to stop—they weren't in our way or anything—yet all four lanes of traffic on Washington Street seemed to be under a cease and desist order.

In a world where few things are sacred, this is something we must hold onto, because it reminds us how precious life is. Very few things would stop traffic on a busy road in the middle of the day, but one family's world coming to a momentary stop was enough to shut it all down. This is significant, because it reminds us of the sanctity of all human life. Funeral processions are not something we do only for the rich and powerful, but to even the most marginalized members of society.

I once heard a story about a funeral procession that was three miles long, much longer than ours was. The response from other drivers, however, was much different. Some people slowed down, some stopped, and others pulled over, got out of their cars, and stood with their hands behind their backs, but then there were those who didn't change the way they drove at all.

I did a little research, and found that vehicles in the opposite lanes of traffic are not obligated to stop for funeral processions in most states. But how far have we fallen when we only pay our respects because we're obligated to? Perhaps I am making a mountain out of a molehill here, but if it were up to me, it would be mandatory for every driver to get out of their vehicle and stand with their hands behind their back. This is about so much more than just funeral processions; it's about a basic respect for human life, something we all seem to have forgotten about these days.

After making our way through the final red traffic signal, we turned onto the freeway, which would take us to the next county over before connecting with the back road that wove through the rolling hills to the cemetery. The cruiser accelerated quickly down the ramp and parked across both lanes of the freeway, allowing our line of vehicles to remain intact as we entered. It was crazy to think that an entire freeway had been shut down for us, even if it were only for a moment.

The cruiser waited until the last vehicle passed, and then turned back toward town as his role of escorting us to the city limits was now complete. We ventured alone into the Missouri countryside where we found that the continual flashing of our hazard lights did not have the same effect as the lights of the police cruiser. The outside world was no longer sharing in our pain as they sped past our convoy in the left-hand lane.

Though we long for a world where more is sacred, we live in a world where not everyone shares this longing. While we are seeking to slow down and hold on to things we feel matter most, others will speed around us and, perhaps, even run us over if we get in their way. This didn't actually happen during the funeral procession, but I think I am talking about more than just funeral processions at this point.

We turned off the freeway onto the back road and drove for another thirty miles. We passed through the little town where my mom and aunt grew up before finally turning onto the gravel road that would take us to the cemetery. The last mile was pretty rough, as our tires began to kick up dust to the point where we couldn't see the vehicles in front of or behind us.

The sun blazed overhead as we exited our vehicles, a stark contrast to the snowy day when we buried Pappa. Grandma's friends from high school were there, a close-knit group that had stood beside one another over the years, most of them having never ventured further than ninety miles from their hometown.

The graveside service was short and sweet. There was a lot of affection and tears, hellos and good-byes, and then everyone turned around and drove back down the gravel road, fanning out to their various homes across the state and beyond. After eating lunch together at a deli in a nearby town, we parted ways with my aunt, uncle, and cousins. We made our way across the state where we spent the night with dad's parents on the farm, before getting up early the next morning to drive the rest of the way back to Texas.

The tires of our family SUV made contact with our driveway mid-evening, and I slowly transferred my belongings to my car. This weekend had felt like the shortest yet, though it was Monday and I had missed a day of camp. I was exhausted by the time I slid into the front seat of my car an hour later. I sat in the driveway for a moment, not wanting to leave. Death had reared its head at the worst moment possible, but I had successfully navigated my way through the process. It was over—for me, at least.

For my grandparents, it was only getting started. The apartment in the retirement community is no longer needed and their house in the little town where my mom grew up hasn't been lived in for years. It's cold and musty and in need of someone to make it a home again. They have a lot of decisions to make and a short window of time in which to make them. Meanwhile, I'm frustrated because I have to go back to camp.

"O death, where is your victory? O death, where is your sting? ... But thanks be to God, who gives us the victory through our Lord Jesus Christ. Therefore, my beloved brothers, be steadfast, immovable, always abounding in the work of the Lord, knowing that in the Lord your labor is not in vain." ~ 1 Corinthians 15:55, 57-58, ESV

CHAPTER 24

TWO WEEKS NOTICE

I used to think my dreams would just happen someday,
but then I realized I would have to chase them down.

Not wanting to go back to camp, I drove aimlessly around town for awhile as night swept across the landscape. I went out of my way to get a good cheeseburger from In-N-Out, then sat in a parking lot for awhile.

The campground was quiet when I arrived, as everyone was gathered in the multi-purpose building for service. I rolled into the parking lot seconds before they dismissed, so the silence was only momentary. As I made my way through the crowd to the media room, several of the other staff members suspended their duties to ask how I was doing. It felt good to know that people genuinely cared about my emotional state, not just the talents I could bring to the table.

It was 2:00 in the morning before I made my way up the stairs to my room in the staff lodge. I turned the key slowly, opening the door to an empty room. My roommate was in another state for a job interview, so I would be alone for at least one night, perhaps longer. It felt good to finally be alone. I needed some time away from the crowd of students, even from my family and friends. I was ready for the whole thing to be over with, ready for the craziness of camp to end—even if that meant returning to my boring, everyday life. There were two weeks remaining, and I knew I had to at least pretend I was happy and as full of energy as I had been during week one. I was determined to do my job to the best of my ability with the little strength I had left, but I knew I couldn't pull it off unless I had some time alone with myself and God.

I honestly don't remember much of what happened that week; I just remember the nights when everything was still, because those were the times when I could feel God speaking to me. The same voice that spoke the world into existence often speaks loudest in the silence. But there are other types of silence that are a bit more unnerving.

The first type of silence occurs when you've been running one hundred miles an hour and finally press pause, when God seems to rush in and refresh your weary soul, which is teetering on the edge of burnout.

The second type of silence hits when you've been running one hundred miles an hour and press *stop*. It starts out the same as the first type of silence. You slow down, this time for two days, rather than just two minutes. You feel refreshed, finally able to breathe. Then, the silence begins to settle in, and the voices start. You begin to wonder what the heck you're doing, why you're running so fast, where you're going. You didn't have time for that with the momentary silence. But now that the fast pace has hit a wall of stillness, you feel very uncomfortable. You don't know what to do with yourself, and the voices certainly don't help.

Pressing *pause* does little to determine the true condition of our souls; only by pressing stop can we get an accurate reading. When we abruptly press buttons without finding a rhythm that leads up to them, we'll end up like a car slamming on its brakes, thrusting everyone forward. What I mean by that is, we all must stop sometime, but when we live fast and furious, without any rhythm, our stops are a lot harder, not unlike running full speed into a brick wall.

During the first portion of camp, I never really pressed pause. I simply went about my tasks and ignored my own emotional well-being. So when the weekends hit, I came to a hard stop and spent much of the weekend in a lethargic state as the weariness of my soul began to catch up with me. The problem was, I wasn't allowing God to restore my soul so I would be fresh for the next week; I was just sitting around watching television all weekend.

Having my own room during the fourth week of camp enabled me to press *pause* a little more often, but the damage had already been done. I still ended up freaking out by Friday and found myself in need of an escape, just like all the weeks before.

Now that I am looking back on this season of my life, I think I see what was going on behind the scenes. Before camp ever started, I was feeling as though my life wasn't going anywhere, that writing a book and working with the youth outreach ministry here and there was just a waste of time. Actually, that's a poor choice of words. I didn't so much feel like I was wasting my time as I did that my life, overall, had no purpose. I didn't have the feeling that *my life matters* waking me up each morning. I also felt like working a normal job was not enough, that I needed to be doing something that made an "eternal difference," or else I was somehow missing my calling and wasting my life. I could probably write an entire book on that topic, so I won't dive into it any further here. [1]

I am trying to write this in a way where it makes me sound intellectual and stuff, but I feel as though it is making things a bit more complicated than they need to be. To put it even simpler, I am trying to say I learned that it's important to slow down a bit each day and let God restore your soul, and take at least one day off a week.

In his wonderful book, *Sabbath*, Dan Allender talks about how we should spend one day a week delighting ourselves in whatever brings us the most joy. [2] But this is hard for us to do, because we are Americans. We would often rather work our tails off to obtain things we think will bring us joy, rather than pursuing what actually brings us joy—even if for only one day of the week.

I had initially planned on spending every weekend at the campground, but once camp started, I began telling myself I would spend at least *one* weekend at the campground. I really thought the fourth and final weekend would be the one; I had even purchased a ticket to a Texas Rangers game, which nearly all of the camp staff would be attending together Friday night.

After lunch on Friday, I stood at a crossroads. Would I go to the Rangers game and stay at the campground for the weekend, or make a clean getaway to the suburbs? I chose the suburbs.

Later that evening, as I sat on the couch in my parent's house (watching television, of course), I got on Facebook and saw pictures of my friends from camp at the game. I suddenly felt left out, as if I had been excluded, even though ditching the game had been my own choice.

I got up off the couch and went into my office, where I taped my unused ticket to the wall above my desk as a reminder that we sometimes make decisions we regret, and spending time with real-life friends is almost always better than trying to live vicariously through the characters on your favorite sitcom.

I wasn't a part of the baseball game because I had chosen not to be, not because I had been excluded—though it certainly didn't feel that way. I wasn't a victim, I was a powerful person who was free to make my own decisions and live with the consequences—good or bad.

I love the way that Dr. Brené Brown puts it: *If you own this story, you get to write the ending. Owning our stories can be hard, but not nearly as difficult as spending our lives running from it.*[3]

Owning your own story carries certain repercussions, both good and bad. If you choose to go against the crowd, don't be surprised when you feel like you're not part of the crowd—because you aren't. That is often the price you have to pay if you want to create your own path.

If you decide you don't want to create your own path, that's perfectly acceptable as well. The whole point in creating a path is to create a way that others can follow. If we were all on our own, we would troop through the underbrush from Point A to Point B without bothering to forge a trail.

The purpose of the path is for those who don't know how to pioneer or have the resources to do so. This isn't so much about willpower. We don't create paths so that people who are too lazy to create their own will have an easier go at things. Some might think something like, "If they wanted it bad enough, they would forge the path." That generalization may be true in some cases, but at best, it is a generalization. Those who desire to walk down a path must still will themselves to do so, and not everyone gets the pioneer gene. This is a good thing, because if we all had it, we would go mad. If everyone forged their own paths in life, there would be no point in doing so. Most people who pioneer do it because they are sick of the status quo. If the status quo suddenly became *each create their own path,* the pioneers among us would be forging paths back to the former status quo of traveling paths that have been created by others. And let's be honest, many of us who think we're pioneers actually aren't. Many of us who think we're forging new paths are only walking down narrower paths than everyone else.

Perhaps the term *pioneer* should be reserved for people who actually crossed the country in covered wagons. Or perhaps it should be reserved for people like Martin Luther King, Jr., who dreamed of a world where all were equal. But what if the original pioneers weren't really "pioneering" anything at all? They were on an adventure, sure, far more risky than any you and I will likely go on, but they didn't "discover" Oregon, just as Christopher Columbus didn't "discover" America—there were people here long before he stepped foot on our shores.

Since I'm already meddling, what if MLK didn't pioneer the civil rights movement? What if he wasn't the first man who "had a dream?" What if he was just the first person to act on his dream? He is certainly one we remember more than others, but to use him to illustrate that *history remembers those who act* would be unfair to everyone else who stood up for civil rights, but were shot down and never recorded in [mainstream] history. Sometimes you step out and no one cares or remembers.

We could go at this all day. Which proves my point—there is always someone that was here first. MLK did indeed make the path wide and smooth, but there were countless others that were picking away at it slowly, when it was nothing more than a bunch of overgrown weeds.

This brings me to another question. What if the only true pioneer is God? I know it sounds trite, but He is the only person in history to ever make something out of nothing. Others chose their paths, and we honor them for their accomplishments, but we must not forget there was always someone before them. Otherwise, we end up turning people into gods and remake the Original Pioneer in our own image.

There are many paths available, both wide and narrow. And when none of the paths seem to be quite right, there is room to forge a new one; this just doesn't happen as often as you might think. Most of the "forging" we do is simply making a narrow path wider for someone else.

Whatever route you choose, own your story. The path isn't yours—it was here before you, and it will be here after you—but your story is yours forever. You are powerful. You are free to choose which path you take. Perhaps you were born on third base, or perhaps you hit a triple. You might be somewhere in between, or just stepping up to the plate. Perhaps you aren't aware that there *are* any bases—or a field, or a game, or even a stadium. Somehow, you've been driving by it all these years, completely oblivious to the fact that this massive brick building is a place where games are played. You saw it, sure, you just never wondered—*what is that*? Perhaps you tried to get into the stadium and were denied entry. Perhaps you were born in a city where there weren't any stadiums, and the bases were set up in a neighborhood park. Perhaps you don't realize that we are no longer talking about sports. Perhaps you don't care at all.

Regardless of the circumstances of your life, you are not a victim—unless you choose to be.

You are powerful.

Choose your path.

Make your decisions.

Own your story.

There will be people that help you along the way, but your story is yours.

If you own your story, you get to write the ending.

If you don't own your story, someone else will write the ending for you, and it will never be the story that *you* were created to tell.

※ ※ ※

Things got dark that night, and God felt strangely distant. I hadn't gone to church all month—not because I was too tired or didn't have time, but because I just wasn't excited about it anymore, which was odd, because I normally love church. I had lost that fire, that fervency, that raw passion for God, and I was hungry for an encounter with Him again. Sometimes we get so caught up in doing work *for* God that we forget to actually spend time *with* God. This is one of the greatest dangers of ministry in my opinion.

Things weren't much better when I rolled out of bed around noon on Saturday. I went for a drive with my dad and we talked about life, openly questioning if we would ever be significant or able to provide our families with the things they need. I think these are two things guys spend most of their lives pondering, and I don't think we ever get to a place where we stop asking ourselves these questions. My dad and I are in totally different phases of our lives—I don't even have a family—yet, the same questions return each night when our heads hit the pillow.

I went to church on Sunday, the first time in weeks. I attended a class before the main service, which was taught by my friend, Beth, the above average freedom pastor. It was one that I attended previously, so I felt my mind drifting as she talked. Halfway through, I realized that there was a disconnect somewhere, because even though I knew and understood everything she was saying, it wasn't hitting my heart. Toward the end of the class, I realized the disconnect had something to do with a simple, yet frightening word called *surrender*. As I pondered what this might look like during this season of working at the youth camp, I attempted to exert my will to bring myself to a place of surrender, but my heart didn't seem to budge. You can't will yourself into surrender; you just have to let go and let God take over.

I know I talked earlier about owning your own story, which is definitely something we need to do, but we must also balance this with an awareness that our stories often get out of control and need to be surrendered to God. This doesn't mean we forfeit ownership of our stories; it simply means we acknowledge God holds the trump card to any of our plans.

God isn't looking to just tell you what to do; He wants relationship with you. He wants you to own your story and hand Him the trump card, and above everything else, let Him form you into the person He created and redeemed you to be. Don't just ask God for a road map; ask Him to take you on a journey. One of these requires you to stay connected to Him, whereas the other gives you a false sense that you can make it through life on your own.

It's probably a good idea to give God the trump card *before* things get out of control, but I often fail to do this. And I don't even realize what's going on until things blow up and I look down to see I'm still holding my trump card with an iron fist, desperately seeking to control my own life.

Ever since the beginning, humanity has been seeking to gain control, but walking with God is about giving up control as you learn to trust. There is a difference between control and ownership. I can't control what happens to me, but I can control how I respond. This is what owning your story is all about.

I was frustrated when I left Beth's class, mostly with myself. I walked from the classroom to the sanctuary and took a seat toward the front a few minutes before worship began. It was nice and everything, but it felt as though only a part of me was present. My soul was disengaged, leaving my body to do nothing but go through the motions. I sang along with all the songs and even lifted my hands, but when I sat down twenty-three minutes later, I felt the same as when I had entered the sanctuary. The video announcements rolled and the sermon was preached. I'm sure everyone else was drawing life from it, but I wasn't, and it wasn't anyone's fault but my own.

A few hours later, I was headed to Maypearl for the final week of camp. My frustration began to lift as I drove, and I began to pray aloud as I drove the empty streets of the campground. As I turned into the parking lot of the staff lodge, I told God I had exhausted all my options and I was ready to surrender. The only problem was, I didn't feel like I knew how to do so. The words had barely rolled off my tongue when an undeniable feeling of peace rushed in, as if the dam between me and God had split wide open. I had no idea surrender could be that simple. Once I stopped trying to figure it out from an intellectual standpoint, it just kind of happened. It's as if God was waiting for me to stop trying to define *surrender*, and instead, look Him in the eyes and say those difficult words: "I trust you."

※ ※ ※

As the first few days of camp unfolded, I was amazed at how refreshed and full of energy I was. I felt like it was the first time since week one that I actually began a week of camp with my tank full. It made me wish I had surrendered to God sooner, but I had been moving too fast the first four weeks to realize I needed to.

Though my tank was full on Monday, by Wednesday, I was ready for camp to be over. I had spent the month before camp longing for it to arrive, so life wouldn't be so mundane, but by the end of it, I was more than ready for life to return to its normal, boring state.

Overall, working at the youth camp was a great experience, and I'm grateful for the opportunity. But, like many things in life, there comes a point when you have to move on. Camp wasn't the pinnacle of my year, it was just another thing I did. It had its highs and lows, of course, but at the end of the day, it was just another phase of the journey. I didn't want to let my identity get wrapped up in being on staff at a camp, because there would be a point when it would be over, and I didn't want my life to end with it.

I have been fortunate enough to have a lot of great experiences at a young age, and I've had a good share of accomplishments as well. But all of that stuff is just that—stuff. It doesn't define who I am, and I don't want it to. Though I am grateful for what has been accomplished, I can't stop looking ahead, because I know I've barely scratched the surface, and I don't want to focus so much on past victories that I become satisfied to stare at a trophy case and ignore the possibilities of the future.

I love the way that Eugene Peterson paraphrases Paul's letter to the Philippians: *The very credentials these people are waving around as something special, I'm tearing up and throwing out with the trash—along with everything else I used to take credit for. And why? Because of Christ. Yes, all the things I once thought were so important are gone from my life. Compared to the high privilege of knowing Christ Jesus as my Master, firsthand, everything I once thought I had going for me is insignificant—dog dung. I've dumped it all in the trash so that I could embrace Christ and be embraced by him* (Philippians 3:7-9a, The Message).

I think a lot of times we let what we do become too much a part of us, to the point that when it comes to an end, we die with it. We think we are only making a difference when we are doing things like working at a youth camp or with orphans in Haiti, and we forget that our everyday lives can make just as big of an impact if we keep our eyes open for situations where God's grace and redemption are needed.

If nothing else, I think the greatest lesson I learned over the summer was that my work doesn't really matter as much as I think it does, but it also matters much more than I think it does. The roles I play in my life are necessary and essential, but at the end of the day, I only play a small role in the larger work of redemption that God is unfolding.

※ ※ ※

One of my favorite people I met over the summer was the night janitor—a guy named John—who lived in a beat-up trailer at the edge of the campground. John would come to the multi-purpose building every night around midnight to empty the trash and clean the bathrooms, and he was usually still there when I would leave to go back to my lodge and sleep for a few hours. Some nights, we only exchanged a simple "hello" as our paths crossed, but most of the time, we would stop and talk for a few minutes.

John was a friendly guy, very open and honest. I remember one night when he told me he used to be homeless, and was grateful to have a job—even though it was a job that few people would be willing to do. He had a much better attitude about his role at the camp than I did. Sure, I worked longer hours, but I was doing work I loved, while John was emptying trash and cleaning toilets.

I think when we get to heaven, we'll be surprised to find the people whom God honors the most are the ones we overlooked here on earth. I think people like John will receive more honor from God than some of the people with big ministries that receive their honor from man instead. I'm not saying God doesn't honor people once their ministry hits a certain pinnacle, because it all comes down to our hearts, you know, and there are many people who have achieved a certain level of attention simply by loving people. These people aren't impressed with the pedestals that are built for them, and I think they will be honored by God right alongside John the Janitor.

I think it's interesting that Jesus rejected every opportunity He was given to be a hot shot and draw attention to Himself. One time, after He had made lunch for five thousand men with five loaves of bread and two fish, the people decided He was great enough to be their king. Jesus realized they were about to force Him to play a role He was never intended to play, so He left the crowd and went off to climb a mountain by Himself (John 6:14-15).

Jesus was given several opportunities to take on a position of great power and influence, but He ended up dying on a cross—so He could have relationship with us. He rejected the crowns of man and drank the cup of suffering, because He knew relationship was more important than power and influence.

※ ※ ※

It was mid-afternoon on the first Friday in August when I drove through the empty campground one last time. As I turned onto the country road away from Maypearl, I felt an overwhelming sense of peace wash over me. I plugged my iPod into the car stereo, immersing myself in the moment as *When the Time Comes* by Jason Upton began to play.

I struggled a lot to maintain contact with God over the course of the month, until one day when I was reading Romans, and I stumbled upon a verse that essentially says whoever loves has fulfilled everything that God requires of man (Romans 13:8).

From that point on, I stopped praying for God to come and do a great work among the students. Instead, I began to pray that He would come and teach me how to love.

Love is tricky, especially since most of us assume we're already good at it. But it's in those moments when you're hot, tired, and beat down, and someone says something that ticks you off, that you discover just how much love you've got in you. Then, you're either blinded by arrogance or your eyes are opened to the reality that, at times, there's more death in you than life, and you're not as deserving of love and grace as you used to think you were.

I need God's love to be stronger than death—because mine isn't. My love is weak and fragile and full of imperfections and selfish ambition.

As I drove into town, I once again asked God to teach me how to love. Silence hung in the air for a moment, and then He responded and told me I was already doing it. I didn't need to keep trying to force myself to love; I just needed to be still, receive His love, and let that love flow through me to the world around me.

I drove from the campground to my friend Seth's house. Several guys from camp were already there, so I had to park a few houses down the street. As I was walking toward Seth's house, I noticed an open garage door and heard gentle worship music quietly playing. Inside, a man was cleaning his motorcycle. Spirituality doesn't have to be as hard as we tend to make it. Sometimes it really is as simple as inviting God to join us in the mundane tasks that make up the majority of our days, turning those otherwise boring moments into moments of worship. Those are moments when heaven bends low and kisses the earth, erupting a well of redemption that touches everything in its path.

CHAPTER 25

THE NEW NORMAL

I used to think a change of scenery would magically improve my life,
but now I know Jesus wants to meet me in the familiar.

Life after camp was a bit of a roller coaster experience. It was full of ups and downs, twists and turns, and many other surprises along the way. I thought things would be different after camp, and they are in some ways. For the most part, however, they're exactly how they were before. That's what happens when we look for a certain moment or event to change the course of our lives. We all have a natural tendency to do this. I haven't met very many people who want their story to be, "I had a great experience, but my life is still average." That's not what we crave. We want experiences that will change our lives, and the bigger they are, the better they make us feel.

Bob the Freedom Guy says changing our circumstances changes nothing, because wherever you go, there you are. [1] In other words, when we seek a change of scenery, a new career, a summer working at a youth camp, or something else to save us from ourselves, it simply doesn't work. We can't change our circumstances and expect to be changed internally. We may be able to create an illusion for a period of time, but it never lasts. But we keep doing it, because changing our circumstances repeatedly is far easier than admitting the real problem might be ... *ourselves.*

Sometimes, there are moments that change our lives forever, but most life change happens in the process of everyday life. God could fix us in a moment, sure, but He often doesn't, because He is more interested in relationship with us than fixing us.

Often, the things that change us the most are the little things, the things we didn't notice as they were happening.

※ ※ ※

I began reading one of Donald Miller's earlier books, *Through Painted Deserts*, when I was alone at my house one night. I was only a few pages in when Don began talking about leaving home and everything he had ever known, with little more than gas money in his pocket. I was immediately caught up in the story, in the ecstasy of adventure. I began to dream of a house on the beach in South Texas, with a big front porch and a hammock. I would fall asleep in that hammock at night, the sounds of the ocean sweeping away every worry and fear.

As I sat in my bed in North Texas, I began to feel an acute sense of loneliness come over me. Part of me wanted to grab my keys, get in my car, and just drive. I didn't have a destination in mind; I just wanted to drive until things made sense again. Another part of me wanted to stay home, plant my roots deep in the soil of everything I had ever known, and cling tightly to whatever life I had left. I was afraid to let go of the familiar, even if to receive something better than what I possessed at the moment.

My parents arrived home after midnight. I turned off the lights and pretended to be asleep as they shuffled past my room. I turned the lights on again after awhile. Still feeling alone, I decided to take a walk. It was around 1:30 in the morning when I slipped out the front door, into the darkness.

I live in a master-planned community that can't decide if it's in the city or the middle of nowhere. A large shopping center was supposed to be built down the street, but then the recession hit five years ago, so it's still an empty field. None of my neighbors leave their porch lights on at night, and since we're [sort of] in the country, there aren't any street lights, except at the corners of the intersections where the streets that all look the same meet. There are a lot of dark patches, especially when you get on the back side of the subdivision where the rooflines meet the tree line of the woods.

As I walked to no place in particular, I thought about this book and how it doesn't have much of a chance of being published. But then I remembered what Elise had told me a few days before, that she was proud of me just because I was doing something; I actually had the guts to get off the couch and turn one of my ideas into a reality, rather than leaving it confined in my head.

I just started working on a book called *Hidden in Plain Sight*.[2] This is my first substantial writing project, which means I will soon be able to call myself a freelance writer—or something like that. The thought of this alarms me, because it's unfamiliar territory.

After I returned from my walk, I filled out an application to work for a large corporation, emptying trash. I used to think that sort of thing was below me, but I don't feel that way anymore.

Most people think being a full-time writer is a glamourous job, because they only see the small part that actually is glamorous. They see the finished product, the printed and bound book with the cool cover and words that seem to come alive and leap off the pages. They see you traveling and speaking and promoting the book, but they never see the struggles that come with the writing process.

They don't know you spent more time surfing the Internet at coffee shops than you did actually writing. They don't know about all the times when you nearly went mad because you couldn't get the words to sound the same on paper as they did in your head. And they definitely don't know about the times you wound up depressed, sitting around watching *Monk* all day, as if watching a show about someone with more issues than you will somehow make you feel better about your own miserable life. On top of all this, there isn't really any money in the business, which is why most writers have to work day jobs. I told myself I needed a day job because I can't seem to bring myself to work on my book for eight hours a day. Four is as good as I've ever done, and even that is a struggle.

A few days into the "freelance writer" thing, I began to think it wasn't going to work out—not at this point in my life, at least. I reasoned with myself that I could get a real job and do my freelance work on the side. But what about my own book? (AKA, the book you're reading right now.) I told myself there would be time in the evenings and on the weekends, even though I knew there wouldn't be. But I convinced myself, because I'm a rather good lawyer, as most writers are. We can talk ourselves into just about anything, no matter how ridiculous it may seem. Why else would anyone pick a career that brings so much frustration and so little income?

Welcome to the wonderful world of writing!

So here I was, on day three of being a freelance writer, and I was already making plans to get a job emptying trash. I filled out the application, praying the whole way through, but my prayers were met with silence.

Since God was silent, I began reading through earlier essays of this book, and I read about how when we step out into the unknown, we often become frozen with fear, which causes us to run back to things that are more familiar. Entry-level jobs are familiar to me. Working full-time as a writer is not. As I sat at my desk, I realized I had a choice to make. I could rip up the essay, or I could rip up the application. I chose to rip up the application.

Every new stage of life brings new insecurities with it, but we must keep moving forward. The insecurities never really go away, they just change into new ones as you continue on your journey. I guess this is just the new normal, and I can't run from it. I have to give this freelance thing a try, and if it doesn't work out, I'll get a day job and push writing to the weekends.

I decided to stay in the game a little longer and I felt at peace, though the feeling was mixed with fear and discomfort. Then I went online and listened to a sermon from a pastor in Florida, and he talked about how most people never begin things because they are afraid of failure. I realized by choosing not to give in and get a day job, I was facing my fear head on.

The janitorial job was something I was willing to do, but not something I wanted to do. (I only wanted it so I would have something to take my mind off of my struggles as a writer.) It was a long commute from my house, would not have paid much, and would have probably exhausted me to the point where I would no longer want to write, essentially putting me back where I started. I still have my job with the youth outreach ministry, which occupies a few hours of my week, but otherwise, the slate is clean and ready for me to fill with words.

If I do end up getting a day job, it needs to be something I am passionate about, something that adds to my life, rather than something I use to escape from what I need to focus on. It needs to be something that leaves me somewhat energized at the end of the day, so I can go to the coffee house and write for an hour or two.

It's astonishing how writing will do strange things to ordinary people, and I am no exception. I now have conversations going on in my head—basically all of the time—and when I write fiction, I can hear the characters conversing in my mind. Writing has a way of making you go mad. It has its rewards, but I am learning that it is not wise to do work solely for the rewards, because they don't always come. Few books become *New York Times Bestsellers*; the vast majority never sell more than five thousand copies. When they do, you still only make a few dollars for each book you sell. You can't really make a consistent, living wage from writing unless you are a copywriter or journalist for a larger organization.

The real money is in speaking engagements. It's funny how people will balk at paying $15 for a book, but will pay someone $15,000 to speak for an hour, and not think twice. If you want to make money as a writer, you have to not only be a great writer, but a great speaker as well. Of course, pay days like this are for the big dogs, and many speakers make far less than that, if anything at all.

I guess there really is no formula for it, and the whole business is a bit of a lottery. Now that I think about it, I guess any business venture is not unlike playing the lottery, on some level, and success in life is rarely guaranteed, unless you're born into a family with enough money to buy you whatever position or status you want in life.

I read a book once that said writers who are serious about writing will give their lives to it and do it full-time.[3] In most cases, however, that is simply not practical—unless you're single and don't mind living in the back of your van. Actually, the writer who works a day job at a coffee house and comes home exhausted out of his mind, yet still makes the choice to break out the laptop and write for a few hours when all he wants to do is sink into the couch and watch television, is just as serious—perhaps more serious—than the professional who tells everyone he works eight hours a day, but spends most of it piddling around the house or surfing the Internet.

There are a lot of people out there who think they are writers, who call themselves writers, but are actually not writers. These type of people tend to over-identify with their work and only work for the rewards. When the rewards don't come, they quit. True writers keep going and don't quit, even in the face of failure. They don't write for the rewards, they write because they are writers and writing is their work and passion. If writing is just work, you'll never put your soul into it. If writing is just passion, you'll never force yourself to sit down and actually do the work. True writers have found the intersection of work and passion.

I used to over-identify with my work, but I quit doing that somewhere in the middle of this book. Now, I just write. There are often voices that make their way into my mind, but I do my best to ignore them. The voices tell me that no one will ever read my work, that it will never change anyone's life. I know these are lies, but I find myself believing them at times. I do my best to keep moving forward, and I remind myself that no matter how great of a writer I become, my value and affirmation will always come from God, not how great a writer I am. This is all very good theory, and I find myself actually putting it into practice about half the time.

ACT V

Redeem

Jesus invites us to find our
life in Him, to enter in to the
life that never stops.

~ Daniel Grothe

CHAPTER 26

EVOLUTION OF AN IDEA

*I used to ask God to give me a blueprint for my life,
but now I just want Him to be with me wherever I go.*

When I heard that my friend, Henry, was putting his art up for sale, I knew I had to be the first to acquire one of his paintings. I knew exactly which one I wanted, a somewhat abstract piece entitled *Evolution of an Idea*.

A few weeks later, a package from Kansas landed on my desk. I tore it open like it was Christmas morning, even though I knew exactly what it was. The painting became a part of me from the moment I held it in my hands. It was like Henry had taken a blank canvas, painted the story of my life, shoved it into a frame, and dropped it in the mail to Texas.

Three quarters of the bright, yellow background was covered with different colored puzzle pieces, each a unique shape. Some were simple squares, but others were crooked and jagged and rather ugly looking on their own, though when paired with the other pieces, they formed a masterpiece. There were four pieces missing, but the outline of them could be clearly seen. Then, there was the entire right side of the painting, which was still blank. It was obvious there were more pieces that needed to fall into place, but it was impossible to tell what they looked like.

Henry described the painting as an idea that starts with a seed (represented by a white square in the right corner—the smallest puzzle piece). As the idea becomes more cohesive, the other pieces begin to connect.

When I look at it, I wonder if some of the pieces formed on opposite ends of the spectrum in the early stages. Perhaps it took some time for other pieces to grow and form it all into one cohesive image. Regardless, the puzzle is not complete. Though many pieces have fallen into place, there are still others missing. The shape and form of some of the pieces is known, but the others are still unknown, and you won't be able to tell how they fit until they become part of the puzzle.

There are times when I feel as though my life is just like this painting—until I realize it isn't. The painting is nearly finished, and you can get a pretty good idea of what it's about by looking at it, though a part of it remains elusive. My life—though it feels like that at times—is still the seed in the corner of the painting, with a few random puzzle pieces splashed onto the canvas here and there. This is frustrating, because I want my life to evolve from just a seed into something rich and meaningful, and I want this to happen by the end of the week, instead of slowly, over time.

I feel as though I've been asleep for the past few years of my life, and I'm just now beginning to wake up. My eyes are still adjusting to the light. At times, I can't even see the seed of what is to come. I feel as though there is something wrong with the blank canvas, until I realize the canvas is not blank.

Henry's painting, even the parts where the pieces are missing, does not have an inch of space that is a blank canvas. The entire thing was painted yellow before the white seed was ever added.

What if we were to say the yellow canvas is the Kingdom of God, and when we receive Jesus—when we're born again (when we're *born from above,* as the Scriptures say)—we become the white seed. It's small and seemingly unimportant on the vast canvas, but at least it's *on* the canvas. There are many people who live their lives off-canvas, and many others who spend their lives trying to find their way to the canvas. As we journey with Jesus, new pieces are added and filled in. The picture begins to make sense, except for when it doesn't—and then you're left staring at an *Evolution of an Idea,* trying to figure out what it means. I'm staring at it now, and I think I know what it means—except for the empty yellow part.

No one told me about this stuff when I first appeared as a seed on the canvas. No one told me I would have to wrestle with tough questions, learn how to love, help others find their way onto the canvas, and even suffer at times.

My life is not progressing as quickly as I want it to, which is pretty frustrating most days. But when I get still and listen for God, He comes. He cuts through all the static, all of my ambition and lofty dreams, and He reminds me to enjoy the journey, to embrace the forming process as each piece is shaped and added to the canvas.

And so, I ask you, when you consider your canvas, when you stare at the vast, yellow emptiness, when you complain about how blank it is—what if that part of the canvas isn't empty at all? What if the yellow portion of the canvas is full of life, love, hope, joy, peace, redemption, and all the other things the Kingdom contains in excess, with Jesus ruling as the world's first and only perfect King?

CHAPTER 27

CATCHING SUNRISE

I used to think I had to position myself just right to catch
a glimpse of beauty, but now I realize beauty is everywhere.

As I read Donald Miller's books, I've noticed he writes a lot about catching sunrises, to the point where it makes me wonder if I'm missing out on something by sleeping in. One day, I decided it was time to start waking up early in order to watch God's beauty unfold across the skies.

The next morning, I got up before 6:00. It was dark and calm as I retreated to my studio to take care of a few mundane tasks. Dawn was beginning to break as I exited my house an hour later; the sky had turned from black to a deep blue. My street was still and quiet. Straining my ears, all I heard was the distant sound of cars on the five-lane highway a mile to the south. Light escaped from behind the curtains, through the windows of a third of the houses, but the rest were still asleep.

I passed a couple of runners, and by the time I reached the main road that cuts through my master-planned community, many cars had sped past, their drivers on their way to their jobs—in downtown Dallas, I'm sure. I remember when I used to get up that early and drive to work, though it was only two or three mornings a week because I worked part-time.

I crossed the main road to a small lake, which was still and smooth—a stark contrast to the speeding cars. By this time, the blues in the sky had begun to give way to a dark, gray color. I made my way around the lake, illuminated only by one or two streetlights several yards from the shoreline, and I noticed the weeping willow trees, which had been mere saplings when I moved into the neighborhood six years prior. They now towered into the sky, but still bent low to kiss the ground from which they came.

Shortly before 7:00, the sky became lighter, and that's when things got ugly. The fountain in the center of the lake sputtered and turned on, shooting water ten feet upward. The once still lake was now rippling as it was filled with artificial sound and beauty, which drowned out the natural beauty I had been enjoying. Dump trucks thundered past. More cars exited the development, headed to closer workplaces in Addison or Plano; I'm sure my dad was one of them. A couple of guys on riding lawn mowers arrived to mow the grass around the lake and entrance to the community. Not because it needed to be mowed, but because it was Tuesday, and the grounds must remain perfectly manicured. The stillness, calmness, and sense of peace had given way to noise, striving, and progress. And the sunrise itself was one of the ugliest I have ever seen in my life.

It quickly became apparent I would not see beauty that morning. I was disappointed, because I got out of bed just for her, and she had failed to show up. It didn't feel right, because the morning had started out on such a good note. I felt cheated, as if the sun rises every day for me and me alone. If that is the case, it is really me who has been cheating.

Standing up from the bench I had been sitting on, I walked to the base of a towering tree, the largest one around, and just stood there. It began to rain, but the drops were few and far between.

I received a text from my friend, Shelby, asking how my morning was progressing. I told her I had gotten up early to watch the sunrise, but it had ended up being ugly, so now there was nothing else to do but go home and do my work for the day.

The next day, I set my alarm for just before sunrise. When morning came, I kept hitting the snooze button, so all I saw were glimpses out the side of the north-facing window above my nightstand. From what I can remember—now that I am awake and have had my coffee—I didn't miss much. I told myself I would try again the next morning.

Thursday came bright and early. I completely slept through my first two alarms, so by the time I woke up, the colors were already shooting across the eastern sky. I watched from my bed, captivated by the glow of the golden sky, before rolling over and going back to sleep. Shortly after 9:00, I stumbled out of my bed, and managed to make it into the loft, a commute of approximately thirty feet. Plopping down on the couch, I picked up Donald Miller's *Through Painted Deserts* and began reading. Before I knew it, I was asleep again. This time, my slumber lasted until noon. The rest of the day was spent on the couch, as I became engrossed in Don's story. I barely budged for the remainder of the day, until the book was finished. Turning the last page, I processed the words and let the book fall into my lap. It was bittersweet. The story was over, but I didn't want it to be. I think that's how it will be toward the end of our lives, and we'll look back on those times when we tried to get God to hurry things up, and we'll realize we should have been more present in those moments.

Friday morning I found my rhythm again. My second alarm got me out of bed just as the sun was preparing to make its ascent into the eastern sky. Skipping my coffee, I quickly slipped out of the house. Within minutes, I was standing on the shore of the lake. The sky was already baby blue at this point, and there wasn't much cloud cover. But the clouds that were there were a light, pink color—like cotton candy—as they stretched across the sky from east to west and back again. I sat down under a weeping willow tree, thirsty for more, but that was all the beauty that came. I suppose the elaborate sunrises only come when you're not expecting them. It seemed that the more effort I put into positioning myself to see beauty, the less beauty I saw.

The day progressed slowly, the kind where you string an hour worth of work out over eight hours. It's now officially Saturday morning, and I'll be leaving for a family vacation in a few hours. I have yet to pack, or even sleep, but the night is still young. What started out as a spontaneous road trip where you wake up in a new town each day has morphed into a nice, but well-structured, four-night stay at a cabin in the woods of eastern Tennessee. I haven't been to that part of the state before—only the areas around Memphis and Nashville—and I hear the mountains of Middle Tennessee are irrelevant when compared to the Smokies. My parents are happy that the trip has become more stable and predictable, and I suppose it's time for me to give up the fight for spontaneity, but it's a shame, because I had everything planned out for a spontaneous road trip that we would remember forever.

As I think back over the past week, one day in particular stands out. That day is

Wednesday. After oversleeping and drinking a cup of coffee, I left to meet two of my friends from church, Sean and Jackson. I enjoyed a healthy breakfast of cookies on the way to Jackson's house, which made me feel like a college student. We spent the morning filming some videos for my job with the youth outreach ministry. One of the locations we used was a park in Frisco, which I had only previously visited once—seven years ago, before my family even moved to Dallas. I thought back to that weekend when we visited from Austin. I thought about how I fell in love with the Metroplex, and how badly I wanted to move there. It was a vast, unfamiliar city at the time, but now it feels much different, as if I have lived here my entire life.

Jackson had to leave for band practice at noon, so we hurried to finish filming. After dropping him off at his house, Sean and I went to grab lunch before we began the process of editing the videos. After waiting in a drive-thru lane far too long, we decided to stop for coffee, so we could begin the afternoon strong. As we were driving away from the coffee shop, I asked Sean to tell me his story.

Sean has lived in one house for most of his life. His family moved to Frisco long before it became the sprawling city of master-planned communities it is today. He didn't grow up in church, but his family believed in the general idea of God, and even attended church for a few months, around the time my family fell in love with Frisco. But then they stopped going for awhile—six years, actually—and it wasn't until recently that they began going again, to the church we both attend now.

I asked why they had stopped going to church six years ago, and Sean told me it was because everyone they talked to was snobby and treated them as less than human, and they quickly grew tired of it.

During this time, Jackson began asking Sean to attend his youth group. He finally caved, and went back to church one Wednesday night. This time, his experience was completely different. He came back the following week, and the week after, and even began attending on Sundays. He then brought the girl he was dating at the time, as well as his sister, and the three of them realized that even though they had believed in the existence of God on an intellectual level for most of their lives, they had never actually given Him their hearts. When they did, things began to change in their lives.

When Sean and his sister told their parents what had happened to them, they were intrigued, so they asked them to begin attending church as well. Sean's mom came, and quickly gave her heart to Jesus, but his dad was much more hesitant. A strong, military man, he had already been wounded by church once, and wasn't quite ready for round two. That didn't last very long, though. I think maybe God was after him, just like He was after me at one point in my story.

Later that afternoon, we were at Sean's house editing the videos, and I got to meet his dad. He said hello, and then went into the other room to fill out job applications. We continued our work and Sean told me his dad had been without work for several months. I could completely relate, because I'm in a similar place. I've been without a consistent job for seven months now, and I would be lying if I told you it has been easy. I can only imagine how hard it must be for Sean's dad. I wonder if he sometimes crawls back into bed in the middle of the morning after everyone has left and the house is empty. I wonder if he stands at the window, staring out into the world that seems to be moving along as normal, oblivious to the fact that his world has come crashing down around him. I wonder if he ever gets in his car and just drives around town aimlessly, looking for a reason to care about, well, anything.

I'll never forget what happened right as we were finishing the video. Sean's dad came into the kitchen and told him he was leaving for a few minutes to run an errand. Nothing out of the ordinary, just a simple errand. But then he looked at Sean from across the room, and when he opened his mouth, four simple, love-drenched words came out. "I love you, son." That was all he said. That was all he needed to say. The moment in itself was quite ordinary, but as he said those words, it felt as though time had stopped, as an ordinary moment became a holy moment.

Suddenly, I didn't feel anxious about my own life anymore, even though the words had not been directed at me. You can never underestimate the power of a father's words; they have the power to build a fortress of love and security, or tear down everything around them, leaving destruction and broken hearts in their wake. Mother Teresa said it like this: *Kind words are short and easy to speak, but their echoes are truly endless.*

I remember when I didn't have any friends at church, even though I had been going there for several months. There were a few people I knew vaguely, and we would see each other every week, but we largely carried on our own separate lives, which never intersected outside of the building where we worshipped on Sundays. It's only when I look back that I realize how shallow that was. Not that the people were shallow—I mean, they may have been, but I think perhaps the problem was more with me. I think I was too afraid of being rejected to get out there and make friends, so I settled for a bunch of acquaintances. I guess I figured if my gross number was high enough, it would make up for the fact that all my friendships were flimsy facades.

CHAPTER 28

FAST FORWARD

I used to think life would become a lot more awkward when I turned twenty,
but now I know awkward seasons are only as awkward as you make them.

I'm quickly running out of room to tell this story, so if you don't mind, we're going to fast forward a few weeks. It's now Saturday morning, September 22, 2012. My alarm sounds at 5:45, with no time to press the snooze button. It's been exactly two months since Mamma's funeral. My grandparents—who have only lived in two adjoining Missouri counties their entire lives—are now looking at houses in Texas.

As we drove south on the highway that connects Dallas to Austin, I couldn't help but relish God's faithfulness. My grandma put her life on hold eight years ago. She stepped in and filled a need. What she did was not overly spiritual in appearance, but she gets it. She understands that Jesus says those with true faith will care for those who can't care for themselves (James 1:27).

We've always talked quietly—almost behind the scenes—about what would happen when my great-grandparent's lives on this earth came to an end. Ideas have ranged from my grandparents moving to a neighboring town, to them moving to Texas. My grandpa never was too keen on the whole Texas thing, so I never thought it would actually happen. But there we were two months after the funeral, going to look at a house they had picked out.

We arrived at Uncle Gregg and Aunt Machelle's house in Round Rock a few hours later, and drove ten miles east to Taylor, a small town of about fifteen thousand. It's the type of town that's in the city, yet in the country at the same time, and it will be the largest town my grandparents have ever lived in.

Standing in the kitchen of their average house in an average neighborhood in an average town, we watched as they signed the paperwork. My grandparents now owned a home in a brand new city in a brand new state. Redemption has occurred in just two short months, though the backstory takes us back eight years, when my grandma first pressed pause on life. Now, she is ready to press play again.

That night, after everyone else had crawled into bed, I stood in my aunt and uncle's living room. I knew that I, too, would soon fall asleep, and when I woke up, I would be twenty. I stood in the dark, staring out the window, even though all I saw was darkness. There was something so bittersweet about the moment. Part of me wanted to be young again, to forget the broken state of the world and just live and breathe in the creation around me. The other part of me wanted to be old and married and successful, having done something that mattered with my life, to live the kind of life that echoes into eternity. But there are no shortcuts. I have to keep moving forward; I have to grow older at a normal pace. I have to try and fail and experience success and rejection and all the other things I'm afraid of.

There are seasons of life where we know God is whispering to us to stay put, and we have to trust Him. Then there are times when God is whispering for us to move forward, and we have to trust Him in that place as well. Finally, there are the seasons where we have to stay put, but move forward at the same time. Those seasons are the hardest. Those are the seasons we look back on twenty years down the road, laugh, and casually comment on how the things that terrified us ended up shaping us into the people God wanted us to become. Those are the seasons where you may not have a job for eight months, but you write a book. They are difficult and painful and frustrating, and it never seems like it will be worth it at the time.

I think a lot of times we look to God to speak through a megaphone, telling us exactly what to do and when to do it—in a voice so loud, it's nearly audible. I used to do this, until I realized that neither God nor myself are robots. He doesn't try to control me, so why should I try to control Him? He sometimes gives me signs that I'm on the right path, but other times, He doesn't. Sometimes, I have no clue whether I'm on the right path or not, I just know that He's there, and that is enough.

※ ※ ※

I woke up on the couch Sunday morning to find my dad looking up at me from his air mattress on the floor.

"Happy Birthday," he whispered before rolling over and going back to sleep.

"Thanks," I replied with a smile. I then got up, tiptoed quietly up the stairs, and stared at myself in the bathroom mirror. I was twenty—which I've always said is an awkward age. I kept waiting for the awkward feeling to kick in, but it never did. I didn't feel any different at all, actually. It didn't even feel strange that I was no longer a teenager, that the door to the rest of my life had just swung wide open.

For most people, twenty is awkward because you're not a teenager anymore, but you don't really feel like an adult. And it's like you've hit some sort of milestone, as if the "every ten years" birthdays suddenly become significant, because we don't really celebrate when someone turns ten more than when they turn nine, so twenty is the first one you arrive at before thirty, which is the age where the reality that your childhood is never coming back usually sinks in. But twenty—twenty is somewhere between all of that.

An hour later, I exited my the house alone, before anyone else had begun to stir. I crossed the street and quietly slipped into the front seat of my family's SUV. I drove across town, past the neighborhood where I grew up, the stores I used to shop at, and the ever-changing skyline nestled on the banks of the Colorado River. Signs marking the way to One Chapel greeted me as I merged off the freeway onto the exit ramp. There were more signs lining the access road, all the way up to the parking lot of the office building where the church met.

I was early, so I waited in the parking lot until a few minutes before the service was set to begin. I then walked into the two-year-old church plant where I didn't know anyone, though many people I passed seemed vaguely familiar. Several people stopped and shook my hand as I made my way to a seat in the corner, about halfway back from the stage. Worship began moments later. After a few songs, Pastor Ross got up and reminded us about how much Jesus loved us—which is good, because we tend to forget—and then we sang some more songs and took communion and recited the Nicene Creed in unison, which was one of the most holy things I have ever done in a weekend church service. There were elements both old and new, joining the past with the present. It was a bit messy, but it was a divine mess, dripping in love and grace.

At some point, Pastor Ross introduced his brother, Pastor Brent, who talked to us about our stories and the tendency we have to believe life is all about us. When we don't know our place in God's story, we create our own story, and then we get insecure and anxious and stressed out from running all over the place trying to prove to everyone that we are someone great, someone worthy of love and acceptance.

My church back home in Dallas was beginning a series on the Lord's Prayer the same weekend that One Chapel was finishing up their series on the same topic. Pastor Brent read from the last verse of the prayer, about how the kingdom and the power and the glory belong to God, which implies that it doesn't belong to us. This life isn't about seeing how much power we can gain or how much glory we can get directed at us, nor is it about building our own personal empires.

Pastor Brent says when we step back from the spotlight and let God take center stage, it frees us to become the people He created us to be. It frees us from striving to make everything come together perfectly, from the burden of everything we are not. We don't have to put on a show and try hard to get God's attention, because we already have His attention and He really likes us, which means that even though we are honestly nothing, we are actually something—because the Creator of the Universe tells us that our lives are precious and valuable to Him.

I quietly slipped out shortly after the service ended, passing all of the people in the foyer who were laughing and talking like they had been friends for ages. A few minutes later, I pulled into a run-down shopping center less than a quarter of a mile away from the church in the fancy office building with all the cool signs alerting passersby to its existence. One of the buildings had a plain banner with three large letters on it. This banner marked the entrance to another church, which you would never know was a church unless you were looking for it. This church is called Open Gate Ministries—or OGM, according to the banner. OGM is a small community of believers, nestled between a gas station and a nightclub in South Austin. My friend, Rocky, who used to be a pastor at a large church outside of Dallas, started OGM a few years ago with his wife, Janice. Rocky told me someone once saw the banner and thought it stood for Old Gangster Ministries, which I find quite hilarious.

I was last at OGM two years ago, on a day much like this one, where I attended the early service at One Chapel beforehand. Back then, there were only a dozen or so in attendance, and everyone sat around three white, plastic tables that had been pushed together to form a makeshift conference table. Rocky stood at the head of the table and preached like he was speaking to thousands. It came naturally for him, he was good at it, and his words seemed to flow from someplace other than his mind. I once heard a theologian say the Church is the place that hosts the *words from elsewhere*, and if we do not host the words from elsewhere, we end up being a shallow reflection of our secular culture. [1]

Worship had just ended when I entered the building. It wasn't very big, so there wasn't a lobby or any sort of generic fellowship space—you're either in the sanctuary, the kitchen, the bathroom, or outside the building altogether. I entered quietly, feeling like I was crashing an old friend's party. I immediately spotted Janice standing off to the side, and moved toward her. She caught me in her arms, like old friends who were seeing each other for the first time since high school. Rocky subtly waved to me from the stage before launching into his talk.

My eyes began to scan the room from the corner where I stood. I quickly spotted the familiar conference table in the center, but there were several others, eight in all. There were the plastic tables, a couple of bistro tables, and a big table that looked like it had previously been in someone's dining room. Each of the tables were packed to capacity; the crowd had tripled since I was last there two years ago. Colorful paintings adorned the walls, most of which had been painted by people in the community. One in particular caught my eye. Though it was nothing more than a yellow background with a red vase containing three green and blue flowers, I recognized it immediately. It had been painted by my friend, Henry, just like the painting that sits on my desk at home.

Our lives used to intertwine more frequently, back when we all lived in Central Texas. But then, my family moved north to Dallas, while Henry and Michell moved further north to Kansas, leaving Rocky and Janice behind in Austin.

While I vaguely remember growing up in this community, I know I never fully appreciated it. But now that I'm older, something in me craves church that functions as a close-knit family and leaves off the extras. The kind of church where hand-crafted art adorns the walls, where people sit around tables drinking coffee, eating muffins, and studying the Scriptures together.

In the last few months, Henry and Michell lost the building their church meets in—the one I visited while they were on the beach in South Texas. They had arrived home to discover they were actually pastoring a mega-church—twenty people accompanied by a few thousand bats. They were everywhere, and there was no way to get rid of them. The giant bat nest was ultimately torn down, so their church now meets at the local zoo. I've heard about a lot of churches that have done crazy things in the name of being culturally relevant, but I have never heard of anyone holding weekly services at the zoo.

Midway through his talk, Rocky shared a story about a man who had an encounter while lying on an operating table in a hospital. He was taken to heaven, and was actually able to recall what he had seen when he returned to earth. The man described heaven as a place with no walls, no ceiling—a place that went on and on, seemingly endless. He was a different man after this, in the years that followed this encounter. He didn't write a best-selling book about it, but he h ad a different look in his eyes, a sort of newness of life. He would stand in his study and stare aimlessly out the window, dreaming of the things he had seen as he lay on that operating table, the very things he would one day see again, things that wouldn't fade back to earth the second time.

Following this story, Rocky launched into the main part of his message, which was about the Lord's Prayer. I couldn't help but smile. Rocky told us he was going to preach on the first verse—the *Our Father which art in Heaven* part—except he never made it that far. Rocky talked for the same amount of time as Brent did at One Chapel, but never made it to the word "our," as his talk hovered on Matthew 6:5-8. Even so, it was one of the best messages on prayer I've ever heard.

On this morning, I visited two churches. They were totally different, but in a way they were exactly the same. One had cool signs and graphics pointing it out to everyone who passed by; the other was in an obscure location where few could find it, but both churches were places of authentic community, places where people from all walks of life were being connected to the story of redemption.

CHAPTER 29

COMING HOME

I used to think I had to figure life out before I finished writing this book,
but now I know that my journey is just beginning.

I've never really been a huge fan of small talk. It's almost a non-human experience, if you really think about it. I say this, because small talk involves two people who, though they may be very different, are both living the same experience of being human. They both have hopes and dreams and fears, and they're both trying to find their place in the world. Yet, for one reason or another, their interaction is limited to mundane topics such as the weather or the price of gasoline.

I was having a conversation with a man named Steve recently. It was just small talk at first, but that quickly changed. Steve began to talk about Jesus, and he talked about Him in a way that would make you think they were close friends. "I can't imagine what it will be like to see Him with my own two eyes, to touch Him, to feel the holes in His hands." Steve wept as he talked. He was full of a passion for Jesus that you don't see in too many people. I wish I had that level of passion, that I would be moved to tears whenever Jesus is brought up.

I was at a church in East Texas once, when I noticed the girl sitting behind me was crying throughout the service. Her mom, who was sitting next to her in the pew, wrapped her arms around her and held her close. After the service, I crossed paths with the family in the foyer. I introduced myself and talked to the mom and dad for a few minutes as she looked on, staring blankly into space. As the conversation came to a close, I looked her square in the eyes and told her that Jesus loved her more than she could ever know, that He saw her differently than she saw herself, and that her life had value and meaning because of Him. She returned my words with a glazed over look. Without words, she stared at me for what seemed like an eternity before nodding slightly.

I lingered as her dad walked her out to the car. As I looked at her mom apologetically, she leaned in and embraced me before I could find words that danced around the tension of the moment. She then told me that her daughter needed to hear what I had said. I found this to be very interesting, since I honestly had no idea where the words I spoke had even come from. Before she left, she looked me in the eyes and asked me to remember her daughter in my prayers, and I told her I would.

It wasn't until later that I found out the girl had just been released from a mental hospital, where she had spent several days after a failed suicide attempt. Though she couldn't receive it at the moment, she desperately needed someone to remind her of her value, to remind her that her life had purpose and meaning.

We all need that reminder, a reassurance that our lives are worth living. We search for it in our relationships, in our seemingly constant desire for affirmation from others. We search for it through sex, drugs, money, power, fame, new cars, shopping sprees—even religious activity, void of the Spirit of God. We experience this every day, a chasing after the wind, as we search for someone or something to save us. These things never will. We were never meant to be satisfied with anything temporary. We were designed to crave beauty, wonder, and life-giving connection with the One who created us and knows us better than we know ourselves. But, for one reason or another, we are quick to settle for cheap imitations.

When Adam and Eve were in Eden, they lived life in unbroken connection with the Father. There was no war or violence or striving. They didn't have to worry about making it to the next level in life; they didn't have to prove themselves to anyone, because the Creator of the Universe knew their names and walked alongside them in the paradise He had created. Everything was perfect, as is often the case before the world comes crashing down.

Prior to the moment when satan entered the story in the form of a snake, the only voice that Adam and Eve knew was the Father's. But at that moment, a new voice entered the narrative—a voice that called into question everything they had ever known.

We sometimes think Adam and Eve had limited options in the garden, but that was not the case. God told them to eat freely; there was only *one* tree they were told not to eat from. Everything else was fair game; everything else was at their disposal. This tells us God was and is quite generous, but the new voice convinced them that He was holding out on them. This voice was so deceitful that it actually convinced Adam and Eve that they were not who they already were; it told them they would become like God if they ate from the tree they had been told not to eat from. As Eve reached out to partake of the tree, she was reaching for what she already possessed. Both she and Adam were already like God; they were created in His image, according to His likeness. Their sin was so much deeper than eating from the tree God told them not to eat from. In that moment, they failed to believe what God said about them was true, which was the deeper issue. Had Eve been conscious of her identity in the moment, she would have rejected the new voice that was trying to force its way into the narrative. [1]

Why do I need to do that to become like God? I'm already like God! Why would I disobey Him to obtain what I already possess? Sin is often an attempt to obtain what we already possess through illegitimate means.

Adam and Eve fixated on this one piece of fruit from this one tree when God had given them endless trees with infinite varieties of fruit to enjoy, which is often our problem. There's so much to enjoy; yet we fixate on something we don't have. This is why gratitude is so key to the life God made us for. Until we center ourselves on what we have, on the life we get to live, we'll constantly be looking for another life. [2]

When Adam and Eve first ate the fruit, it wasn't about the fruit, it was about their dissatisfaction with the world God had placed them in. Creation wasn't good enough for them. ... And so they ate the fruit and everything fell apart. They were tempted with something that promised what it couldn't deliver, and they lived with the consequences. [3]

God made man, put him in a garden, and told him that all he needed to do was live and move and draw his life from their connection, which at the time was unbroken. But man chose to stop partaking of the beauty of sweet communion with the Father. He disconnected from the one and only source of life and soon after, found himself in need of a Savior. And then low and behold, as he was walking through the garden with his wife, he noticed some fig leaves and thought to himself, "Perhaps these will save me ..."—when all he needed to do was run back to the beauty he had left. But he was content with the leaves, with his own imitation over the real thing.

How could someone who has tasted and seen the goodness and glory of God be satisfied with cheap imitations? Yet, we see it all the time. In fact, I think one of the biggest cheap imitations of the wild and wonderful Kingdom of God is religion. I think there are a lot of people out there like Mamma who grew up in church, attended faithfully, perhaps even served in ministry—but never actually gave their heart to Jesus. Instead, they settled for the cheap imitation of trying to get to God through dead religion.

Some think all you have to do to get to God is go to church, confessional, or just simply be a good person. The good news is, the Gospel is easier than that, because Jesus has already done everything necessary to restore us to the life we lost in Adam. All we have to do is give Him our hearts and receive His life. The bad news is, the Gospel is harder than that, because in order to receive the life God offers, we must realize there is nothing we can do to earn it. We must come to the end of ourselves; we must surrender. We don't like this, because most of us would rather do something for our salvation than receive it freely, which is why we must humble ourselves and receive God on His terms. It's not just an act of faith, but an act of humility as well, to receive something we don't deserve and can't obtain on our own. We can't work to obtain the life and love of the Kingdom of God, but we can receive it as a gift. We don't have to worry about trying to get our feet in the door, because even though we couldn't get anywhere near the door, God in Christ has brought the door to us and flung it wide open. All we have to do is make the choice to step through the door.

I used to be dead.

I was physically alive, sure, but I was dead inside.

I needed the life of God to be breathed into me.

I needed the power switch to be turned on.

I needed Jesus to come and make the dead things in my life alive.

I needed Him to exchange the death in me for the life in Him.

I needed Him to take my heart and give me His heart.

I believed in the existence of God.

For much of my life, I tried to be religious.

... it didn't work.

I tried to do more good things than bad things.

I tried to make God like me.

I went to church.

I read the Bible.

But I never gave Him everything.

I never gave Him my heart.

I never cried out, "Here I am, God! I can't do this on my own!"

Except for this one time—at 6:00 in the morning—when I did.

It was a few months after I turned eighteen. I was sitting at my desk in the dark after being up all night. I remember the ache in my soul, how God continually pursued me. I remember kneeling at the foot of my bed, and I remember that this was the moment when everything changed.

Religion made me a better person, at least in theory. It even made me think I had been made new, though it failed to transform my heart. In fact, in many ways, it left me more broken than I was previously.

I know what it's like to be broken—and I know what it's like to be made whole. It's strangely liberating—realizing I'm not perfect and I don't have to be, because Jesus was already perfect on my behalf. I just had to allow Him to exchange the death in me for the life in Him, as Bob the Freedom Guy would say.

You can spend your entire life in church, celebrating God amongst the crowd, but never really know Him. It's possible to be in a church service and not be any closer to God than when you're throwing back shots and smoking weed at a seedy night club.

It's all about the heart, you see. Where is your heart? Where are you drawing your life from?

Have you ever seen a guy or girl from across the room and been immediately attracted to them, even though you know nothing about them? Perhaps you follow them around for awhile, going to all the places they go, hoping to run into them.

You may even convince yourself you know them, when you've never had more than a passing conversation. FYI, that's not a real relationship.

All God wants is for you to truly know Him. He isn't shocked by your story. He isn't concerned about where you've been or who you've become—He just wants you! He wants your heart above everything else; He wants you to be alive and engaged with Him. He'll take care of the mess you've gotten yourself into; He just wants you to come home, so He came make you new.

Perhaps your story will be like Mamma's. Perhaps you will come alive for the first time as you read this in your living room on a Saturday morning.

I'm not going to give you a formula. I'm not going to give you a card to fill out. I'm not going to give you a twelve-step plan. I'm not even going to give you a prayer to pray. You don't need my words; you just need Jesus to come into your life and make all things new.

Call on Jesus. Cling to Jesus. Let Him give you a little taste of redemption—on earth as it is in heaven.

I like how Elise says God has been right beside us our whole lives, regardless of whether or not we were aware of His presence, and how the Apostle Paul says He is not far from us (Acts 17:27).

Romans 10:13 tells us, *Everyone who calls on the name of the Lord will be saved.* This is a powerful Scripture. Not just because of what it says, but what it *doesn't* say. It doesn't say you have to *call on the name of the Lord and figure the Bible out* in order to be saved. It's okay if you don't understand the entire Bible. I don't either! What truly matters is your willingness to humble yourself, let go of everything you've been clinging to so tightly, and lay everything at the feet of Jesus—your sin, your shame, even your doctrinal views.

As you take Jesus with you on the journey, you'll begin to understand things in the Bible that you don't understand right now, but you will never understand everything there is to know about God. Just trust Jesus with your life, and trust the Holy Spirit to lead you into all Truth. Find a community of people you can belong to, and allow their stories to intersect with yours as you grow in grace and the knowledge of God together. Read the Bible—not because you have to or want to prove you are right about something—but to fall deeper and deeper in love with the mystery of the God who wrapped Himself in flesh and ran after us while we were still running away.

CHAPTER 30

REDEMPTION

I used to think God operated on my schedule,
but now I know I have to embrace the process.

The word *redemption*, in the literal sense, means to *buy back*. In other words, Jesus' death on the cross and resurrection from the dead secured our redemption, bringing us back to God. However, Scripture also uses the term in a much broader sense, pointing toward the future redemption and restoration of all things when Jesus returns. This is the vision that John saw on the island of Patmos—Jesus making all things new (Revelation 21:5). To *redeem* is to *repair, restore, heal, make all things new*.

We know that God will someday make all things new, but we also see Him at work making all things new even now. The paradigm that the Kingdom of God is *now, but not yet*, was first developed by Princeton theologian Gerhardus Vos shortly after the turn of the century. Professor George Eldon Ladd of Fuller Theological Seminary would later expound on this in the 1950's. *Now, but not yet*, states that we, as believers, are actively taking part in the Kingdom of God through the power of the Holy Spirit, but the Kingdom of God will not reach its full expression until some point in the future. This would explain why living as children of God in a fallen world is not without tension. Our spirits have been redeemed and brought to life in Christ now, but our physical bodies will not be redeemed until some point in the not yet.

Both John the Baptist and Jesus proclaimed *The Kingdom of God is at hand!* (Matthew 3:2, 4:17; ESV) more than two thousand years ago, but we have not yet seen Revelation 21-22 fully manifest. We live between the advents of Christ, in the land of the *now, but not yet.* We see this in many places throughout Scripture. One example would be 1 John 3:2, which tells us we are *now* children of God, and at some point, when the *not yet* comes to pass, we will become something else. We don't know what that entails exactly, but we know it has something to do with looking like Jesus.

Throughout the course of this book, I have referred to the dawn of this age (described in Genesis 1-2) as *creation,* and the end of this age and the beginning of the age to come (described in Revelation 21-22) as *redemption.* And right now, we are living within the pages of The Story—in the overlap of the ages. The Kingdom of God was inaugurated by Jesus two thousand years ago, but it will not reach its full consummation until He returns.

The story begins in a garden where humans live in unbroken connection with God, and the story ends in a city that bears similar, garden-like characteristics where humans live in unbroken connection with God. It would be fair to say that, in many ways, the story ends where it begins.

We are in the overlap of the ages, but if you think about it, we are not fully in one place or the other. *Redemption* is really all about getting us back to *creation,* which we've defined as life fully connected to God, before the fall of man and the entrance of sin into The Story (described in Genesis 3). We are in an age where we are experiencing a little bit of creation as we were designed to experience it, and we are also experiencing glimpses into the age to come, when redemption will be complete. That's the whole point as to why Jesus came—to restore us to the life we lost. What the human race lost at the fall is restored to us in Christ, and we will see the full manifestation of this reality when we see Jesus face-to-face. Until then, we live between creation and redemption, which is why we need help finding our place in a fallen world.

❋ ❋ ❋

The week after I turned twenty, Elise and I met on a Thursday afternoon to discuss the state of our stories. That morning, out of nowhere, I received a phone call that just might change the course of my life. I skipped a few weeks of events that led up to this phone call when I hit fast forward on the story, so let's back up a bit.

I was on my way home from Tennessee when I received an email from my friend, Beth (who is above average), about a full-time job opening at my church in Southlake, a position that had my name written all over it. I quickly filled out an application and turned it in. Three weeks passed with no word on the status of my application. I had given up on the idea that I would even get an interview, let alone the job. Then, on the Thursday after my birthday, the call came—I had an interview first thing the following morning.

I was filled with joy as I went about several mundane tasks that morning. I then got in my car and drove to Lewisville where Luke and I ate Chinese food and caught each other up on the last few months of our lives, everything since before the youth camp. I drove him back to his office afterward, and he prayed for me in the lobby before I left.

I then drove across town to meet Elise. We talked about life for two hours in a little coffee house around the corner from her house, which wasn't far from the tiny apartment where my family lived when we first moved to Dallas seven years ago, years before Elise and I's lives intersected.

We also talked about how both of us would love to leave our lives behind and move to the Pacific Northwest, to a fantasy city like Seattle or Portland. I told her that if we lived in either of those cities, we would have had our conversation in a 24-hour diner in the middle of the night, and it would probably be raining, adding to the ambiance. We would both take the bus or the subway to get there and there would be mood lighting, just like in the movies. Except if this were a movie, we would fall in love; even though she is dating Chase, she would realize that I am the one she really wants to be with. But our lives are not movies. They are more boring and a lot less vivid, but at least they are real.

In real life, I don't actually want any of this to happen. I don't want to leave my life behind to chase a fantasy. I don't want to live in Seattle or Portland—I've never even been to either of those cities; I just like the idea of them. I've fallen in love with a world I've read about, a world I've watched movies about. The only problem is, that world does not exist. The cities themselves exist, but the idea that those cities can somehow save me from the struggle is pure fantasy.

I am okay with the conversations in the middle of the night part of the story, and we could probably replicate it if we were willing to drive to Dallas' Uptown district, but that's nearly an hour away. There might be rain, perhaps, but no subway, because we don't have one.

And I don't want Elise and I to fall in love, either. I want her to keep dating Chase, and not me, and I want to invite the right girl into my story someday. I don't want our lives to turn out like the movies, because I've seen the sequels where things don't end up as perfectly as they appeared to be at the end of the first film.

※ ※ ※

I woke up at 6:30 on Friday morning. After spending the first moments of the day taking in the silence, I sat in the big, leather chair in my office and talked to God for a bit. I then took a shower and got dressed—in a nice shirt, slacks, and my pointy shoes. I left my house and made the drive to Southlake, pulling into the parking lot of my church's office complex thirty minutes ahead of schedule. I sat in my car for a few minutes, working up the courage to enter the building. When I did, I immediately recognized the receptionist. It was Linda, an older woman whom I had worked with at the coffee shop for several months before she quit due to the physical toll the job was taking on her aging body.

"Jared!" she exclaimed. "What are you doing here?"

I just smiled. We hugged from across the counter, which was quite awkward, actually. I then sat down in one of the comfortable chairs to wait for the person who was scheduled to interview me.

"This is it," I thought to myself. *"This is my chance to redeem myself. Perhaps this will be the door God will open for me."*

It's interesting that I had this thought, because there is a big difference between redeeming myself and God breaking in on the scene to turn the storyline in a new direction.

It had been eight months since I had stopped working at the coffee shop, and this was the only job I had been able to apply for in good conscience since. I wanted a job within two months, perhaps three, but God had a different plan—a plan that involved me walking through some dark, lonely places. I would emerge a different person—a person with more confidence and less fear, ready to step into the next season of life with my head held high.

The interview went well. Friday, September 28, 2012, might very well be the first day of the rest of my life.

I was in a worship service that night, at an event held by the youth outreach ministry. It was rare for me to actually be able to worship at these events, because I was often busy making sure everything ran smoothly.

I remember lying on the floor by the stage that night, soaking in the presence of God as the band played. I remember telling God that I trusted Him, regardless of what happened, even though I wanted the job very badly. And then, a thought made its way into my mind, and I realized that even if I didn't get what I thought I needed, God is faithful and He is for me. When He frustrates my plans, it's often because they're too small. Sometimes, He doesn't give me what I want, so He can give me what I actually want, but aren't yet aware of, because I'm thinking too small. As the Apostle Paul says, God is able to do *immeasurably more than all we ask or imagine* (Ephesians 3:20).

※ ※ ※

I walked into the middle of a field one morning while I was still at my grandparent's farm in Missouri. Something began to happen as I absorbed the creation that surrounded me. I began to sing and jump and leap and shout. I lost connection with any earthly reality as a new, heavenly reality invaded the space my body occupied. This lasted a few minutes. When I turned back around, I saw a dozen cows, perfectly lined up in a row, staring at this two-legged freak show.

It began to rain. I stretched out my arms as far as they could reach, until I could almost feel my feet lifting off the ground. I turned my head to the sky as drops of water gently splashed my face, washing me clean. I took my glasses off and held them by my side, knowing that I did not need them to truly see. The sky was blue and gray and gold. It was raining, but light was shining through the clouds. Though there was no rainbow visible, God's promises felt more alive than ever before.

A neighbor was burning trash somewhere over the tree-lined horizon, causing thick smoke to ascend into the sky. Water and fire and billows of smoke. I think at one point, the moon even turned to blood. [1]

It was as if God Himself had shouted into the silence with the same voice that spoke the world into existence. In that moment, His Kingdom collided with earth in a beautiful symphony of grace. Life swallowed up death and perfect love cast out all fear. All things were being made new. As I stood in the middle of creation, I didn't find myself longing for redemption anymore. Instead, I opened my eyes and simply experienced it.

EPILOGUE

It's hard to believe three years have passed since I wrote the manuscript that would become *Creation & Redemption*. I was originally going to publish it in September of 2014, but life threw me for a bit of a curve last summer, and I now split my time between Texas and Pennsylvania—when I'm not on the road.

A few years back, I was in a cabin in the woods in Tennessee when I realized that all of the stories I wanted to share would not fit in this manuscript. I never set out to write more than one book of this style, but I am excited to say that I now have plans for at least seven more books that talk about the ups and downs of finding your place in the world. Hopefully, this one will sell, so that there will be a reason for me to write the others. Be on the lookout for part two in *The Early Essays* series—*Life, Love & Good Coffee*—which will be available at some point down the road.

I write this as I sit in the upstairs loft at my friend's house, nestled at the foot of the Bridger Mountains in Montana. I come here when I need to clear my head, but I no longer feel as though a change of scenery will magically change my life. In fact, there are a lot of things in this book that don't quite reflect the person I am today. Not that I am taking back anything I have written or that any of it is untrue, I'm just in a different season of life.

I run a moderately successful business now, but I know that my job does not define me, and I certainly don't look to my career path as the source of my redemption as I alluded to in the final chapter. However, in my rounds of edits, I have left much of the original manuscript intact, because I want it to reflect where I was at in life when I wrote it. It makes me cringe at times; when I read the story about Ashley, I can't help but laugh at myself. At the same time, I realize the parts of my story that I'm not as excited about sharing could be the parts that impact people the most. It's not often that a Christian book gets down in the dirt and lingers there for a bit, and I want my story to be an authentic expression of the reality that life is hard sometimes, but also full of so much beauty if we stop to take it in.

It's funny how so much can change in such a short period of time. Elise and I aren't that close anymore, mostly because our lives have taken us in opposite directions. I've come to realize that some things in life will only remain for a season, though we may want to hold on to them forever. I was in Southlake this past January, and I got to see Elise and Chase tie the knot before I got on a plane back to the East Coast. I spend a lot of time these days in states I had never visited when I wrote this book. In this way, it almost feels as if this book is about an entirely different person, because so much has changed so fast.

Danica is growing so fast that I barely recognize her. My mom's parents are thriving in their new home in Texas. Christina has dropped off the map, but she's still alive somewhere in Florida. She recently got engaged and will be married in October. Jeremiah and Nicole are doing well, I think. Henry and Michell left Central Kansas for Central Texas where Henry has gone back into real estate. Dave and many of my friends in Oklahoma have moved their missions base to Harrisburg, Pennsylvania. Kyle (from the lake) married Kacie Asper and is now a father. I was there when he proposed to her, and cried seven months later at their wedding. Both Bob and Alan are no longer at Gateway as one has gone back into private practice; the other, to plant a church. The students in my old youth group in Frisco have graduated and fanned out to colleges across the country, and I moved on from working with the youth outreach ministry after four wonderful years.

John Ondrasik of Five for Fighting talks about how we need to enjoy every stage of life, because we've only got a hundred years to live [1] and Kenny Chesney tells us a hundred years goes faster than we think. [2]

Just a few weeks ago, I was riding a bus through the back country of Mexico, a few hours south of the border crossing at Nogales, Arizona. I was listening to a podcast from Daniel Grothe at New Life Church in Colorado Springs [3] on the topic of the apocalypse (stay with me; it's not what you think). In many Christian circles, we often think of really bad Hollywood movies that should have never made it out of Nashville. These movies often claim to depict biblical prophecy. The only problem is, in the Bible, *apocalypse* has a totally different meaning.

Translated from Greek into English, *apocalypse* means something more along the lines of *revelation, manifestation, enlightenment, disclosure*. In fact, the very first word in the book of Revelation is *apocalypse—the apocalypse of Jesus Christ*. The image we are meant to see is that of the pulling back of the curtain, which reminds me of how the veil was torn at Calvary, giving mankind access to God (Matthew 27:51). All that we see is not all that is true; a far greater reality is at work behind the scenes. If you want to see what is true, allow God to pull back the curtain and give you an apocalypse (revelation) of the age to come, to uncover something that is presently true, but has been hidden from public eye (Matthew 13:13-17). John the Baptist said it like this: *Repent, for the kingdom of heaven is at hand!* (Matthew 3:2, ESV).

For the creation waits with eager longing for the revealing of the sons of God ... For we know that the whole creation has been groaning together in the pains of childbirth until now. And not only the creation, but we ourselves, who have the firstfruits of the Spirit, groan inwardly as we wait eagerly for adoption as sons, the redemption of our bodies (Romans 8:19, 22-23, ESV). All of creation eagerly awaits the revealing—the apocalypse—of the children of God. All of creation is longing for our apocalypse, for us to step into what is most true about us and walk in our authority as sons and daughters of God. Or, as Eugene Peterson puts it in his translation of the Scriptures: *You're sons of Light, daughters of Day. We live under wide open skies and know where we stand. So let's not sleepwalk through life like those others. Let's keep our eyes open and be smart. People sleep at night and get drunk at night. But not us! Since we're creatures of Day, let's act like it. Walk out into the daylight sober, dressed up in faith, love, and the hope of salvation* (1 Thessalonians 5:5-8, The Message).

Daniel says the Church is the group of people who understand what God is going to do at the end of the story, and strive to pull it into the middle. Because we know what God will do in the end, we know what we are called to do now.

I suppose this is why how we view the end matters. If we think God's primary purpose at the end of this age is to blow up the world and start over, we will live in this manner ourselves. I've seen a lot of angry Christians spend more time "blowing up" the world than they do loving the world. But if we believe God's primary purpose at the end of this age is to restore and renew creation, we will focus our attention on being agents of restoration and renewal in the here and now.

It's important that we understand what God is doing; otherwise, we might mistake what we are called to do. Creation is longing for the people who know what's going to happen at the end of the story to rise up and pull it into the middle of the story. Or, as Jesus taught us to pray: *Thy kingdom come, Thy will be done in earth, as it is in heaven* (Matthew 6:10, KJV).

The Church is the apocalypse that the world has been waiting for. God is righting the wrongs of a world gone mad by sending His peculiar people into the world to heal it through Him, to usher in the age to come when He will heal the world in full and make all things new.

God's peculiar people are those who live in the world, but look different from the world. Not in the sense of moral superiority or Christian t-shirts, but in the sense that they are sons of Light and daughters of Day who clothe themselves in faith, hope, and love and refuse to sleepwalk through life in survival mode.

I shall close with a few thoughts from Bob the Freedom Guy: *In the visible creation, God has expressed His invisible attributes, but we can look and miss it. ... I am aware this morning that all of creation is groaning—eagerly awaiting the unveiling of the heirs of the Creator. ... Utter peace and perfect love; no more tears and no more inflicting pain on one another. The Perfectly Loving One generating His nature through those designed to receive, contain, and broadcast Him to all of creation. The sting of death and fear removed, and nothing but endless expression of the Greatest Father ever. Striving will cease and the government of His peace will cover the creation like the waters cover the sea.*[4]

That, friends, is a little taste of what redemption looks like. We are invited to experience it here and now, though not in full. But there will come a day when we return to the tree we were designed to eat from for all of eternity—the tree of life.

Jared Stump
Bozeman, MT
April 6, 2015

Contact Jared

As Bob Goff says, "It will be our accessibility, not our words, that will be our legacy." While I'm not quite as brave as he was when he put his cell phone number in the back of *Love Does*, I want to be available to anyone who'd like to get in touch with me.

Feel free to explore my website or follow me on Twitter for more thoughts on life and faith. If you'd like to talk to me directly, the email address below is a good avenue. I will do my best to respond, unless you are a Nigerian prince in need of $10,000.

Web: jaredstump.com
Email: jaredstumpauthor@gmail.com
Twitter: @jaredstump

Acknowledgements

First off, I'm grateful for everyone who has invested in me over the years; I wouldn't be who I am today without your love and guidance. I know I will miss many people who deserve to be mentioned, but here it goes ...

Mom and Dad - Thanks for giving me life and everything else, for pointing the way to the True Father in both the bad times and the good.

Henry and Michell - Oh, gosh. Where do I even begin? You both seem to always have just the right words, even when you actually don't. We're not in Kansas anymore. That pretty much sums it up.

Ron and Sue - Thanks for your continual encouragement and provoking me to believe in myself.

Kyle Embry - I don't mean to brag, but you have likely made the biggest impact in my life in recent years. I wouldn't be writing or speaking today if you had not taken a risk and pushed me forward when I was content hiding in the shadows. Thanks, mate!

Beth Helton - You believed in me before I believed in myself, and that made all the difference. Thanks for being above average, friend!

Bob Hamp - Thanks for the forward to this book. Oh, and helping me discover who I was created and redeemed to be.

Pastor Charles - Thanks for leading so well and being a continual example of joy and optimism. You are a treasure to the Body of Christ.

Uncle Gregg - Thanks for encouraging me to go after my dreams and not worry about what anyone else thinks.

Grandma Stump - Thanks for telling me it was okay to do what God wanted me to do instead of what people wanted me to do.

Grandpa Joe and Grandma Darlene - Thanks for allowing me to so candidly tell your story. Welcome to Texas.

The Battle Family - Thanks for being my home away from home in Central PA.

The Tripode Family - Thanks for inviting me into your lives, as well as into your booth at the Frisco Chili's.

Wayne and Lee - Thanks for giving me opportunities to grow in my gifts, as well as opening your home to me on so many occasions. The forgotten villages of Mexico and sweeping vistas of The Last Best Place have given me enough inspiration to last a lifetime.

Josh and Elizabeth - Thanks for opening up your home to me time and time again, in both Oklahoma and California. When I hear the phrase "hospitality," I often associate it with you without hesitation. I love you both, as well as Elia, Ethan, and my BFF for life, Cookie. Liz, I promise to recognize you next time you say hello to me in passing at a church in Shawnee.

Mark Royalty - I don't know where to begin, because there are so many things I respect about you. I think I'll just throw my laptop over the fence and you can watch it on CNN.

Kyle McMurray - You helped me walk through one of the most difficult seasons in my life, and you didn't even realize it at the time. Seriously, bro, I couldn't have done it without you.

Josh McGready - Thanks for always calling me on my crap and telling things exactly as they are.

Tyler Palomares - Hey, I need you to walk to the top of the hill with me, so I can scream some stuff.

Cody Swarny - I still drink coffee out of the mug you bought me in Sacramento.

Luke Gajary - I would have never met Kyle had it not been for you, Twitter, and the

Upper Room. Thanks for still meeting me for lunch after all these years.

Elise Pittman - You're in this book a lot already, but I thought I should mention you here as well. You were the first one to read my entire manuscript, and your feedback kept me going when I thought everything I was writing was total crap.

Sam Miller - I have no idea where you are right now, but I remember the days when I was first trying to be a writer. I would come to Buon Giorno for the atmosphere, and you would serve me delicious coffee with a side of encouragement. You were my first real fan. Thank you.

Wayne Drain - We've never met, but the prophetic word you gave me at the Gateway NRH Presbytery service in August of 2011 changed my life. It was the spark I needed to pursue writing, and I don't know where I'd be without that.

Donald Miller - We've also never met, but I feel as though we've had many coffeehouse conversations together through your books. Thanks for modeling what vulnerability in writing looks like. You're great.

Jason Upton - Your albums were my soundtrack on many lonely nights in my studio as this book was being composed. Thanks for sharing several little pieces of yourself with the world.

To my creative team: Mom, Kat, Christy, Chanel, and Amy—this book would still be an unattractive document on my MacBook if it wasn't for you guys.

To all of my financial backers and supporters, both on IndieGoGo and behind the scenes. Tony Fouts at Four Story Creative and Planet 316, you are an inspiration. Ricky Allen, I thoroughly enjoy our conversations about Jesus and your heart to follow Him when it's not popular. And Lorie, I know you would probably prefer not to be mentioned, but I couldn't have done this without you. Thanks for diving in head first with me in my endeavors to manifest the Kingdom on earth.

I have grown and been challenged by the ministries of Gateway Frisco and Life Center—my church family in Texas and Pennsylvania, respectively. Thanks for your love and support. Pastor Randy Cochran and Pastor Robert Morris at Gateway played key roles in shaping who I am today—in totally different ways. The North Texas Assemblies of God gave me a place to get my feet wet while I was still figuring life out, and the Burn 24-7 Crew kept the fire for God burning bright in my heart, especially in the dark times. Dave, Tannon, Cristina; I wouldn't be who I am today without you and so many others. And of course, I can't forget the cafe crew: Alana, Amy, Andrew, Annie, AJ, Cathy, Elise, Jennifer, Jordan, JR, Kayla, Keith, Lina, Linda, Martha, Megan, Neeli, Nicole, Tony, and Thomas. I can't wait to see how each of your stories unfold.

Though I no longer believe you need a special environment to write a book, *Creation & Redemption* was written at the following locations:

- My studio at the far end of Dallas suburbia
- The 333 House in the inner-city of Harrisburg
- My grandparent's farmhouse in Missouri
- The Bartolomucci's living room in Shawnee, OK
- The Wolverton's dining room in Waxahachie, TX
- The Royalty's back deck in Rapid City, SD
- The Hanson's house in Bozeman, MT
- The Battle's house in Lebanon, PA
- A cabin in the mountains of Tennessee
- A cabin on the Clinch River in Virginia
- A dock on Lake Grapevine in Texas
- On Southwest Airlines Flight 520—Baltimore to Dallas
- On Spirit Airlines Flight 720—Denver to Dallas/Fort Worth
- In an RV while traveling the back country of Sonora, Mexico
- Various coffee houses in Texas, Oklahoma, Missouri, and Washington, D.C.
- And several other locations while on the road in Arkansas, Indiana, Montana, Pennsylvania, South Carolina, and Tennessee

ENDNOTES

Chapter 1 - Creation
1. Genesis 1:1, ESV.

Chapter 2 - The Struggle
1. Donald Miller says something similar to this in his book, *Searching for God Knows What* (Nashville: Thomas Nelson, 2004), 162.
2. This is a reference to 2 Corinthians 4:6-7.

Chapter 4 - Depression and Worship
1. Writing has been in my heart for as long as I can remember, but I was terrible at it in my early days. Until one year, when I wrote a short story called *Oklahoma Nights* for school. Then, in August of 2011, I was at a Presbytery service at my church in North Richland Hills when I got a prophetic word from Pastor Wayne Drain. Wayne and I had never met before, but he told me that I was asking God for direction in my life (which I was), and I needed to do what was in my heart—the one thing that stood out from everything else. That was when I knew I needed to be a writer, so I went home and started writing a book called *Grace is Enough*, but it wasn't very good, so I quickly gave up on it. A few months passed; Christmas was quickly approaching. I was really struggling at the time, so I started writing another book called *Confessions of a Struggling Evangelical*. This one was even worse than the first, and was abandoned by January. A week later, I got the idea for this book, and on February 17, 2012, the first words were typed into my computer.
2. Fun Fact: I used to attend Gateway Church in Southlake, but I attend the Frisco campus now.
3. Translation: Around $500.
4. Blaise Pascal, *Pensées* (Public Domain, 1669).
5. My adaptation in these next few paragraphs is taken from Mark 8:31-38.

6. Mark 8:36-37, NASB.

7. This story is found in Luke 2:41-47.

8. My recollection of a story Pastor Don Johns told during the Maundy Thursday homily at Springhill Presbyterian Church (Bozeman, Montana), April 2, 2015.

Chapter 5 - Longing for Adventure

1. Donald Miller, *A Million Miles in a Thousand Years* (Nashville: Thomas Nelson, 2009).

2. I love how Ephesians 1:23 refers to God as one who "fills everything in every way."

3. This thought was borrowed from Rob Bell's book, *Sex God* (Grand Rapids: Zondervan, 2007), 39-40.

Chapter 6 - Life on the Farm

1. This story is found in John 3:1-21.

2. I was visiting Servant's Heart Community Church in Weatherford, Oklahoma (now Liberty Church) in 2009, when I heard Pastor Scott Page give this analogy.

3. This principle is found in several places throughout Scripture. A few examples include Colossians 2:13 and Ephesians 2:5.

Chapter 8 - Wrestling with God

1. Isaiah 58:8

2. John Eldredge says something similar to this in his book, *Waking the Dead: The Glory of a Heart Fully Alive* (Nashville: Thomas Nelson, 2003), 34.

3. Yes, this is a cheesy John the Baptist reference. You're welcome.

4. Luke 2:30, 2:14, respectively.

5. This story is found in Mark 9:17-27.

6. The Bible is actually kind of funny at times, if you really pay attention to what's happening. You can read about this in Genesis 28:16-19.

7. Genesis 14:18-20 talks about Abraham and his tithe.

8. Thoughts on Jacob wrestling with God were developed in part thanks to Brian Zahnd, Pastor of Word of Life Church (St. Joseph, Missouri). For further study, check out BZ's sermon *Jacob's Limp,* which was preached on October 6, 2013. This sermon is available at no charge in the archives at wolc.com.

9. This is a joke.

10. Genesis 32:20 states that Jacob's intention was to bribe his brother. This time,

he sent his messengers ahead with the actual possessions, not just talk of them.

11. 2 Corinthians 3:7-18, particularly verses 16-18.

12. C.S. Lewis, *Letters to Malcolm Chiefly on Prayer* (San Diego: Harcourt, 1992), 116.

Chapter 9 - Seasons

1. Phil Wickham, *You're Beautiful,* from the album *Cannons* (INO Records: 2007).

Chapter 10 - Hallways

1. When I talk about working extra hard to make up for time off, I'm not referring to making coffee. That was a part-time job, and in my spare time I wrote books and trained for ministry, which was the area of my life where I put too much pressure on myself.

2. Donald Miller, *A Million Miles in a Thousand Years* (Nashville: Thomas Nelson, 2009), xiii.

3. My very loose paraphrase of Jeremiah 29:4-14.

Chapter 11 - Ripped Out and Torn Apart

1. This pastor was Jimmy Evans, who has written a book on healing emotional pain. *Life Hurts* (Grand Rapids: Baker, 2013).

2. If you don't know what this is, you're probably not from Texas.

Chapter 13 - Answers

1. This occurs numerous times throughout the Gospels, including John 12:16.

2. I love the emo Michael W. Smith song, *This is Your Time*, which is about Cassie Bernall—one of the victims of the Columbine shooting, which occurred in 1999 in the suburbs of Denver. I've been drawn to studying Columbine for awhile now, for a number of reasons. It's one of those things that we don't really have any answers for, but there is a lot we can learn from it.

3. For this chapter, I researched Columbine extensively on the Internet and through the following books: Brooks Brown and Rob Merritt, *No Easy Answers: The Truth Behind Death at Columbine* (New York: Lantern, 2002), and Misty Bernall, *She Said Yes: The Unlikely Martyrdom of Cassie Bernall* (New York: Pocket Books, 2000).

4. Quoted from The Nicene Creed, modern wording (Public Domain).

5. Many of the thoughts in these last few paragraphs on the reality of pain and God answering our pain by becoming human were developed from the teachings of Brian Zahnd, Pastor of Word of Life Church (St. Joseph, Missouri). For further study, check out BZ's sermon series *Jesus in a World of Hurt,* which was preached in September/October of 2013. These messages are available at no charge in the archives at wolc.com.

Chapter 14 - Silence

1. Quote attributed to Cheri Cochran, via Twitter (emphasis added).
2. I can't recall where I first read this, but you can find lots of information and even see Hitler's paintings on the Internet by searching "Hitler artist."

Chapter 17 - Community

1. Meaning I have no idea where we were located.
2. *Iglesia Nuevo Pacto* is Spanish for *New Covenant Church.*
3. Bill Johnson, *Back to Kindergarten.* Bethel Church (Redding, California), August 14, 2011.
4. The internship I referred to was called *Burning Ones,* and it was located in Shawnee, Oklahoma. In 2013, Dave and most of his team re-located to Harrisburg, Pennsylvania. Today, Tannon and Cristina Herman (who were mentored by Dave) direct *School of the Heart,* which is what the internship has evolved into. The ministry trip that I was a part of is called the *Burn Wagon.* They take students and young adults on similar trips across the country every summer. All of these ministries are a part of a larger organization called *Burn 24-7.* For more information, visit burn24-7.com or burnwagon.com.
5. Idea inspired by Ross Parsley's book, *Messy Church* (Colorado Springs: David C. Cook, 2012).
6. Rick McKinley, *A Kingdom Called Desire* (Grand Rapids: Zondervan, 2011), 133.
7. Ibid., 135.
8. Ibid., 138.
9. Adapted from Ibid., 137-138.

Chapter 18 - Confession

1. I've heard some pastors cite James 5:16, saying that if we confess our sins to God, He'll forgive us, but we have to confess our sins to others in order to be

healed. The traditional view is if we struggle with a certain sin (usually a "big sin"), we should confess to someone, have them pray with us, and it will go away. But the text from James clearly states that we should "confess our sins *to each other*"—implying mutual confession instead of one person confessing their crap to someone who has their act together.

Chapter 19 - Fitting In

1. Rob Bell, *Grace*. Mars Hill Bible Church (Grandville, Michigan), November 6, 2011. While I do not agree with everything Rob teaches, he is not a heretic like some say he is. Many of his older teachings are quite rich in terms of Scriptural knowledge and soundness of doctrine.

Chapter 20 - The Time of Our Lives

1. For a balanced introduction to the Holy Spirit, my pastor has written a book that I recommend: Robert Morris, *The God I Never Knew* (Colorado Springs: WaterBrook Press, 2011).
2. Lake Lewisville in North Texas.
3. This isn't the same Kyle that I talked about in *Hallways*, who is a youth pastor. I went out searching for friends one time, and I came back with five Kyle's. It can get pretty confusing.
4. I'm unsure of the validity of this statistic, but I read it on the Internet somewhere, so it must be true.

Chapter 21 - Maypearl

1. When I say "my boss," I mean my boss with the youth outreach ministry, which is a branch of the same ministry that did the youth camp.
2. Tullian Tchividjian preached a sermon series called *In the Beginning ... Grace* at Coral Ridge Presbyterian Church (Ft. Lauderdale, Florida) from August to November of 2012.
3. Quote attributed to Tullian Tchividjian, via Twitter.
4. http://goodreads.com/author/quotes/847789.Timothy_Keller — Accessed April 29, 2015.
5. Luke 2:8-10, NLT.
6. References for translation of Greek: http://scripture4all.org/OnlineInterlinear/NTpdf/mat5.pdf, http://biblehub.com/greek/teleioi_5046.htm (both accessed April 29, 2015) and other sources.

7.   1 Corinthians 14:20, Philippians 3:15, Colossians 4:12, James 1:4.

8.   http://brianzahnd.com/2012/07/oh-mercy/ — Accessed April 29, 2015.

9.   Micah 6:8

10. James 2:13

11. Matthew 9:13, quoting Hosea 6:6.

12. Luke 5:32

13. G.K. Chesterton, *Saint Francis of Assisi* (Seattle: CreateSpace Independent Publishing Platform, 2011), back cover.

14. Quote attributed to Burk Parsons, via Twitter.

15. I am not saying I literally never step foot in a bookstore or enjoy a good read; I just make a conscious effort to ensure that my enjoyment of books, particularly theology books, doesn't turn into a replacement for a living and vibrant relationship with God.

16. In his book *Addiction & Grace* (New York: HarperOne, 1988), Gerald G. May, MD explores the reality that we all have addictions, and our addictions come in many different forms.

17. 2 Corinthians 5:21, among countless other Scriptures.

18. Sometime after my initial conversation with Annie, I read John 16:8-11 with a fresh set of eyes. This revelation was right in front of me the whole time, hiding in plain sight within the text. Since then, I've heard many people teach John 16 correctly (and many more incorrectly). If you'd like to know more on this topic, I'd encourage you to do your own research.

Chapter 23 - Amazing Grace

1.   C.S. Lewis, *A Grief Observed* (London: Faber, 1961).

2.   Brian Zahnd, *A Tapestry of Grace*. Word of Life Church (St. Joseph, Missouri), October 27, 2013.

3.   Ibid.

4.   Brian Zahnd, *Peter's Tears*. Word of Life Church (St. Joseph, Missouri), October 13, 2013.

Chapter 24 - Two Weeks Notice

1.   In Chapter 4 of his book, *A Journey Worth Taking* (Phillipsburg, New Jersey: P&R Publishing Company, 2007), Charles D. Drew eloquently explains how all work is sacred and important.

2. Dan B. Allender, *Sabbath* (Nashville: Thomas Nelson, 2009).

3. Attributed to Brené Brown. Compiled from two quotes, which were edited for proper grammatical structure. Taken from http://goodreads.com/author/show/162578.Bren_Brown — Accessed January 10, 2014.

Chapter 25 - *The New Normal*

1. For more on this topic, I highly recommend Bob's teaching *Levels of Change,* which is part of the *Foundations of Freedom* series. You can watch the entire series at no charge here: bobhamp.com/media.

2. Kyle Embry, *Hidden in Plain Sight* (Dallas: Battle Ground Creative, 2013).

3. Stephen Pressfield, *The War of Art* (New York: Black Irish Entertainment, 2002).

Chapter 28 - *Fast Forward*

1. Dr. Walter Brueggemann, *The Prophetic Imagination.* Faith & Culture Conference at Word of Life Church (St. Joseph, Missouri), April 14, 2015.

Chapter 29 - *Coming Home*

1. Thoughts about Adam and Eve were developed in part thanks to Erwin McManus, Pastor of Mosaic Church (Los Angeles, California), from his sermon *Who Told You You Were Naked?,* March 9, 2014.

2. Rob Bell, *Sex God* (Grand Rapids: Zondervan, 2007), 74.

3. Ibid., 73.

Chapter 30 - *Redemption*

1. This is a joke. It did not actually happen.

Epilogue

1. Five for Fighting, *100 Years,* from the album *The Battle for Everything* (Aware Records: 2004).

2. Kenny Chesney, *Don't Blink,* from the album *Just Who I Am: Poets & Pirates* (BNA Records: 2007).

3. Daniel Grothe, *Apocalypse Now.* New Life Church (Colorado Springs, Colorado), June 8, 2014.

4. Bob Hamp, posted on Facebook. First line taken from the blog post *Seeing the Invisible God,* posted online, May 17, 2009 — Accessed June 23, 2015.

Made in the USA
Middletown, DE
14 July 2015